A HISTORY OF THE AUSTRIAN
MIGRATION TO CANADA

A HISTORY OF THE AUSTRIAN
MIGRATION TO CANADA

Edited by
Frederick C. Engelmann, Manfred Prokop
and Franz A.J. Szabo

Carleton University Press

Canadian Cataloguing in Publication Data

Main entry under title:
    A History of the Austrian migration to Canada

Includes bibliographical references.
ISBN 0-88629-283-2

    1. Austrian Canadians—History. I. Engelmann,
Frederick C., 1921- II. Prokop, Manfred, 1942-
III. Szabo, Franz A. J.

FC106.A9H58 1996   971'.00436   C96-900281-5
F1035.A9H58 1996

Cover Illustration: This photograph of an Austrian immigrant, taken in the
summer of 1955 in Montreal's Jeanne-Mance Park at the foot of Mount-Royal,
captures the loneliness and isolation of the immigrant experience.
Source: Private collection.
Cover Design: Your Aunt Nellie
Typeset: Mayhew & Associates/Chisholm Communications, Ottawa, Ontario

Carleton University Press gratefully acknowledges the support extended to its
publishing program by the Canada Council and the financial assistance of the
Ontario Arts Council. The Press would also like to thank the Department of
Canadian Heritage, Government of Canada, and the Government of Ontario
through the Ministry of Culture, Tourism and Recreation, for their assistance.

CONTENTS

PREFACE

ANNIVERSARIES FREQUENTLY provide scholars with inspiration to re-examine familiar subjects or to bring less familiar ones into focus. It will therefore come as no surprise that the research project presented in this volume was inspired in the first instance by an approaching eminent anniversary in European history. Austrians have been in Canada in any substantial numbers for only the last century, but in 1996 Austrians in Europe are recalling a passage in a medieval document which confirms that their ancestral homeland's name is over a thousand years old. This medieval document, dated 1 November 996, speaks of an area on the southeastern periphery of the old Holy Roman Empire "popularly known as *Ostar-rîchi.*" The Latin version "Austria," which is also used in English, only begins to crop up in documents in the twelfth century, and all that the 996 document confirms is that the word *Ostarrîchi,* medieval forerunner of the modern German *Österreich,* was by then already in usage. These ambiguities notwithstanding, Austrians are celebrating their "millennium," and the occasion provides scholars in a variety of disciplines with stimulus to examine the nature of Austria and Austrians, and to cast a fresh look on the many chapters of Austrian history.

One of those chapters is also a chapter of Canadian history: it is the history of the Austrian migrants who have come to this country and have woven their own particular strands of experience and culture into the diverse texture of the Canadian social fabric. Numerically, they are a modest group, and in their public profile, they have indeed been, as E. Wilder Spaulding said of the Austrians in the United States, "quiet invaders." It may very well even come as a surprise to the Austrian migrants themselves to discover the extent of their impact on their adopted home. It is, in any case, a chapter of Austrian as well as Canadian history which has to date hardly been explored at all, and what little has been said of them has been fraught with analytical difficulties.

Austrians speak German, and their history was till the nineteenth century an integral part of German history. It is therefore not surprising that, for many observers, Austrians are to be understood under the German ethnic umbrella, and should be counted as Germans in the Canadian ethnic spectrum. Yet the Austria of today is a sovereign state, and most Austrians there think of themselves as a distinct nation, not a mere regional or dialectal subset of the Germans. The complexities of this problem are explored in the introductory essay of this volume, but the ambiguities associated with it have certainly played no small role in the neglect of the specific history of Austrian migrants. "Austrians," as Canadian immigration authorities kept complaining, were notoriously difficult to define, and it is understandable that non-Austrian scholars might find the problem not worth the effort. What is more, unlike many other ethnic groups in Canada, the Austrian immigrant community has not produced any Canadian immigration historian of note from its own ranks. When one considers, furthermore, that Austrian immigration to this country has declined dramatically in recent decades and that it may now very well be a closed book, the history of this particular migration might never have been written had the much-touted anniversary not served to focus attention on Austria.

If the millennium has made many Austrian-born Canadians and their descendents focus on their Austrian identity, their collective reflections might still not have resulted in any concrete balance sheet, had it not been for a series of fortuitous coincidences. In the fall of 1993, a new Austrian ambassador, Dr. Walther G. Lichem, was accredited to Canada. Lichem happened to be a political scientist interested in Austrian emigration and had had occasion to focus on Austrian migrants in the New World in his previous posting in Chile. Seeking to brief himself on Austrian migrants in Canada upon his arrival in this country, he soon discovered the lamentable paucity of the scholarly literature in this field. He began to query Canadian scholars—and particularly those of Austrian origin—about this lacuna, and out of these discussions a research project was born. In conversations with the editors of this volume, the idea soon crystallized that perhaps the occasion of the Austrian millennium could provide an impetus for the publication of a book on Austrian migrants to Canada.

Since that anniversary was fast approaching, it was clear that no single individual could undertake a research project on this subject and hope to publish a volume in time for the millennium celebrations. Several narrowly focussed scholars, however, could reasonably hope to produce a series of narrower essays which together would represent a fairly comprehensive compendium. The study of migration is, of course, one with two faces—it is both an emigration and an immigration. Just as Canadians would be interested in the latter, so Austrians would be interested in the former. Recruiting interested Canadian scholars into the project was thus only half the story. The project organizers were also fortunate to draw Austrian scholars into the venture from the beginning. Much of the credit for this is due to Oliver Rathkolb, Director of the Bruno Kreisky Archive Foundation, and an associate of the Ludwig Boltzmann Institute of the University of Vienna. Rathkolb was able to persuade the Boltzmann Institute to lend its institutional backing and to extend preliminary financial credits to the project while funding was being sought. He also coordinated and supervised the activities of the young Austrian scholars we were able to welcome to this publication—Anna Maria Pichler, Michaela Schober and Bettina Steinhauser—and he recruited and trained a team of Austrian graduate students who came to Canada as researchers and interviewers.

As a result, in May 1994, an inter-disciplinary team of both Canadian and Austrian scholars and researchers was assembled with the objective of compiling a systematic survey of Austrian immigration to Canada. The broad themes, which are presented as chapters in this volume, were sketched out, and writers and researchers assigned to each. To review and assess these research findings, an international symposium was planned, and a call for additional papers went out to the scholarly community both in North America and in Austria. By the time the conference was held at Carleton University in May 1995, this call had yielded such a positive response that a companion volume of selected conference proceedings was assembled and is now being published, in conjunction with this study, under the title *Austrian Immigration to Canada: Selected Essays.*

The stimulus of the millennium anniversary may in the first instance have spurred scholars to venture into this relatively uncharted territory, but it also served to inspire the Austrian community in Canada to think of an assessment of itself as a timely enterprise. One of the research tools designed for this project was a comprehensive questionnaire which was distributed to Austrian immigrants and their descendents through Austrian societies across Canada, as well as through various other channels. We were highly gratified by the response from the community to this survey, which far exceeded all reasonable expectations. Members of the Austrian-Canadian community also proved highly co-operative with Rathkolb's research team of Austrian graduate students, and so many individuals proved helpful at every turn that to name them all would require more space than a publication of this scale could accommodate. This co-operation of individual Canadians of Austrian origin all across the country, combined with the yeoman labours of the group of graduate students, consisting of Michael Melzer, Camilla Nielsen, Anna Schober, Alexander Schröck, and Georg Tillner, is to be thanked for assembling an extensive research collection which includes well over one hundred taped interviews. This collection of research materials and taped interviews is referred to in the text that follows as "The Austrian Immigration to Canada Collection [AICC]." It will, in due course, be organized, indexed and deposited in archives for future use by scholars. Agreement has already been reached, for example, to deposit a copy of this collection with the Multicultural History Society of Ontario.

No research project of this scope, operating within the time constraints set by the millennium celebrations, could hope to succeed without financial support. Here the project team was very fortunate indeed to engage the enthusiasm and full support of Ambassador Lichem himself. Thanks to his tireless efforts, critical initial funding to launch the project was secured from the Government of Canada's Secretary of State for Multiculturalism and the Status of Women, Department of Canadian Heritage, from the Presidential Fund for Innovation and Development of the Social Sciences and Humanities Research Council of Canada, and from the Austrian Federal Ministry for External Affairs (Bundesministerium für Auswärtige Angelegenheiten). The research team profited not only from Ambassador Lichem's indefatigable energy, but also from the generous diligence of all the Embassy's personnel, which was forced at some points to cope with the almost daily intrusion of this project into their regular duties. Over the course of the months, additional funding, which allowed this project to be continued, and made the publication of this volume possible, came from both the Department of Canadian Heritage and the Austrian Federal Ministry for External Affairs. We are particularly grateful to the Heritage officials who expedited our requests: Mark Curfoot-Mollington, Judy Young, Susanne Samson and Austin Cooke. The completion of the project, however, would have been inconceivable without a very generous research grant from the Austrian Federal Ministry for the Sciences, Research and Culture (Bundesministerium für

Wissenschaft, Forschung und Kunst) and the personal enthusiasm of its Assistant Deputy Minister for International Cooperation, Raoul F. Kneucker, whose backing was secured by our colleague, Oliver Rathkolb. Finally, various meetings at Carleton University, and especially our May 1995 symposium, were supported substantially by G. Stuart Adam, Dean of the Faculty of Arts.

As much as on financial support, this study relied on the intellectual support and advice of numerous individuals. At our initial organizational conference, we profited from the advice of colleagues, including Oliver Rathkolb, Fraser Taylor, Assistant Vice-President (External) of Carleton University and Head of Carleton International, and Karin MacHardy of the University of Waterloo. We also welcomed the input of the Ambassador, as well as Ulrike Billard-Florian and Jutta Szep-Kroath, Austrian consuls in Montreal and Toronto respectively. Prominent members of the Austrian community who participated in this initial organization included Ernst Waengler of Toronto, Friedrich Istl of Islington, Karl Gyaki of Willowdale, and Roland Pirker of Ottawa. In the subsequent organization of the research, the project directors were particularly grateful to the executives of all of the Austrian societies across Canada, and to the Austrian consuls (in addition to the two already mentioned, these included Graham Clarke in Vancouver, Hans Ockermüller in Calgary, Anthony Merchant in Regina and John Klassen in Winnipeg) who facilitated meetings with them.

In dispatching our team of Austrian graduate students to various points across the country, we received the invaluable advice and help of the Multicultural History Society of Ontario. We are particularly grateful to its director, Paul Robert Magocsi, for organizing an orientation seminar for our young Austrians, and to Roberto Perin, Lillian Petroff, Gabriele Scardellato, Franc Sturino and Harold Tropper for participating in this excellent discussion. An indispensable stage in the evolution of this manuscript was our international symposium, "Austrian Immigration to Canada," held at Carleton University on 19-21 May 1995. We are not only thankful to all our academic colleagues from across Canada and from Europe for taking the time and energy to prepare for and attend the conference, but we are especially appreciative of the many members of the Austrian-Canadian community who travelled from many points in the country to attend. Their comments and discussions were as invaluable as the critiques of our colleagues, and their presence not only helped make the conference a success but contributed in no small part to the making of this book.

We also wish to thank our Canadian research assistants, who laboured in various parts of the country on this project. These included Andrea Benes, Angela Jo Bradford, Karin Fuerst, Marcia Goldberg, Grace Moore, Graham Rawlinson, Richard Schaefer, and Judith Zander. We are grateful that portions of the manuscript were read by Norman Hillmer of Carleton University and John Hilliker of the Canadian Department of Foreign Affairs and International Trade. Preparation of the final manuscript profited from the work of John Flood, General Editor and Director of Carleton University Press and the watchful eye of our copy-editor, Jennie Strickland. Above all, however, we are indebted to the thousands of unnamed Canadians of Austrian descent—not only the subjects of our study, but also the participants in the research process—without whose enthusiasm and support this project would not have been possible. It is to them that we dedicate this volume.

Frederick C. Engelmann
Manfred Prokop
Franz A.J. Szabo

INTRODUCTION
REFLECTIONS ON THE AUSTRIAN IDENTITY IN THE OLD WORLD AND THE NEW

Franz A.J. Szabo

TO PROPOSE SURVEYING the history of the Austrian migration to Canada would at one level seem to be a simple enough matter. The Republic of Austria may be a small European country, and the number of its citizens who have made this country their second home may be relatively modest, but like any other group they have contributed in their own special way to the pluralistic identity of modern Canada. Yet the most fundamental question which faces anyone who would approach this subject is how to define "Austrian." The one-time existence of a multi-lingual central European Austrian Empire has left a legacy of ethnic ambivalences and confusions which require some sorting out before it can be made clear whose immigration is actually being studied in this volume. In this country, where Ukrainians were sent to concentration camps for being Austrian citizens in the First World War, and where immigration authorities long rationalized their ethnographic and geographic ignorance by devising the simple category of "Austrians unless otherwise specified" for a multitude of central Europeans whom they could not readily classify, it would seem obvious that the very word Austrian would need some explanation.

From a practical point of view this study has attempted to be open-ended without being peremptory in its approach. We were certainly not going to claim people for "Austrian origin" simply because of the one-time existence of the Austrian Empire. On the other hand, it was clear that "Austrian" had to be used in a more flexible way than simply meaning citizens of the present Republic of Austria. Of course, Austrians from what is now Austria form the core of this study, but German speakers from German-language speech islands in other parts of the old Monarchy who thought of themselves as "Austrian" in the old imperial way could certainly not be excluded; nor, for that matter, could anyone else who insisted he or she was Austrian, no matter what the ethnicity. In the final analysis our study had to settle on self-definition: He or she is Austrian who thinks he or she is Austrian, though, of course, we are not unaware of the subsequent irony—namely, that there are German-speaking citizens of the Republic of Austria whose families have lived there for generations, but who nevertheless do not think of themselves as "Austrian" but as German. Polls indicate that this is now a very small minority, but its existence not only cannot be denied but brings us to the very heart of the problem of the Austrian identity.

Austrian, Austrian identity, Austrian consciousness, these are by no means simple matters. There is a Republic of Austria, but within that Republic there are also two provinces called Austria (Upper Austria and Lower Austria, who together once constituted a distinct medieval Austria). There was, of course, an Austrian Empire, and later an Austrian half of an Austro-Hungarian Empire. There was also a House of Austria, and we may recall that two successive Kings of France married *Spanish* princesses who were styled "Austrian" (Louis XIII married Anne of Austria, and Louis XIV married Marie-Therese of Austria), and that one of the most famous Spanish admirals, the victor of the fabled Battle of Lepanto, was none other than Don Juan of Austria! As the historian Erich Zöllner has pointed out, the concept of "Austria" has had, variously, historic, political, dynastic and even constitutional dimensions. Over the centuries there have been dramatic changes not only to the borders of what has been called Austria, but also to the meaning of its internal form and content. Not surprisingly, therefore, as the definition of Austria changed, so did the sense of what it meant to be Austrian.

That is why it is perhaps best to begin with the two anniversaries that served as the impetus for this project: April 27, 1995 was the fiftieth anniversary of the proclamation of the Second Austrian Republic; November 1, 1996 is the 1000th anniversary of the famous medieval document which marks the first recorded use of the term "*Österreich*" (the German word for Austria). Austrians thus moved seamlessly from celebrating their fiftieth anniversary to celebrating their millennium! This, in itself, might be easy enough to explain were it not for the fact that Austria had only recently celebrated its "millennium" in 1976, and had even issued an impressive set of commemorative stamps for the occasion. One may well ask: how many millenniums can one legitimately celebrate, and exactly what is it that was being celebrated in 1996? The answer to the first question is not as simple as it may appear, and, indeed, there may be several legitimate Austrian millenniums to celebrate. I will explain what I mean by turning to the second part of the question: namely, what exactly was celebrated in 1996.

On 1 November 996 the German Emperor, Otto III, issued a land grant to the Bishopric of Freising, making over a place called Neuhof an der Ybbs and thirty hides of land (as the Latin document says) "*in regione vulgari vocabulo Ostarrîchi ...*" —that is, in the land popularly known as "*Österreich.*" Some medieval historians question the date because the seal on the document actually dates from 1002, though others argue the date is indeed accurate and that a new seal was only affixed after the old one had fallen off. In any case, in the bigger picture the matter is not that important since the term "*Ostarrîchi*" occurs several more times in other documents dating from 998 and thereafter. What the document confirms is that, at the very latest, the term "*Österreich*" was already commonly used in the second half of the tenth century.

What was celebrated back in 1976, on the other hand, was a more clear-cut political millennium. In the year 976 Emperor Otto I severed the south-eastern border regions of the Holy Roman Empire from the Duchy of Bavaria and established defensive border territories under loyal lieutenants there instead. A Carinthian March (roughly encompassing present-day Carinthia and Styria), already established as a border march by 970, was raised to the rank of an independent duchy. In the same year a certain Leopold of Babenberg was given an eastern march along the Danube (initially merely a narrow corridor along the banks of the Danube between Linz and Vienna, but gradually expanding to a territory roughly encompassing present day Lower and parts of Upper Austria). Under the Babenbergs this area was identified by various Latin and German names—though, significantly, the name "*Ostmark*" never occurs in any medieval document—and by the middle of the 12th century the Latin word "*Austria*" begins to supersede all the others. The establishment of the Babenbergs in what was to come to be called Austria is important because this dynasty over several centuries began the process of gradually accumulating neighbouring Alpine territories through inheritance. After the extinction of the Babenbergs and the acquisition of their lands by the Habsburgs, the name Austria was then increasingly applied by the new rulers to describe their entire dynastic patrimony. By the later Middle Ages this conglomerate largely took a geographic shape roughly equivalent to the present-day Republics of Austria and Slovenia. What kind of "millennium" this made 1976 is therefore not all that unambiguous, especially when one considers that Emperor Charles the Great had also established eastern marches to his empire in the ninth century and colonized them with German speakers. These earlier Carolingian foundations had already led a number of Austrian historians at the beginning of the twentieth century to argue that Austria was celebrating its 1100th anniversary (some argued in 1901 and others in 1906), which in turn resulted in the mounting of the famous relief on the exterior wall of the Church of St. Peter in Vienna in 1906 which hails Charles as the founder of Austria. By that measure Austria has already celebrated its millennium not once, but several times over the last two hundred years.

What makes the *Ostarrîchi* document of 996 particularly interesting, however, is that it served Austrian President Karl Renner well in the founding years of the Second Republic, and was given great play in 1946 (including another commemorative stamp) as confirming the 950th anniversary of Austria. In a sense the *Ostarrîchi* document was used to confer a certain genealogical and political legitimacy on the Second Republic, tying the birth of the latter to the longer historical tradition of the former. However, the two are also tied together in another sense. Cynical observers see Renner's use of the document as a perfect illustration of the creation of an artificial Austrian identity or Austrian nation by the Second Republic as a perfect way to distance itself from Germany and to escape responsibility for collusion with German criminality in the Second World War. Here it is important to retort that while it is true that the leading political figures of the Second Republic have gone a long way to encourage the development and created the firm political framework of not only an Austrian state but also an Austrian nation, they did not invent it. Austria and the Austrian identity, as Zöllner has well emphasized, were not created by a political act—not in 1945 or in 1918 or in 976 for that matter—they were the products of an ongoing evolutionary process. That process had both a political and cultural dimension.

Before beginning with the political dimension, it is important to stress unequivocally that this evolutionary process was an integral part of German history, and that until 1866 it is a mistake to see Austrian history outside that German context. Understanding the evolution of a distinct Austrian nation, however, lies less in comprehending the peculiar dynamic of Austrian historical developments per se, and more in situating these developments in the larger German historical evolution—or, to put it another way—comprehending the distinct Austrian identity is less a matter of understanding the specific steps Austria took to nationhood than a matter of understanding the important steps of the larger development of German history. Thus, when we see how over the centuries Austria grew in political stature and might, how it acquired increasing degrees of political autonomy and eventually of sovereignty within the framework of the German Empire, and how it made increasing political and dynastic connections with territories outside that Empire, we only see the most successful variant of what was happening everywhere in Germany.

The Holy Roman Empire of the German Nation as it emerged in the tenth century was a political association of very distinct tribal entities—Saxons, Franks, Thuringians, Swabians, Bavarians, and so forth—whose tribal identities were never fully submerged in a single integrated German identity. Austrians at this point constituted no separate tribal entity but were, on the whole, part of the Bavarian tribal group. The central government of the Holy Roman Empire of the German Nation, after some initial successes in creating an integrated and reasonably unified Germany, soon came to grief in the Middle Ages. The lesser dukes and princes of the Empire increasingly appropriated aspects of the royal prerogative, and acquired ever greater degrees of independence until, at the end of the Thirty Years War in 1648, they became fully sovereign. By then "Germany" became (to use a term Canadians will easily understand) a very loose sovereignty-association arrangement, not between two, but among some 365 political entities. Austria's medieval road from border march to duchy and (thanks to a skillful forgery) to archduchy, and even its several failed efforts to raise the Austrian lands to the status of a kingdom within the Holy Roman Empire, thus all followed a classic pattern within German history. Even the Habsburg acquisition of a vast non-Germanic Empire was only the most successful variant of what all German princes were trying to do. Thus, for example, the dukes of Hannover were kings of Great Britain and the British Empire for 120 years, and the dukes of Saxony were kings of the Polish-Lithuanian Commonwealth for 60 years.

Insofar as any "Germany" existed in this loose sovereignty-association arrangement, Austria was its leader, and Vienna—the only really substantive urban center in the entire German-speaking world until well into the nineteenth century—was, in the words of the eighteenth-century poet and writer, Johann Pezzl, "the capital of Germany, much maligned and envied by the small-town hicks of the rest of Germany." The death-blow to this arrangement was delivered by the French Revolution and

Napoleon, who turned a substantial portion of the German-speaking political community of central Europe into French puppet states. Here again, it is important to emphasize that when the Austrian ruler of Germany, Emperor Francis II, abdicated the crown of the Holy Roman Empire of the German nation in 1806, it was less a matter of Austria turning away from Germany than of the other Germans turning away from it. Francis simply faced reality by abdicating the crown of an empire that no longer existed. The Kingdom of Prussia had long become a law unto itself, and the rest of the smaller German states were herded by the French into the Confederation of the Rhine. The act that brought about the destruction of the Holy Roman Empire, however, was not so much Francis' abdication of 1806, but rather the much less well-known formal secession of the Confederation of the Rhine from Germany which preceded it. Many Germans in the last hundred years or so have expressed open resentment that the crown jewels of the Holy Roman Empire of the German Nation should, of all places, be in Vienna! But in the context of the historical reality it is only fitting. The smaller German states seceded from Germany leaving the Austrians holding the bag, as it were—only in that bag were the great medieval crown jewels of the old Germany.

The destruction of the Empire, of course, gave impetus to the great German national revival of the nineteenth century. In those decades there was much soul-searching about exactly what "Germany" was—highlighted, most famously, by the poem of Ernst Moritz Arndt, "*Was ist des Deutschen Vaterland?* (What is a German's Fatherland?)." Arndt's answer, that Germany was wherever the German language was spoken, made some sense as a cultural assertion, but as a political agenda it was absurd from the start. Not, of course, that this prevented many people—including many people from Austria—from dreaming this political dream, and from being frustrated with the new political arrangements which were made after the collapse of the French imperium in 1814. Those new arrangements for Germany that emerged at the Congress of Vienna, largely at the behest of the Austrian State Chancellor, Prince Clemens Metternich, were a variation of the sovereignty-association of the Holy Roman Empire, again under Austrian leadership. Not only did this new German Confederation not satisfy the growing number of nationalist dreamers and poets, it also did not satisfy the second largest member of the Confederation, the Kingdom of Prussia.

Prussia was not content (to again use some Canadian terminology) to be merely a kingdom like the others in the German Confederation; it wanted special status and parity with Austria. When the Austrians refused to capitulate on this point, Prussia simply wanted to split the assets—in short, to divide the German Confederation. If it ended up with a larger share of the Confederation in 1871 than even the architect of this division, Prince Otto von Bismarck, originally had dreamed, it was not because Prussia wished to fulfill the German nationalist dream of Arndt and others, but rather because Prussia wanted, as Bismarck so succinctly put it himself, "to put an end to the German swindle." Again, it is important to remind ourselves of the actual sequence of events: When Austria wished to strengthen the bonds of the German Confederation, Prussia refused to participate in the process. When Austria then summoned the Federal German Parliament, the clear majority of German states declared Prussia to be an outlaw, and voted to have this recalcitrant member of the Confederation brought back into line by force of arms if necessary. This led Prussia to secede from the German Confederation and to declare war on it. The catastrophic defeat of Austria and the rest of Germany at the hands of Prussia in 1866 was thus not the first step in the fulfillment of the German nationalist dream, but the fulfillment of the Prussian political agenda. Naturally, Bismarck skillfully played with German nationalism, but for all the propaganda about reviving a second German Empire to succeed the defunct Holy Roman Empire, the reality was that Prussia had conquered large portions of the German Confederation and bullied others into associating with it precisely in order to make sure that Arndt's dream would never come true.

Many people are accustomed to thinking of nationalism as a sort of inexorable force whose logical and inevitable culmination is the creation of the modern nation-state. It is thus not unusual to encounter people who still think that nineteenth-century German or Italian nationalism, for example, grew to such strength that the so-called unifications of Germany and Italy were inevitable. Here one might cite an instructive statistic with respect to the Italian case—namely that many more people died *resisting* the so-called unification of Italy than died trying to achieve it. What historians have increasingly come to recognize is that the so-called unifications of Germany and Italy in the nineteenth century had more to do with fortuitous political factors favouring Prussia and Piedmont, than with the inexorable triumph of any putative national will to unity. Nationalism did not create the states that were known as Germany and Italy; rather those states, once in existence, set about trying to create a concomitant "nation" in order to consolidate their conquests. This is especially important to remember in the German case. What was created in 1866-1871 was not the first step of a "united Germany" encompassing all German speakers, but an entirely new country, which, under Prussian tutelage set about creating an *entirely new* Prussian-German identity. In an age of rapid industrialization such identity formation involved hitherto unknown technological and sociological dimensions, which, in turn allowed this process to occur with unprecedented rapidity. By the time the Bismarckian edifice collapsed in 1918, the creation of the new identity was largely complete. 1866 had really been a "*Stunde Null* (Zero Hour)," as prescient observers such as Jakob Burckhardt saw only all too clearly: the hitherto existing German political community was destroyed forever, and there was no going back. The famous comment of the papal secretary of state, "*Casca il mondo!* (the world has collapsed)" was a truer summation of the reality than we are accustomed to acknowledging.

It took a long time for Austrians to wake up to this reality. Some, like the aged poet, Franz Grillparzer, saw it immediately: As early as November 1870 he recognized that the new German polity coming into existence had nothing to do with the imagined German national state which had been dreamt of, and confessed to an intimate: "Wie es heute bei uns aussieht muß ich sagen, ich bin kein Deutscher, sondern ein Österreicher." ("The way things look around here these days, I must say that I am not a German, but rather an Austrian.") Many others who dreamed the German nationalist dream in Austria persisted in the illusion that Bismarck's German Empire was only the first step in the fulfillment of their dream. Some were even openly treasonous to their own country and fawned shamelessly over Bismarck's putative achievement of the first step of the grand dream. In some places eager burghers went so far as to name Austrian town squares after Bismarck! Their only regret was being left out. These sycophantic acolytes were blind to just how much the Prussian Germany of Bismarck was forging a whole new German identity because they would have happily submerged any distinct Austrian identity within it as well. Indeed, even the Germans of the new Germany themselves often had only an imperfect sense of their new identity; but for all the political, military and economic power of this new Prussianized "Germany," it was clearly a parvenu identity suffering from a massive inferiority complex (the most obvious symptom of which, as Friedrich Nietzsche observed, was its loud and strident but hardly convincing assertions of superiority).

Meanwhile the Austria that continued to exist during this same period certainly did not lack cultural confidence—one might even say "smugness"—and what is especially important about Austro-German relations in the period after 1866 is the gradual divergence of their respective cosmologies as the century wore on. As Hans Kohn showed persuasively 30 years ago, the mainstream intellectual tradition of Germany was marked by a gradual alienation from the West in this era. This did not happen in Austria. While many *individual* German-speaking Austrians followed in the footsteps of the new Germans, the *mainstream* Austrian cultural and intellectual tradition remained rooted in and increasingly committed to the neo-classical, empirical, positivist tradition of the Enlightenment. As Karl Pribram observed, by the late nineteenth century Austria became "the only outpost of nominalistic reasoning east of the Rhine." One need adduce here only Carl Menger and the whole Austrian school of economics; Ernst Mach, Ludwig Boltzmann, Moritz Schlick and like-minded philosophers of science; the abiding strength of neo-classical structures even in Romantic Austrian composers from Schubert to Mahler, not to mention the cerebral precision of the New Viennese School or the assertive twentieth-century neo-classicism of an Egon Wellesz or Franz Schmidt.

For all the naïveté of the notion, perhaps Austrians and some Germans can nevertheless be forgiven, in the aftermath of the great catastrophe of the First World War, for thinking that the pre-1866 question, "What is a German's fatherland," was still open and susceptible to pre-1866 solutions: that the discussions and negotiations could be carried on as if the fifty-odd years between 1866 and 1918 had never happened. As we know, both Austrians and Germans were simply prohibited from pursuing this logic by the terms of the peace treaties imposed by the victorious allies after the war. In this context it is interesting to note how reluctant Austrians were to accept the name "Austria." Austria had come to mean something bigger, and what had come into existence in 1918, as the midwives of that birth insisted, was "*Deutschösterreich* [German-Austria]." Here, too, fortunately, the victors gave the Austrians no choice. Of course, prohibition frequently has the opposite effect intended, making what is prohibited more attractive than it might be if it were not. Naturally, proponents of *Anschluss* (annexation to Germany) on both sides of the border had no idea that their integrative model no longer had any foundation, but, like so many individuals with the lessons of life, so Austrians collectively could apparently only learn this the hard way.

When the *Anschluss* came in 1938, the Nazis used the motto "*Heim ins Reich!* (back home to the Reich)," deliberately cultivating the notion that the exercise would be akin to re-entering the German Confederation or even the Holy Roman Empire—that there was some organic continuity between those older German polities and the so-called Second Reich (of which the Weimar Republic and the Third Reich were political offsprings), and that an amputated limb could now be sewn back on. But the Reich to which Austria was annexed bore the very distinct stamp of the Prussian new Germany created by Bismarck, and the limb was to be sewn on to a different body than the one from which it had been severed. This may not have been immediately apparent because, after all, Hitler was born in Austria. But he was one of those Austrians alienated from everything Austria had become and had come to mean—one of those admirers of Bismarck mentioned above. In any case, all too many Austrians happily but naively climbed on the bandwagon, only to have it gradually dawn on them: this was no longer home. The gradual awakening was something which became increasingly apparent even before the hardships of war and defeat accelerated the process. By this I do not mean to suggest that Austrians were simply victims: Austrians must be prepared to acknowledge that the percentage of their population which was guilty of collusion in the crimes of the Nazi regime—whether out of opportunism or conviction—was no different than the percentage of the German population which was. But at the same time it is also true that *Anschluss* turned out to be nothing like what its proponents had imagined.

Fortunately, the Austrians were given a second chance. In the new *Stunde Null* of 1945 they finally understood what kind of *Stunde Null* 1866 had been, and now systematically set about excavating the Austrian reality from the rubble, and from their own past. As Gerald Stourzh so aptly put it, now the sense of recovering something lost, something whose value only became apparent for having been lost, provided the animating drive to define the Austrian nation. But, again, please note, I say to *define* it, not to *create* it. Well before Austria became a nation politically, it had gone a long way to becoming a nation culturally, and the meaning of the establishment of the Second Republic was simply to give political form and structure to this reality. Among Austrians this was never, and is not now, a unanimous enterprise, though if we place any faith in the successive polls undertaken over the past few decades, it is the enterprise of an overwhelming and still growing majority. That this consciously involved what the Germans call a "*Verschweitzerung*" (turning oneself into a kind of Switzerland: learning to live with being small and neutral) was certainly part of the political equation, but Austrians could never acculturate to a

Swiss social and cultural ethos any more than a Prussian-German one. In this realm they had to turn to their own history, and perforce to the much maligned Habsburg Monarchy—painful though that could sometimes be for many Austrians.

No one who has lived in Austria for even a short period of time can fail to detect its pervasive sense of hierarchy, its obsession with rank and title, with forms and properly affixed seals and stamps. Where else could one possibly insult the honour of someone's *office*—all the way down to the uniformed train conductor!? What this land of "*Amtsehrenbeleidigung* (defamation of office)" is, of course, is the twentieth-century child of a profoundly aristocratic culture—a culture of forms, of manner, of grace. On the negative side we can see this preoccupation to be nothing but a pathetic anachronism and an irritating nuisance, but this old aristocratic culture was also something more. To quote Carl Schorske, "profoundly Catholic, it was a sensuous, plastic culture which viewed nature as a scene of joy, a manifestation of divine grace to be glorified in art. The culture was not moral, philosophical or scientific, but primarily aesthetic. Its greatest achievements were in the applied and performing arts: architecture, theater, and music." As Schorske has shown, this may not have been the culture of the lesser classes initially, but since social assimilation to the aristocracy was virtually impossible, the only road to the ethereal realms of the elite left open to non-nobles was that of culture. Perhaps the aping of the aristocracy was at first merely mimetic, but with time "the receptivity of all educated classes to the life of art, and concomitantly at the individual level, a sensitivity to psychic states, ensured that even the moralistic bourgeois culture in Austria was overlaid and undermined by an amoral *Gefühlskultur.*" The aristocrats themselves may have lost their grip on power, and individual nobles may have degenerated into pathetic and philistine caricatures of their ancestors, but the old imperial Habsburg aristocratic culture has left an indelible imprint on Austria, and provided it with one of its abiding identities.

The failure of the *Anschluss* experiment showed another thing: language alone does not a culture make. Philosophers and poets like Arndt, who worked with language, were quite naturally prone to conceive of integrative structures primarily in linguistic terms. Further, as one of the most important historians of the phenomenon of "nation building," Paul Robert Magocsi, argued recently, their definitions of nationality were ascriptive (that is, "viewed as a fixed and unchangeable [mutually exclusive] phenomenon ostensibly predetermined by blood ties, shared descent, and a particular language and culture"). They also tended to see the normal fulfillment of the "nation-state" in the context of the model provided by the French Revolution, which demanded the supreme loyalty of the individual over all other loyalties, including familial ones. This is not how people naturally behave. Few of us are loyal to one object. Most of us operate within what Magocsi calls "a network of loyalties," and as we see only all too well in the Canadian context, in a multicultural framework where children are quite frequently the products of inter-ethnic marriage, it is quite natural to find individuals who feel perfectly comfortable with one or more "national" loyalties. What is more, as social scientists have begun to argue, "situational or optional ethnicity, in which an individual's identification can be consciously emphasized or de-emphasized as the situation requires," is quite widespread.

Such patterns of behaviour were the norm in the old Habsburg Monarchy. Indeed, as the imperial military establishment attempted to keep ethnic statistics they frequently encountered the problem that the recruits themselves were not conscious of their nationality. They were from "there" or "that place," and literally millions spoke two or more languages indiscriminately. On the whole it was the sub-national loyalties— to village, town, region or province—and social loyalties—to religious faith, guild, estate, family—that predominated individual consciousness. Tolerating such patterns of multiple loyalties could be thoroughly inimical to the national project, as we can see from the reaction of nationalists who derisively describe such sentiments as "parochialism." The French Revolutionaries were certainly clear on the matter, and as a prelude to intensifying their national passions, they abolished the provincial entities of old France altogether. Because the Habsburg Monarchy had no real interest or ability in pursuing such policies on its territories, sub-national loyalties remained strong in central Europe, and one of the main pillars to which the Austrian Second Republic could appeal in its excavation of the "Austrian" was the strong sense of provincial loyalty which could still be tapped. Local loyalties proved to be one of the great antipodes to the *Anschluss* momentum, and the shared local loyalties of the Austrian provinces, parochial though it may undoubtedly have been on one level, proved paradoxically to be a centripetal force in the new Republic after 1945.

It has often been observed that people whose primary focus tends to be sub-national also feel much more comfortable on the trans-national plane. This was a second legacy of the Habsburg Monarchy which could now be emphasized as a desirable quality in the Austrian Republic: its universalism, its broad European rather than narrow German vision of the world, its conciliatory, bridge-building capacity—in short, its cosmopolitanism. If one is to seek the roots of this cosmopolitanism, one must give credit where credit is due, and admit that Austria owed its universalist vision, first of all, to its long-ruling sovereigns: the Habsburg dynasty. Soon after the Habsburgs begun their 400-year stranglehold on the imperial crown of the Holy Roman Empire in the fifteenth century, they began to interpret the imperial tradition in the broad Carolingian and imperial Roman sense, rather than making it the mere dutiful servant of narrower German policies as the Saxon, Salian and Hohenstaufen emperors had done in the Middle Ages. From Frederick III's "A.E.I.O.U." (*Austria Erit In Orbe Universo:* Austria is destined to rule the world) motto, through Maximilian I's spectacular marriage arrangements, to Charles V's conscientious absorption of the broad imperial gospel from Mercurio Gattinara, the Habsburgs were never content to be merely German.

Then, overlapping this in the seventeenth century, came the Catholic Counter-Reformation with its compelling cosmopolitan vision of the Universal Church militant, which became so deeply ingrained in Austria that not only its physical but also its psychological features are still clearly recognizable today. Finally, and most important of all, is Austria's long and integral connection with its non-Germanic neighbours. Even in the early Middle Ages, when Austria was a mere border march, we must remember that this meant not only that it sometimes was on the front line of conflict with the non-Germanic world, but, more frequently, on the front line of cultural contact with other nations. The Habsburgs systematized this by striving to integrate the multi-national Austrian-Bohemian-Hungarian core triad of their empire, especially after 1740. And while we are accustomed to focusing on their failures, it would do well to focus also on their successes. Robert Evans has recently made a very eloquent and forceful case for this point, showing how the Habsburg Monarchy *did* evolve a "common culture, ... common habits of thought, ... common patterns of creativity," and even "similarity of vocabulary, idiom and structure" despite the linguistic diversity of the area. The Austrian identity, in short, was defined as much by its Slavic, Magyar, Latin, and, yes, Jewish dimension as by its German one. One needs but look at Austrian food—such a baffling cornucopia for Germans that a recent German cookbook on Austrian cuisine felt it necessary to preface the volume with a fifteen-page closely-packed double column dictionary of Austrian terms and German translations in order to decipher everything from "Fisolen [G. grüne Bohnen]" to "Marillen [G. Aprikosen]," from "Topfen [G. Quark]" to "Erdäpfel [G. Kartoffeln]," not to mention the completely untranslatable "Gulasch," "Letscho," "Buchteln," "Datschkerln," "Kolatschen," "Potitzen," "Palatschinken" and "Cevapcicij"! The genetic basis of this culinary excursion can be confirmed by looking at any Austrian telephone directory under A for Adamicka, B for Blazevic, C for Czizsek—not to mention V for Vranitzky—and so on. I'm always gratified to find dozens of Szabos, and I see that the Vienna directory has 27 columns of Swobodas!

What these realities reflect are *kinships:* both in the literal sense of the word and in the broader symbolic and cultural sense of the word. Even where individual Austrians might be reluctant to recognize and resist the imputation of kinship with their eastern and southern neighbours, nothing is more obvious—and, I might add, *more distinctive and characteristic—* about the Austrian identity than precisely that kinship. It may be disconcerting for people who dislike one another for linguistic, national or even racial reasons, to be told how similar they are to the very objects of their antipathy. As a historian it certainly has always amused me how many nineteenth-century German nationalists had Czech names and how many Czech nationalists had German names! The filaments of that very fundamental kinship with the family of nations once under the scepter of the Habsburgs are, of course, most easily recognizable in non-linguistic areas, but as has been pointed out above, those are precisely the areas which come closest to the aesthetic central European soul. Architecture is the most-often cited example, for by that index it is even today still possible to discern where the borders were a hundred years ago. But, just as they had played a great integrating role ever since the Baroque, it was the arts in general that were long held up as the last great integrator of the future.

In 1899 the Imperial Austrian government founded a new Arts Council whose role, as then Minister of Culture, Wilhelm von Hartel (1839-1907), clearly stated, was to give formal recognition and support to the common identity of the peoples of the Monarchy as a *Kunstvolk.* "Although every development is rooted in national soil," Hartel said, "yet works of art speak a common language [in this monarchy] ... and lead to mutual understanding and respect." It may appear to us that the arts were unable to bear this daunting burden and fulfill their designated role in the face of the intolerant nationalisms which gripped central Europe in the decades that followed, but one can hardly imagine the recovery and crystallization of the Austrian identity in the Second Republic without them. *This* was the cultural legacy upon which the Austrian identity was built first and foremost. *This* was the precious treasure which the Second Republic could exploit, the golden reservoir from which it could draw its own most flattering and distinctive self-images. But, to return now to the question of kinship, this was an Austrian achievement in the larger imperial sense of the word. If the Austrian identity is determined in large measure by basking in this achievement, then that pride is contingent on the recognition of the kinships which created it. And here it becomes necessary to touch upon the most painful and tragic wound of all in the tragic history of twentieth century central Europe: the extermination and expulsion of its Jews. As Steven Beller has been at pains to point out, the great cultural legacy which is the heart of the Austrian identity owes so much to Austria's Jews—both in its creation and in its preservation (often only in emigration!)—that no Austrian should fail to acknowledge this most fundamental kinship of all. One cannot fail to be impressed how often over the past century pan-German nationalism and anti-Semitism in Austria went hand in hand. If Austrians now reject the former as absurd, they must be equally vociferous in rejecting the absurdity of the latter. If Austrians are who they would like to think they are, they must always keep before their eyes that this is so because of their very peculiar pluralistsic historical tradition. Ironically, it is perhaps a lesson more easily learned in emigration, and for this reason I would like to turn to a number of points that are more conclusions from rather than an introduction to this study.

Now, it may seem that an immigrant from the lush sybaritic central European hot-house of epicurean and aesthetic pluralism would be very much out of his or her element in this majestically elemental frontier society with its relatively straight-forward English and French pieties. Yet this is not so. For Austrians the migration process simply tends to add additional layers of loyalties to the network of loyalties already in place. But Austrians seldom seem to perceive the acquisition of incremental layers of identity as an assimilationist threat; rather they perceive positive value in integration. There is sometimes nostalgia for the old country, but little alienation in the new. Long accustomed to the ambivalences of multiple identity, Austrians are indeed, as E. Wilder Spaulding said of those who emigrated to the United States, "quiet invaders." They appear to resist advocacy-group lobbying on their own behalf, partly, it seems, because they feel quite confident that the host society will be more than eager to adopt what Austrians have to offer without prompting or advertisement. Ironically, therefore, despite their own multicultural legacy, or perhaps because of it, Austrians do not seem to respond well to official multiculturalism as articulated in the current social science modes of "identity politics."

There is no doubt that Austrians who come to Canada, especially at first arrival, have a sense of linguistic community with Germans, Swiss, Danubian Swabians and other German-language groups. This sense of larger linguistic community, however, is muted by strong sub-national loyalties (that distinctive provincial patriotism mentioned above). The Burgenländer in particular have developed a most impressive array of organizations that almost never hear the "German" siren song. As suggested earlier, this sub-national ethos shades easily into a trans-national one, and this too seems to be reflected in Austrian organizations in this country. Austrian clubs everywhere are very heterogeneous, and seem to be magnets for the entire central European family of nations. Ironically, the only instances where Austrians felt themselves swamped by all these outsiders were instances where so many Germans joined extant Austrian societies that the Austrians left. This ties in directly with my next point.

Emigration has a way of facilitating the recognition of kinships. It has been argued by one historian that one of the fundamental errors of Thomas Masaryk was that he built his vision of a future Czechoslovakia on his American experience, and particularly on the observation of how similar Czech and Slovak immigrants in the Pittsburgh area were, how well they got along with each other. There was, of course, a particular emigration dynamic at work here which did not necessarily apply in the homeland. Related minorities in a totally alien environment must bury their differences in order to preserve more successfully what each in turn values. Emigration compels, first and foremost, the acquisition of a new language. But the moment all agree to speak a common second language, the solitudes imposed by linguistic incomprehension frequently melt away. Then one suddenly recognizes who does things in one's own familiar way: the Czech tailor, the Hungarian butcher, the Slovenian gardener, the Slovak electrician, the Croatian shoemaker. Austrians in emigration seem to recognize their true kinships with their former central European neighbours better, and they do so much more readily in Canada than they ever did at home.

Whether one chooses to call it assimilation or merely integration, it is undeniable that with each successive generation the process gradually strips away layers of the original Austrian identity. What is particularly interesting to observe, however, is that it does so on a hierarchical basis. One tends to jettison liabilities first; this is followed by matters of indifference, and only reluctantly do we surrender the things that truly warm the cockles of our hearts. It may very well be that in the present pluralistic Canadian reality which tolerates and even encourages diversity, one could cling to these last poignant vestiges indefinitely. Like the Germans, Austrians are quick to lose the language, and have one of the poorest second-language retention rates in Canada. This is certainly partly linked to the fact that speaking the German language openly was, for obvious historical reasons, a clear liability for many generations of immigrants in this century. But because Austria was not, as I have indicated, primarily a literary culture, it is easier for Austrians to maintain a larger spectrum of identity elements despite the erosion of the language. This is certainly true on the aesthetic side, with art and with music, and it seems even to be true on the folkloric side. But is it, of course, particularly true with material culture, and above all with food. In emigration one clings longest to what matters most. And in the end it is perhaps the stomach that is the most tenacious.

This dynamic process of shedding layers of identity and acquiring new ones over generations is, of course, common to all immigrant groups. The very existence of these immigrant groups, at whatever stage of the assimilation or integration process they may find themselves, in turn not only becomes a fundamental demographic, social and cultural reality of the host country, but in often subtly subversive ways, transforms the identity layers of the original hosts themselves. In time, no one can imagine life without the concrete elements of these many foreign cultures. Austrian migrants may be proud that among these Canada counts many things that are peculiarly Austrian. But perhaps the most important thing that the Austrian culture at its best can bring to distant lands is its own experience of the impoverishment that comes from xenophobia and the enrichment that comes from openness and pluralism. It is one of the noblest Austrian traditions of all, and one could do worse than to call its North American devotees simply "Canadians."

CHAPTER I
THE GROWTH OF AUSTRO-CANADIAN
RELATIONS TO 1968

Robert H. Keyserlingk and Bettina S. Steinhauser

CANADA IS THE SECOND-LARGEST geographical state in the world after Russia, but its modest population and colonial status long kept it from developing an independent state personality. Meanwhile, Austria-Hungary could boast of centuries of power and international influence. After 1918 the two countries found themselves to be on a more equal footing as Austria was reduced in size and Canada began to adopt the trappings of sovereignty. Currently, both countries live in the shadow of culturally-related but much more powerful neighbours.

This introductory chapter on Austrian-Canadian relations reflects past differences and more recent changes in the two countries' status. Before the 1950s, official relations between Canada and the Austro-Hungarian Empire and its successor republic—both here referred to simply as Austria—were weak and asymmetrical. For over a century, official ties stretched from Vienna to Canada, but were not reciprocated by Canada. Austrian consuls, at first honourary, existed in Canada since 1856—in other words, even before Canadian Confederation began to consolidate British North American colonies into a new unit called Canada. However, Canada possessed no official representatives in Austria until the mid-1950s.[1] While Austria had a long and proud diplomatic experience, Canada remained firmly embedded in the British Empire into the 1930s. External relations continued to be administered by Great Britain. British Imperial policies or treaties such as the 1876 Anglo-Austrian commercial treaty automatically applied to Canada.[2]

British Imperial unity, Canadian provincialism and regionalism, and the French-English division long precluded the evolution of a specific

Canadian identity and independent foreign policy.[3] Before the 1931 Statute of Westminster, Canada was not a sovereign state but rather a self-governing colony within the Empire.[4] In some practical areas of direct interest to Canada, such as commerce and immigration, Canadians were encouraged during the late nineteenth century to develop gradually some tenuous direct administrative relations with other states, especially Great Britain and the United States. A few Canadian immigration and trade representatives, together with a High Commissioner without any diplomatic status, came to be stationed in Great Britain. From time to time, others appeared on the European continent. None was sent to Austria before 1945. Free movement of immigrants, often without passports and minimum border controls, was encouraged by the miniature Canadian bureaucracy, while private agencies such as the Canadian Pacific Railway or shipping companies did the practical work.[5]

A separate Canadian Department of External Affairs was not set up until 1909. But even then it did not develop independent policy, long serving instead merely as an archive with a small staff of three, housed over a barber shop in Ottawa. Not until the 1920s did Canada begin to name and receive diplomatic representatives. In the meantime, other countries were sometimes represented within Canada by consuls. When the first External Affairs office was opened, the list of foreign consuls in Canada ran to 32. These foreign agents were granted their authority by writs of exequatur, or certificates of recognition, to operate in Canada by the British government in London. Most were permanent residents of Canada rather than career officers and their offices were situated in Montreal and Toronto instead of in the federal capital, Ottawa. Those few professional foreign consuls were not treated as diplomatic officers. They might at times be consulted on an informal basis by Canadian officials, but they never gained the diplomatic recognition they desired.[6]

Before 1900 Canadians, mainly in the major eastern seaports of Halifax and St. John, New Brunswick, acted as honourary Austrian consuls.[7] William Cunard of Halifax, founder of the famous shipping company, became the first honourary Austrian consul in Canada in 1856. A second honourary consul was later named in St. John. Then in 1900 began the huge wave of Austro-Hungarian immigration to Canada, which in the space of a decade and a half climbed to a quarter of a million. About 15% of these were termed Austrians, the rest Austro-Hungarian, of whom the largest group was Ukrainian.[8] As a result, an Austro-Hungarian Consulate

General was established in Montreal staffed for the first time by members of the Imperial and Royal Habsburg diplomatic service.

This new breed of Austrian consuls were men of great experience, most of it in eastern Europe and the Ottoman or Turkish Empire, possessing command of many languages.[9] Ferdinand Freyesleben, who opened the Montreal Consulate General in 1902, came from New York after five postings in the United States and was to go on to Calcutta after Montreal.[10] His 1907 successor, Alexander Pescha von Kis-Zsam, had served mainly in the Ottoman Turkish empire before coming to Canada, after which post he retired. He was fluent in a dozen Germanic, Slavic and Near Eastern languages.[11] Upon his return to Vienna in 1909, Pescha fell into a serious dispute with his successor, Hans Schlegel, over money, which at first cut into his pension and stopped royal thanks for his service upon his retirement. The case was settled in his favour and Dr. Schlegel was moved briefly to Winnipeg, where he opened the consulate.[12] Schlegel's successor the same year in Winnipeg, Nikolaus Ritter von Jurystowski, a lawyer by education, also had spent many years in the Near East before coming to Winnipeg.[13] Hermann Hann von Hannenheim, the last Consul General in Montreal before the outbreak of war, also spent most of his career in the Ottoman Empire before coming to Montreal.[14]

When Great Britain declared war in August 1914, Canada automatically was at war as well. Canada's active participation in World War I saw some movement towards a national identity and international status.[15] A Canadian delegation attended the Paris Peace Conference; Canada signed the Treaty of Versailles and was recognized as a separate member of the League of Nations. An important development came in 1931 with the British Statute of Westminster, which formally recognized the various British Dominions' right to full legal freedom. In 1927 Vincent Massey was named the first Canadian diplomatic envoy extraordinary abroad. He did not come from the seven-man staff of the small Department of External Affairs. Canada's non-diplomatic representation in Paris, established in 1882, acquired diplomatic status in 1928, and Tokyo was next in 1929. There were still no Canadian consulates abroad.[16]

The small post-1918 Austrian republic at first laboured under its enemy alien status and extreme poverty. A small embassy was opened in London, England, in 1919 under Georg Franckenstein, who was to remain there to the end of World War II. Only in 1925 was the Montreal consulate reopened as one of three Austrian consulates abroad.[17] In early 1930, because of growing trade between Canada and Austria, Austria decided to establish its first Consulate General in Ottawa and appointed Ludwig Klein-wächter, who had previously served in Chicago and Washington, to run it.[18] Kleinwächter's reports home from Ottawa indicated that Austrians were exceptionally well viewed in Canada. For upon his arrival in Ottawa, he was immediately invited to the Governor General's private drawing room, some-thing only to be dreamt of by other consuls in Canada.[19] He dwelt on Cana-dians' distrust of Germans, despite a clear improvement of Canadians' atti-tudes in this regard. For instance, Canadians blamed the Germans rather than the Austrians for the failed 1930 Austro-German customs union.[20]

Opened with such great hopes in early 1930, the Consulate General was again closed in December 1931 because of the Depression.[21] Until the 1938 *Anschluss,* Austria was again represented in Canada by an honourary consul in Montreal, a Canadian citizen of Irish background.[22] During the 1930s all but a fraction of Canada's political and commercial relations continued to be with the United Kingdom and the United States. A most-favoured nation treaty was reluctantly signed by Canada with Austria in the mid-1930s.[23] Canada chose to drift along its comfortable path of iso-lationism and appeasement, a policy guaranteed to exclude real interest in Hitler's expansionist plans concerning Austria.[24]

Canada's hands-off policy towards the deteriorating international scene hardly changed at all. Although some Canadians cautiously recog-nized that membership in the League of Nations could be useful for con-sultations, collective security and sanctions were not generally viewed as effective. Without their own diplomatic representatives in major Euro-pean capitals, Canadian politicians and officials continued to gain their information about European affairs through optimistic British sources such as Sir Neville Henderson, the British ambassador in Berlin.[25]

When the March 1938 *Anschluss* took place, the Canadians adopted the same attitude as the British and Americans, displaying less shock at the action itself than at Hitler's brutal and illegal methods of achieving this goal. Many Canadians, too, had long believed that such a union was inevitable and they were delighted that it took place without endangering the general peace.[26] As Canada had no diplomatic relations with Austria, it was not forced to react publicly to the event.[27] After the *Anschluss,* when the Austrian state disappeared, its official files in Canada were handed over to the German embassy in Ottawa, which shipped them to Germany the next year. Apparently, they were almost totally lost during the course of the war.[28] Kleinwächter, who had returned to Vienna in 1931, was tem-porarily jailed in 1938 by the Nazis.

Once war started the Canadians appeared to discover their international conscience. The government could claim to the public that Canada had never recognized the *Anschluss de jure*.[29] At a more confidential level, however, the government agreed with the British that restoration of Austria should not become an Allied war aim.[30] Austrians in Canada were classed as enemy aliens and German citizens, and ten were interned as dangerous enemy aliens. Ex-Austrians in Canada since 1922 were also forced to register with the police. Canada held several thousand German and Austrian nationals in internment camps for the British government, which during the Fifth Column scare of 1940 had sent these civilians to Canada for safe-keeping.[31] Following representations by Austrian refugees in Canada, the Canadian government considered making a distinction between Germans and Austrians, but in the end turned this idea down.[32] However, in the fall of 1942 it decreed that all enemy aliens, except the Japanese, would be treated as friendly aliens if they agreed to take out papers towards Canadian naturalization.[33] The government admitted that most Austrians in Canada "have shown their hostility to the Nazi regime and their loyalty to Canada."[34] By the end of that year, Austrians and Italians were freed from the duty to register, even though they still legally remained enemy aliens.[35]

Little serious attention was paid to Austrian exiles in Canada as a group. The British, for propaganda purposes, encouraged the establishment of friendly governments-in-exile, but chose not to do so for Austria.[36] The British did send an Austrian exile, Hans Roth, to Canada to set up the Free Austrian Movement, a moderate monarchist group. But it received no official recognition in Canada, despite some Canadian sympathy, and in 1942 moved its center of activities to the United States.[37] A friend of Roth's, a certain Dr. Klein, was permitted to put out an English-language Austrian exile news magazine called *Voice of Austria,* and a group of private Canadians formed the "Canadian Friends of Austria."[38] However, the British and Canadian governments agreed that the various bickering Austrian exile groups, which refused to unite in a common cause, were too divided to be useful to the war effort or to be granted political influence.[39]

During World War II, psychological warfare considerations played a large role in the Western Allies' military strategy. Learning false lessons from the Central Powers' 1918 defeat, which was termed a morale rather than military collapse, and Hitler's apparent use of psychological means to gain power and overwhelm his military opponents, Western planners

throughout World War II calculated that bringing about the internal collapse of German morale might be the most feasible way to bring the war
to an end without the need to invade the continent militarily and suffer
another bloodbath as had taken place in World War I.[40] Canadian
wartime studies identified Austria as an excellent target for propaganda
warfare, a conclusion agreed to by the British and Americans.[41] As the
Allies moved up Italy towards Austria in 1943, psychological warfare
experts convinced their governments to issue a declaration to the effect
that the *Anschluss* was null and void, that Austria was to be liberated and
restored as a state, and that Austrians should co-operate with the Allies in
order to expiate any guilt they may have gathered upon themselves
through their co-operation with the Nazis. This declaration was issued in
late 1943 and became known as the Moscow Declaration on Austria. Its
aim was not to put forth an Allied war aim, but to try to bring about
rebellion in ex-Austria.[42]

Consequently, the Moscow Declaration had no influence on Canadian—or Anglo-American—post-war planning.[43] Wilhelm Wunsch, newly-
elected head of the Free Austrian Movement in Canada, appealed in 1945
to the Canadian government and public opinion for a more positive view
towards post-war Austria, but in vain.[44] As far as the Canadian government was concerned, Austria had in fact disappeared as a state in 1938. It
might possibly be recreated after the war—but only if its security and
well-being could be guaranteed in some way and European security was
not compromised. If this were not possible, one would have to fit it into
some larger type of Danubian federation, or if all else failed, even con-
template leaving it inside a greater Germany. To again set up a weak,
failed state as Austria had been before 1938 could only lead to another
Anschluss or to Soviet expansion.[45] Certain influential public voices were
raised in Canada pointing out that most Austrians had been anti-Nazi
and deserved special treatment. But these voices, too, grew fainter when
it became clear in 1944 that the Moscow Declaration had not triggered
the hoped-for rebellion in Austria against the Nazi regime there.[46] The
future for a positive post-war Austrian-Canadian relationship looked
bleak indeed.

At the end of World War II, the two countries' international positions differed radically. As part of the victorious Allied coalition, Canada
had established itself as a middle power and undergone economic
growth.[47] Austria, on the other hand, had become an integral part of Nazi
Germany after 1938, and in 1945 was left in a disastrous economic and

political situation.[48] The country was to remain divided and occupied for the next decade. During this period, Austria struggled to gain recognition and support against the Soviets from Western countries such as Canada. However, Canada remained remarkably deaf to Austrian pleas. It preferred to remain free of the Big Four occupation of Austria, not because it was blind to Austria's fragile position, but because it did not wish to become a client of the occupying powers. Canada, like other smaller Allied powers, had found with some disappointment that its wartime military participation did not lead to real political influence on Allied occupation or peace policies. As a result, between 1945 and the conclusion of the Austrian State Treaty in 1955, Canada chose to ignore Austrian pleas for diplomatic recognition.

In this period, Canada was run by Liberal governments beginning with that of Mackenzie King and ending in 1957 with the defeat of the St. Laurent government. After 1945, the Canadian Department of External Affairs still concerned itself largely with British and American affairs, although the influence of the United States became stronger both economically and politically. This newly emerging superpower hoped for loyalty and support from its northern neighbour on the North American continent. Canada's new-found prosperity allowed it to aid the war-torn European countries, such as Austria and in particular Britain.[49]

In April 1945, Soviet troops moved into Austria, the first contingent of the Allied armies to occupy Austrian territory. American, British and French troops began to move into western Austria a month later. Austria, like Germany, was divided into four occupation zones. The Soviets administered the northeastern fourth of the country directly, and confiscated major industrial plants in Lower Austria and Styria as reparations.[50] Soviet occupation policies and strong internal Communist pressure acted as serious sources of instability for the country's weak economy. The first post-war Austrian government was elected in November 1945,[51] with the Communists polling 5% of the vote. In an attempt to build up its independence and to gain assistance in providing the necessities of life to its people, the fledgling republic was eager to win help from the Western powers. Therefore, one major Austrian foreign policy goal was to establish diplomatic relations with as many of the Western democratic states as possible.

A first overture to Canada was made very quickly by the Austrian representative in Washington, Ludwig Kleinwächter. As mentioned above, Kleinwächter had briefly acted as Austrian Consul General in Canada in the early 1930s. After World War II, he was appointed to Washington and was commissioned by the Austrian government to represent his country not only in the United States but also in Canada. In the years following, Austrian diplomats in Washington and London approached the Canadian Department of External Affairs repeatedly, but in vain, with requests that diplomatic relations be opened with the new Austrian republic.[52]

Despite the Canadian cabinet's negative stance towards Austria, influential members of Canada's younger generation of diplomats like Hume Wrong, Lester Pearson, and Norman Robertson were in favour of helping the young republic strengthen its ties to the West by opening diplomatic relations. In 1948, following further communications from the increasingly frustrated Austrians, Lester Pearson told Louis St. Laurent, then the Secretary of State for External Affairs, "that our Ambassador in Washington [Wrong] and our High Commissioner in London [Robertson] both expressed regret that we did not accede to the Austrian Government's minimum request ... for a Consulate General."[53] Wrong felt that Austrian representation was needed in Canada to provide consular services so that information could be accessed more easily in connection with Canadian subsidies provided under the Marshall Plan. He added that he was "rather loath to undertake to explain to my Austrian colleague here the reasons for our reluctance when we have in Ottawa, let us say, a Haitian Consul General, a Lebanese Consul, and a Finnish Minister."[54] From London, Canadian High Commissioner Norman Robertson understood the Cabinet's reluctance to open a Canadian office in Vienna under the occupation regime, but suggested that Canada accept an Austrian representative without sending a Canadian to Austria. "[O]ur general policy in the past has been to put no obstacle in the way of friendly countries establishing Consulates in Canada, particularly if there was no implication of reciprocity in such arrangement. I think it would be difficult to make an exception in this rule against Austria."[55]

However, despite these arguments, Canadian prime ministers Mackenzie King and then Louis St. Laurent continued to postpone any decision to open relations with the Alpine republic.[56] In the summer of 1948, following another rejection, Pearson echoed his colleague Wrong's embarrassment. He commented bitterly that "I need hardly say how reluctant I am to pass on a decision of this kind. It is embarrassing ... to tell the Austrian government that we will not receive a consular representative."[57] In 1948 St. Laurent claimed that finances were the problem: "[w]e are not able to expand at the moment."[58] Staff shortage was also given as another reason preventing Canada from setting up a diplomatic mission in Austria. But the most important factor was that Canada preferred not to become powerlessly associated with the occupation of Austria, as it had not been given any role in negotiations for a peace treaty. The Canadian government wanted not only to be consulted by the great powers but also to participate meaningfully in decision-making. As this was not possible, Canadians refused to become involved in U.S.-Soviet friction over Austria.[59] Austria's final fate continued to be unclear and it appeared likely that Soviet influence in Austria would become stronger. So Canadians hesitated until Western policy towards Austria and Austria's future became clearer. As St. Laurent wrote, "I prefer to wait until I can suggest something more obvious in the way of advantages of a grouping of the Western powers."[60] Meanwhile, in 1947 Canada opened legations in Czechoslovakia, Poland, and Yugoslavia because in the growing Cold War these posts became important sources of information.

But Austria was still ignored. Finally, as a result of a constant flow of letters from the Austrian legations in Britain and the United States, Canada agreed in 1949 to the establishment of an Austrian consulate general in Ottawa.[61] A few years later, Canada haltingly established similar consular relations with Austria. In part, this shift resulted from an improved fiscal situation within the Department of External Affairs.[62] Canadians also came to realize that Vienna, still occupied by the four powers and close to the Iron Curtain, had become the center of Eastern and Western intelligence services. Arthur Andrew, the first Canadian diplomat to set up a mission in Austria, soon realized that one officer was not enough to cope with the increasing workload. Following a trip to Europe in mid-1953, R.A. Mackay, a senior bureaucrat in the Department of External Affairs noted: "[a]t the very least this is a two-officer post."[63] He also emphasised that he was "highly impressed with the importance of Austria and particularly Vienna in the Cold War."[64] Furthermore, MacKay wrote to Charles Ritchie, another senior official, that Canadians were under the moral obligation to support a democratic Austria. As well, it was imperative for Canadians to develop their own sources of information about Austrian affairs, including relations between the occupying powers, the other Danubian states, trade possibilities and immigration.[65] Still, Canada hesitated to open full diplomatic relations with the Austrian republic. In Ottawa the two Austrian consuls, Friedrich Riedl-Riedenstein and Kurt F. Paümann, continued to try to convince the Canadian Department of External Affairs to permit the exchange of ambassadors.[66] Their successor, Walter Peinsipp, who became Chargé d'Affaires in 1952, seemed to be less active in this regard.[67]

Things began to move again in the mid-1950s. In 1955 the Austrian State Treaty was signed between the occupying powers and Austria. As a result, Austria was freed of foreign troops and regained its full sovereignty and independence. In addition, the International Atomic Energy Commission, of which Canada was a permanent member, came to be located in Vienna.[68] A successful visit to Canada by the Federal Chancellor of Austria, Julius Raab, underlined the priority Austria put on full diplomatic recognition by Canada.[69] With the arrival in Canada of Kurt Waldheim in early 1956, Austria gained an forceful spokesman for the improvement of Austrian-Canadian relations. Arthur Andrew, who had met the Waldheims during his mission in Vienna, wrote that "I was delighted to hear that the Austrian Government has asked for our agreement for the appointment of Kurt Waldheim as Austrian Minister to Ottawa. Both he and his wife ... are charming people in the best Viennese tradition."[70] Waldheim was eager to strengthen Canadian-Austrian ties. Not only did he quickly make himself familiar with Canada's domestic and foreign affairs, he became a frequent visitor to the Canadian Department of External Affairs in order to obtain first-hand information about Canadian policies and push for full ambassadorial recognition. Reports from the Canadian legation in Vienna suggesting an urgent need to enlarge and upgrade Canadian representation, finally convinced External Affairs to allow Vienna and Ottawa to move towards full diplomatic relations.[71] Finally in 1958, during Waldheim's Ottawa period, Austria was permitted to change its legation to an embassy. Waldheim became known in Vienna for his intelligent reports to the Austrian foreign office, informing his colleagues about Canadian and North American perspectives on international politics.[72]

However, Canada still hesitated to sign the Austrian State Treaty. Canada went along with other smaller states like the Netherlands, Belgium and the Scandinavian countries, which at that point had also not yet signed it. Waldheim's main task now was to convince Canadian officials to accede to the Treaty. In January 1959 Waldheim reported, after a meeting with Davis, then in charge of the European Division of the Canadian Department of External Affairs, that "Ottawa consulted the Dutch and the Belgian governments, which had decided not to sign the Austrian State Treaty because of legal problems about property. Davis explained that these countries had to be consulted so that the opposition's critique could be rejected."[73] Another factor delaying a decision were the results of the 1957 Canadian election, which brought the Conservatives to power after two decades of Liberal rule. The Conservatives did not trust bureaucrats, whom they saw as Liberal appointees, and were at first unwilling to follow External Affairs' advice, which now had become favourable to signing the Austrian State Treaty. As a result, a backlog of foreign policy decisions grew.[74] Only in 1959, following renewed efforts by Waldheim, did the Canadians sign the treaty.[75]

Canada regarded neutral Austria, a small state in the middle of Europe, with respect and admired its stable political and economic condition. Canadian Ambassador, J.S. MacDonald, wrote in September 1959:

Indeed, apart from the South Tyrol[76] and reparations questions, Austria has few problems with any country. Even the problems which often disturb and divide other nations internally are here entirely absent. There is no race or colour problem—they are one people. There is no linguistic problem—they all speak German. There is no sectarian problem—they are practically all Catholics together. Moreover, as a nation which has accepted military neutrality, they have no armament problem.... Austria is becoming the Welfare State par excellence."[77]

In 1960, Waldheim's work in Canada came to an end. The Department of External Affairs judged his stay in Canada to have been very successful. In a very detailed departmental memorandum about Waldheim it was noted that "in his dealings with the Department he has shown himself to be dedicated to his work and an effective exponent of his government's policies."[78] At the same time, Waldheim drafted his own perceptive final judgement about Canada. He reminded Vienna that Canada's and Austria's identity problems and relationship with their larger neighbours bore a certain similarity. "The country is eager to keep its distinct identity. Nothing hurts the Canadians more than identifying them as Americans." It was therefore vital to "deal with Canadian political, economic and cultural affairs from a Canadian post.... Imagine how we would react, if foreign offices situated in Germany would deal with Austria, just because we speak the same language as our neighbours do."[79]

Waldheim's successor in Ottawa, Eugen Buresch, focussed his attention on encouraging trade between the two countries. At the same time, he was very sympathetic to Canada's sometimes difficult relations with the United States, resulting from massive American investments in Canada and Canada's criticism of American foreign policy.[80] Like his predecessor,

Buresch emphasized that relations between Canada and the United States were of particular interest to Austria, as Austria faced similar problems with West Germany. When the Liberal Party, now under Lester Pearson, returned to power in 1963, Buresch believed that Canada, after some years of unstable domestic and foreign policy, would regain some of that strong international reputation it had built up for itself after the war. In 1964, shortly before Buresch left Canada, he reported that "our correspondence with the Canadian foreign office is very frank.... I am convinced that this mission, now that the Pearson government has strengthened its position, will regain its former importance as a listening post."[81]

But in spite of their similar identity problems and their utility as listening posts, neither Canada nor Austria saw any pressing reasons to deepen political ties with each other.[82] Many other factors drew them in other directions. Geography, economics and ideology generally determined that Canada associate itself more with American foreign policy, while Austria struggled to maintain its neutrality and sovereignty within Europe. Their respective large neighbours, the United States and Germany, were necessarily of predominant interest. Although trade between Canada and Austria increased, these commercial relations were almost negligible compared with other trading partners.[83] Whereas Austrian immigration to Canada had played such a large role in the 1950s that the Austrian government had tried to regulate it, by the 1960s the trans-Atlantic surge died down. In 1968 the Canadian Department of External Affairs described Austrian-Canadian relations as friendly, but "not close and ... limited mainly to consultations from time to time on various issues facing the UN and the international financial and trade organizations."[84]

In conclusion, although Austria was represented in Canada by consuls even before 1867, Canada opened up consular and then diplomatic relations with Austria reluctantly after 1945. Not until the 1950s did Canada slowly begin to take any real interest in Austria. On the other hand, post-World War II Austria began its requests to Canada to establish diplomatic relations with it almost immediately after the end of that war. The urgency sprang from a sense of pressing necessity to tighten its ties to the Western democracies against the Soviet threat. Yet Canada held back, afraid to become a pawn in great power politics. Only in the 1950s did the two countries gradually develop full diplomatic relations and did Canada accede to the Austrian State Treaty. What resulted from this flurry of activity were friendly, but perhaps increasingly divergent, interests as subsequently the two countries' priorities shifted elsewhere.

AUSTRO-HUNGARIAN/AUSTRIAN
CONSULS IN CANADA TO 1953*

Year	Halifax	Montreal	Maritimes	Winnipeg	Ottawa
1856	William Cunard to 1877				
1870		Alfred Hasche? Edward Schutzle to 1902			
1878	All Offices Vacant				
1881	W.H. Hart to 1896				
1882			St. John, NB Vice-Consul H. Thompson to 1900		
1897	H.L Chipman to 1914				
1900		Becomes a consulate general			
1901			St. John, NB Percy Thompson n.d. **Pictou** Consular Agent C. Dwyer to 1906		
1903		Dr. Ferdinand Freyesleben to 1907			

* Based on the annual British publications, 1865-1953, *Imperial Calendars* and *Foreign Office Lists,* "Foreign Embassies, Legations and Consulates in British Dominions," found in reference sections of the Public Records Office, London, England.

Year	Halifax	Montreal	Maritimes	Winnipeg	Ottawa
1908		Alexander Pesche von Kis-Zsam to 2. 1909 Hans Schlegel to 12. 1909	Sydney, NS Consular Agent Alex Neil McLennan to 1914		
1910		Hans von Hannenheim to 1914	Hans Schlegel to 1911		
1911				Nikolaus Ritter von Jurystowski to 1914	
1914-19	All Offices Closed				
1919		Frederick Franke to 1925			
1925		Vice-Consul Albert Müller to 1929			
1930					Consul General Ludwig Kleinwächter to 1931
1931		Honorary Consul Thomas Guerin to 1938			
1938-48	All Offices Closed				
1948					Consul General Friederich Riedl-Riedenstein to 1952
1953					Minister Max Loewenthal Chumecky. Hon. Vice-Consul K.F.G. Paümann

ENDNOTES

1. Pamela A. McDougall, *Report of the Royal Commission on Conditions of Foreign Service* (Ottawa, 1981), lists of Canadian officials overseas from the 1880s to 1940, pp. 95-105, Table FST-2.
2. After 1880, Canada could ask to be excluded from British treaties if it wished.
3. Until 1914 aliens naturalized in Canada remained aliens in the rest of the British Empire. M. Hancock. "Naturalization in Canada," *Proceedings of the Canadian Political Science Association* 6 (1934), 33.
4. George Parkin Glazebrook, *A History of Canadian External Relations. The Formative Years to 1914* (Toronto, 1966) I, 82ff.
5. The list of Canadian officials in charge of immigration services in Britain and Europe can be found in Canada, Department of Manpower and Immigration (unpublished draft), "Canada's Immigration Overseas Service: A Summary History and List of Overseas Posts, 1867-1987," Ottawa, 1987, Appendix 1. The first Agent-in-Chief for Britain and Europe was named in 1872 and stationed in London, England. No Canadian immigration representatives were stationed in Austria before 1945. Other Canadian emigration offices on the continent existed from 1870. Antwerp was the first, followed by Paris and Hamburg (1872), LeHavre (1874), and Copenhagen (1914). After World War I others were established in The Hague, Danzig, Riga, Bucharest, Warsaw, Bremen, Gdynia, Hong Kong, and Lisbon. The first Austrian office was in Salzburg, which opened in 1949. *Ibid.,* Appendix 3. For consular representation, see John Hilliker, ed., *Canada's Department of External Affairs,* Volume I: *The Early Years, 1909-1946* (Ottawa, 1990), cf. index entry "consular representation."
6. See Sir Wilfried Laurier's 1910 unsuccessful attempt to give consuls higher status in Canada. Canada, *House of Commons Debates,* 1909-10, p. 853.
7. See attached list of Austrian consuls in Canada to 1945 in the Appendix.
8. Austrian Immigration to Canada Collection, "Austrian Immigration to Canada: Statistical Highlights."
9. We are grateful to the archivist, Dr. Hutterer, of Vienna's Österreichisches Staatsarchiv [hereafter ÖStA] for excerpts from the consuls' personnel files and the official *Austro-Hungary. Jahrbuch des K. und K. Auswärtigen Dienstes 1914* (Vienna, 1914), hereafter cited as *K. und K. Jahrbuch.*
10. Born in 1864, Freyesleben had a trade and commercial training before being sent to his first post in Pittsburgh in 1893. *K. und K. Jahrbuch,* p. 277.
11. Born in 1852, Pescha went to the Oriental Academy before being sent to his first post in Alexandria in 1874. Before taking over the Montreal Consulate General, he served in Belgrade, Mostar, Adrianople, Sarajevo, Constantinople, Scutari, Prisen,

Widden, Petras, Allepo and Liverpool. *Ibid.,* p. 376. His languages included French, English, Italian, Turkish, German, Hungarian, Rumanian, and all South Slav languages as well as writing Russian and getting by in Norwegian. ÖStA, Gruppe O1: Auswärtige Angelegenheiten, Bundesministerium für Auswärtige Angelegenheiten [henceforth BMAA], Pescha, "Sprachkenntnisse," Petras, 25 June 1898.

12. *Ibid.,* Pescha to Foreign Minister Alois von Aehrenthal, 12 December 1910. Born in 1875, Schlegel also graduated from the Oriental Academy and before his Montreal and Winnipeg postings was sent to Chicago, Buffalo, Pittsburgh, Zurich, Capetown, Salonica and New York. He was sent from Montreal to open the Winnipeg consulate in October 1909, but probably because of his 1910 differences with Pescha, was relieved in December 1910. He later went to the consulates in Denver and St. Louis. *K. und K. Jahrbuch,* p. 410.

13. *K. und K. Jahrbuch,* pp. 319-20. He was fluent in German, French, Polish, Russian, English and Italian and had some Serbo-Croatian. ÖStA: BMAA, "Qualificationstabelle," 15 March 1911.

14. Born in 1868, Hann von Hannenheim also studied at the Oriental Academy and was stationed in Trieste, Alexandria, Cairo, Bucharest, Crajova, then again in Cairo and Belgrade before coming to Canada. *K. und K. Jahrbuch,* p. 298.

15. Canadian historian Arthur Lower's famous statement that "Canada entered the war as a colony, she emerged from it close to an independent state" seems overly optimistic. Arthur R.M. Lower, *Colony to Nation. A History of Canada* (Toronto, 1946), p. 470.

16. Hugh L. Keenleyside, "Forward [sic]," in Keenleyside, et als., *The Growth of Canadian Policies in External Affairs* (Durham, NC and London, 1960), p. 4.

17. Consul Frederick Franke ran the office until 1925 when Vice-Consul Albert Mueller took over. The other two Austrian consulates in 1925 were in Melbourne and Bombay. See pp. 37-38, this volume.

18. Kleinwächter reappeared in the United States in 1946 as Austria's first post-war representative there. See below.

19. ÖStA, NPA, 571. Liasse GB 2/11 (Kanada), 2115. Kleinwächter to Johann Schober, Bundeskanzler and Bundesminister für Auswärtige Angelegenheiten, Ottawa, 26 March 1930.

20. *Ibid.,* Kleinwächter to Schober, (n.d.) 1930. He also may have revealed his sympathies for a monarchical revival in Austria by claiming that such a development would be acceptable to Canadians.

21. Kleinwächter's personnel file in *ibid.,* F4. AA memo, 10 November 1931, to the *Wanderungsamt* to the effect that Kleinwächter was to return to Vienna.

22. The honourary consul was a private businessman, Thomas Guerin.

23. National Archives of Canada, Ottawa [hereafter NAC], RG 25, Department of

External Affairs, A12, 2094. Austria imported mainly Canadian wheat and some cars. Austria was not happy with mutual trade relations because Canada restricted the entry of Austrian goods to Canada. In 1934-36, Canada exported $254,000 worth of goods to Austria, but imported goods valued at only $24,000.

24. James Eayrs, *In Defence of Canada: Peacemaking and Deterrence* (Toronto, 1972), p. 168. Cf. Robert H. Keyserlingk, "Invisible Austria: Canada's View 1938-1959," *Austrian History Yearbook* 19-20, (1983-84), Pt. 2, 149-77; and "Grundsatz oder Besatzung: Kanada und Österreich," *Zeitgeschichte* 10 (1983), 227-39.

25. Felix Gilbert, "Two British Ambassadors: Perth and Henderson," in Gordon A. Craig and Felix Gilbert, eds., *The Diplomats 1919-39* (Princeton, 1955), p. 543; James Eayrs, "'A Low Dishonest Decade': Aspects of Canadian Foreign Policy 1931-39," in Gillespie, ed. *Growth of Canadian Policies*, p. 59ff.

26. NAC, RG 25, G1, 1556, Note to His Excellency, the Governor General in Council, 8 April 1938, and Canadian Secretary of State for External Affairs to the British Secretary of State for Dominion Affairs, 19 January 1939.

27. *Ibid.,* 1876, Departmental legal adviser J.E. Read memorandum, "Summary of the Note Concerning the Position of Austria," 6 March 1939.

28. A few scattered papers do exist in Bonn, but they are too anecdotal to be useful.

29. NAC, RG 25, G1,1876, O.D. Skelton, Under-Secretary of State for External Affairs to Philip F. Vineburg, 4 September 1939.

30. *Ibid.,* 197, Secretary of State for Dominion Affairs to Department of External Affairs, 9 November 1939.

31. *Ibid.,* G1, 1964 for the 1940-41 internment statistics. See also: J.J. Kelly, "The Prisoner of War Camps in Canada 1939-47," (unpublished M.A. thesis, University of Windsor, 1976), chapters 1-4; Keyserlingk, "Invisible Austria," pp. 157-60.

32. NAC, RG 25, 773-F-40, Secretary of State for External Affairs, N.A.R. Robertson, to RCMP Commissioner Wood, 21 April 1942.

33. NAC, MG 26, J4, Mackenzie King Papers, 249, Conference Bulletin, 17 October 1942, Department of External Affairs.

34. NAC, RG 25, 2915-40C, press release, 24 December 1942.

35. *Ibid.* Also, Keyserlingk, "Invisible Austria," p. 161.

36. David Stafford, *Britain and the European Resistance, 1940-45* (London, 1980), p. 2ff; Robert H. Keyserlingk, "Austrian Restoration and Nationalism: A British Dilemma During World War II," *Canadian Review of Studies in Nationalism* 9 (1982), 289-90.

37. NAC, RG 25, D1, 822, Prime Minister's instructions to cabinet on political refugees, 16 July 1942. On the Free Austrian Movement, see *ibid.,* 3241-40C, "Organization and Status of the Free Austrian Movement in Canada," 3 July 1941 and 20 January 1942.

38. *Toronto Globe and Mail*, 16 November 1944. The editor of the influential magazine *Saturday Night*, B.K Sandwell, was a leading member of this pro-Austrian group.

39. NAC, RG 25, 7-P9s, Canadian Secretary of State for External Affairs to British Secretary of State for Dominion Affairs, 14 December 1943. National Archives, Washington, RG 59, Department of State, 863.01/782, Office of Strategic Services, "The Austrian Scene," 30 June 1943.

40. This Anglo-American Combined Chiefs of Staff military-psychological strategy, called "Plan Rankin," existed into 1945.

41. NAC, MG 26, 462, Most secret memorandum to the Prime Minister on psychological warfare and the Moscow Declaration on Austria, 25 August 1943; NAC, RG 26, 5353-S-40C, T.A. Stone memorandum, "Psychological Warfare Directed at Austria," 18 December 1943; *ibid.*, post-war Canadian report "Psychological Warfare [in Canada]," 3 July 1946.

42. For more on the Moscow Declaration as a military-psychological rather than a political tool, see Robert H. Keyserlingk, *Austria in World War II: An Anglo-American Dilemma* (Kingston and Montreal, 1988), pp. 87-156.

43. *Ibid.*, p. 123ff.

44. NAC, RG 25, 4697-S-40, 6 March 1945.

45. *Ibid.*, legal adviser J.E. Read still held the view in 1953 that the Allies had taken the Austrian area in 1945 into their complete control through unconditional surrender, that they could deal with the area as they wished and that Austria had been an enemy country which should sign a peace treaty in the same way as Germany must. J.O. Perry, External Affairs Legal Division, 21 December 1953.

46. The *Toronto Globe and Mail*, 12 September 1944, wrote "at present, in the eyes of the world, they [Austrians] are involved in deep complicity with Hitler and his gangsters. If they did nothing for themselves, the country should be treated 'as a defeated Nazi vassal.'" *Ibid.*, 14 October 1944.

47. Robert Bothwell, Ian Drummond, and John English, *Canada Since 1945: Power, Politics, and Provincialism* (Toronto, 1981); Norman Hillmer and J.L. Granatstein, *Empire to Umpire: Canada and the World to the 1990s* (Toronto, 1994).

48. Erika Weinzierl and Kurt Skalnik, eds., *Österreich: Die Zweite Republik* (Vienna, 1972); Manfried Rauchensteiner, *Der Sonderfall: Die Besatzungszeit in Österreich 1945 bis 1955* (Vienna, 1987).

49. J.L. Granatstein, *How Britain's Weakness Forced Canada Into the Arms of the United States* (Toronto, 1989), pp. 43-62.

50. Manfried Rauchensteiner, *Die Zwei: Die grosse Koalition in Österreich, 1945-1966* (Vienna, 1987), pp. 201-02. The United States stopped requesting reparation payments from Austria in 1947, whereas the Soviet Union did so in 1953.

51. *Ibid.*, pp. 59-66.
52. NAC, RG 25, V. 2094, f. AR 36/4, containing several letters written by the Austrian representative in London, Heinrich Schmid, and Ludwig Kleinwächter in Washington.
53. *Ibid.*, V.6285, f. 8447-40, Memo to the Secretary of State for External Affairs (SSEA) from Pearson, 14 July 1948.
54. *Ibid.*, Wrong to Read, 28 May 1948.
55. *Ibid.*, Memo to the SSEA from Pearson, 14 July 1948.
56. *Ibid.*, Pearson to Robertson, 29 July 1948.
57. *Ibid.*, V. 2094, f. AR 36/4, Pearson to Robertson, 29 July 1948.
58. *Ibid.*, V. 6285, f. 8447-40, Memo to SSEA, 1 January 1948.
59. Charles Percy Stacey, *Canada In The Age of Conflict*, Volume 2: *The Mackenzie King Era 1921-1948* (Toronto, 1981), pp. 386-91; John Hilliker, "No Bread at the Peace Table: Canada and the European Settlement, 1943-7," *Canadian Historical Review* 61 (1980), 82.
60. NAC, RG 25, V. 6285, f. 8447-40, Memo to SSEA, 4 April 1948.
61. John Hilliker and Donald Barry, *Canada's Department of External Affairs. Volume 2: Coming of Age, 1946-1968* (Montreal, 1995), p. 12.
62. Arnold Heeney, who became Under-Secretary of the Department of External Affairs in 1949, reorganized the structure of his department, and consequently financial matters improved. *Ibid.*, pp. 49-57.
63. NAC, RG. 25, V. 4337, f. 1136-80-40, R.A. MacKay to Charles Ritchie, 19 August 1953.
64. *Ibid.*
65. *Ibid.*
66. Marina Decker-Paümann, "Kurt F. Paümann and the Establishment of Austro-Canadian Diplomatic Relations in the Post-War Era," (paper read at the international symposium, *Austrian Immigration to Canada*, Carleton University, Ottawa, 20 May 1995).
67. ÖStA: BMAA, Pol II, Kanada 1955, General Secretary of the Foreign Ministry to Federal Chancellor and Foreign Minister, 8 June 1955. Before this period, materials in the Austrian archives are unfortunately very sparse.
68. John W. Holmes, *The Better Part of Valour: Essays on Canadian Diplomacy* (Toronto, 1970), p. 7.
69. NAC, RG. 25, V. 4337, f. 1136-80-40, Memo to R.A.D. Ford from J. Ethier Blais on the Austrian representation in Canada, 13 December 1954.
70. NAC, RG 25, V. 6504, f. 8447-40, pt.2.1., Arthur Andrew to European Division, 18 January 1956.
71. *Ibid.*, V. 4337, f. 1136-80-40, Memo of the European Division of the Department of External Affairs on Canadian Representation in Austria, 28 June 1955.

72. Waldheim sent political reports to Austria at least twice a month. ÖStA: BMAA, Pol II, Kanada 1956-1960.

73. *Ibid.*, BMAA, Pol II, Kanada 1959, Waldheim to BKAA, 16 January 1959. Also, *Ibid.*, Ottawa 1956, Peinsipp to BKAA, 6 February 1956.

74. Hilliker and Barry, *Canada's Department of External Affairs*, pp. 154, 166.

75. Canada. Report of the Department of External Affairs. *Annual Report, 1959* (Ottawa, 1960). Canada acceded to the Austrian State Treaty, and a direct Canada-Austria air service was inaugurated.

76. Austria's relations with Italy were marred in the post-war years by a dispute concerning the special status within Italy of the German-speaking majority in the province of South Tyrol (Alto-Adige).

77. NAC, RG 25, V. 4248, f. 8447-40, pt.3, MacDonald to SSEA, 29 September 1959.

78. NAC, RG 25, V.4248, f. 8447-40, Memo for the Minister: Farewell Call of the Austrian Ambassador, 17 June 1960.

79. ÖStA, BMAA, Pol II, Kanada 1960, Waldheim to BKAA, 20 June 1960.

80. *Ibid.*, Kanada 1962, Buresch to BKAA, 3 January 1962.

81. *Ibid.*, Kanada 1964, Buresch to BKAA, January 1964.

82. NAC, RG 25, V. 3170, f. 36-1968-3 Vol. I, Special Task Force on Europe: Austria, November 1968: "Purely bilateral Canadian interests in Austria are minor. There are no bilateral political issues having a bearing on important or specific Canadian national interests."

83. *Ibid.*, "Austria is still a small Canadian export market. In 1967 it ranked as Canada's 45th export customer, accounting for slightly less than 1% of Canada's total exports to continental Western Europe. The best year for Canadian exports to Austria so far was 1966 when sales reached $11.6 million."

84. *Ibid.*

CHAPTER II
AUSTRIAN IMMIGRATION TO CANADA
IN THE IMPERIAL PERIOD

Michaela C. Schober

IMMIGRANTS FROM THE AUSTRO-HUNGARIAN EMPIRE began to arrive in Canada as early as the seventeenth century. They were soldiers, enrolled in French regiments which came to New France, sojourners, and settlers.[1] However, their number was insignificant. From the 1880s on, more Austro-Hungarians immigrated to Canada and, after the turn of the century, they were arriving on a large scale.

AUSTRIAN EMIGRATION REGULATIONS AND
CANADIAN IMMIGRATION POLICIES

The attitude of the Austrian government towards emigration was mainly passive. The right of individuals to emigrate, with the exception of those who had to serve in the army, was proclaimed in the constitutional law *(Staatsgrundgesetz)* of 1867. Formal restrictions were not introduced until March 1, 1914, when the government upon an initiative of the Imperial Ministry of the Interior and the War Administration established the so-called *Kontrolldienst* (control service) to observe and supervise emigration, primarily to prevent men liable to military service from crossing the border.[2]

Canadian immigration policy gradually shifted from one of "at least theoretically laissez faire" to a selective policy between 1896 and 1910.[3] Political considerations, in particular a "White Canada policy," and economic factors became more and more important. Clifford Sifton, Minister of the Interior in the Liberal government of Sir Wilfried Laurier from 1896-1905, was determined to settle the Canadian West with "experienced farmers from the American Middle West and Britain (if available), peasant farmers from Europe, or simply people who had been born on the land, preferably in northern regions, and who were accustomed to a pioneering life."[4] In 1899, the Canadian government concluded a clandestine agreement with the North Atlantic Trading Company for the systematic and responsible recruitment of continental European farming classes.[5] In 1905, W.S. Fielding, Canadian Minister of Finance, wrote to the Austrian Minister of the Interior, Count Bylandt Rheidt: "While we welcome the arrival of all healthy emigrants of good character, we especially desire emigrants of two classes for whom employment can always be found. The two classes ... are those engaged in agricultural pursuits and domestic servants."[6]

The agreement between the Canadian government and the North Atlantic Trading Company—although preferably aimed at Scandinavians and Germans—was given up in 1906, because it had encouraged, in the opinion of some, too many immigrants whom they considered "undesirable," in particular Ukrainians ("Galicians" or "Ruthenians"). The opponents to Sifton's immigration policy accused him "that his immigration policies were non-selective and indiscriminate, and that he was admitting 'illiterate Slavs in overwhelming numbers.'"[7] Two years later, in 1908, the Canadian government emphasised due to an economic crisis that "experienced farm workers, farmers financially able to take homesteads or to purchase land, and female servants" were the only ones wanted. Furthermore, it was pointed out that there were no jobs left for railway workers for 1908.[8] In spite of the former opposition against bringing too many Ukrainians into Canada, the Canadian Department of the Interior informed the Consul General of Austria-Hungary in Montreal that "homesteads may be taken by any person, irrespective of nationality."[9]

However, new immigration acts in 1906 and, in particular in 1910, increased the powers of the immigration officers to refuse the entry of "undesirable" immigrants.[10] The immigration regulations required that all immigrants, including family members who travelled along, had to bring a certain amount of money as well as a ticket to their "final" destination. Immigrants over 18 years of age had to have $25, and minor immigrants over five years of age half that amount, if they arrived between March and October. Arrivals during the rest of the year had to be in possession of $50 and $25, respectively. Immigrants who were travelling to naturalized and well-off immediate relatives, who were also willing to receive them, were exempted from this regulation. Anyone who had prearranged employment needed only a ticket and appropriate

money for provisions. Scandinavians and Germans, who had been classified as "desirable" immigrants, were exempted from this regulation in
1912.[11] Although immigrants from Austria-Hungary were not classified
as "desirable" they came to Canada in large numbers until the outbreak
of World War I. The supposition that immigration and economic prosperity were linked enabled the Canadian government to ignore largely
any prejudice against some white immigrants.[12]

AN APPROACH TO AUSTRIAN IMMIGRATION
BY STATISTICS AND CENSUS DATA

The data on Austrian immigration to Canada often show many inconsis-
tancies. According to Canadian statistics, 104,716 immigrants from the
multinational and multilingual Austro-Hungarian Empire arrived between
1900 and 1910.[13] However, Austrian statistics report 131,247 people
exclusively from the Austrian part of the Dual Monarchy (Cisleithania) for
the same period.[14] Immigration statistics on Austrians, or Austrians and
Hungarians are difficult to evaluate because there are major discrepancies
in figures not only between Austrian and Canadian sources, but also
between sources from the same country.[15] According to Samuel Altmann,
who was Representative General of the Canadian Pacific Railway Company in Austria, 241,065 Austrians and Hungarians immigrated to Canada
from 1876 to 1914.[16] Official Canadian statistics show the entry of
200,026 Austrians and Hungarians between 1900 and 1920.[17] If Altmann's
figures are accurate, about 40,000 would have arrived before 1900. Such a
large number is highly questionable. However, according to Austrian
sources,[18] 61,400 Austrians and Hungarians immigrated until 1897. This
number is even more doubtful because the Austro-Hungarian Consulate
General in Montreal reported just about 80,000 Austrians and Hungarians living in the Prairie provinces and in British Columbia in 1905,[19] while
other Austrian data show the immigration of 55,830 Austrians between
1898 and 1904. Although the last number does not include Hungarians,
who came in small numbers anyway, it would mean that about 117,000
people from Austria-Hungary had come to Canada until 1904.[20] Considering the reported 80,000 Austrians and Hungarians in western Canada, it
is not very likely that about 37,000 Austrians and Hungarians lived in the
eastern provinces of Canada at that time, since most immigrants were
lured to the Prairies. Other sources confirm this improbability. In 1901,
only 919 immigrants from the Habsburg Monarchy lived in Ontario and

159 in Quebec, respectively.[21] The difference between Austrian and Canadian data results partly from the fact that registration of immigrants by the Canadian authorities was based upon fiscal years, whereas European port statistics were based on calendar years. Another source of errors inherent in the statistics are those Austrian and Hungarian immigrants who moved to Canada after some years in the United States. In 1912-13, 4,747 Austrians and 224 Hungarians emigrated from the United States to Canada. However, this number does not include Austrians and Hungarians who had already taken up American citizenship or had been born there.[22]

The classification of immigrants who came from that part of the Monarchy which corresponds with present-day Austria is quite complex. Of course, neither Austrian nor Canadian statistics did or could categorize them separately. In 1903-04, 9,307 or 93.9 percent out of 9,914 immigrants from Austria were Poles from Galicia or Ukrainians (Ruthenians) from Galicia and Bukovina. A total of 516 German-speaking immigrants were subsumed in the group "other Austrians."[23] The vast majority of them came from the German-speaking enclaves in Galicia and Bukovina. This leaves only a very small number from the geographic area of post-1920 Austria. However, it does not include Austrians from Burgenland which then was the westernmost part of Hungary and where the vast majority was German-speaking.

Ascertaining the number of immigrants from present-day Austria is complicated by the fact that most of the available data do not distinguish sufficiently, if at all, between the different groups from Austria. For instance, the 1901 Census of Canada for Winnipeg City has columns for the country of birth, racial origin, and nationality. Most people who came from anywhere within the Austrian part of the realm gave Austria as country of birth. No doubt, a large number of those who had either a German family name or gave German or Austrian as mother tongue, which—apart from regionally different dialects—is basically the same, did not come from the area of post-1920 Austria. Many of them were Presbyterians, Methodists, or Lutherans. This indicates that a majority probably did not emigrate from the territory of post-1920 Austria where more than 90 percent of the population were Roman Catholics. Yet, we cannot even establish that all German-speaking Catholic immigrants came from post-1920 Austria.

None of the members of the Salem United Church of Christ in Winnipeg who emigrated from "Cisleithania" (the "Austrian" half of the Austro-Hungarian Empire) came from Austria in its present-day borders.

Since this is not a Catholic church, one would not be very likely to find many or any post-1920 Austrians among them, but it confirms the assumption that most of the Austrians in Winnipeg, at least those belonging to the Protestants, did not come from post-1920 Austria. This is most probably also true for other parts of Canada, though it is likely that some of the immigrants from post-1920 Austria had come as Protestants or had converted from the Catholic Church to one of the Protestant churches.[24] Apart from few exceptions, parish registers show the place and country of birth; the latter usually was given as Austria but sometimes also, more specifically, Galicia. Nevertheless, almost all of them came from Galicia, since villages like "Felsendorf in Austria" were in the province of Galicia.[25]

Since the term "nationality" was used either in the meaning of citizenship or ethnic origin, it is not surprising that immigrants frequently confused these terms when asked for their nationality. The 1901 census used "nationality" to refer to citizenship, and this was difficult to misunderstand since "racial origin" was a separate question. Yet, Woodsworth used "nationality" also in the meaning of ethnic origin.[26] The 1901 census shows an Austrian living in Toronto who was more specific with regard to the place of birth: it was given as Tyrol, a province of Austria.[27] On the other hand, many Ukrainians deliberately spoke of themselves as being Austrians.[28] Since the vast majority of immigrants from Austria-Hungary were Slavs, the term "Austrian" was closely linked to the term "Slavic." Even after the dissolution of the Austro-Hungarian Empire some immigrants from what was no longer Austria, in particular Ukrainians, still called themselves "Austrians," and a fair number continue to do so. In the consciousness of the Canadian public, chiefly in the western provinces, "Austrian" was therefore often synonymous with "Slavic."[29] According to Canadian statistics, 29,725 "Austrians" immigrated to Canada between 1900 and 1914.[30] This number is much too small to cover all immigrants from the Austrian part of the realm, but is much too large to account for those who came from post-1920 Austria where emigration was only marginal. From such data as we have, we can estimate that probably no more than 5,000, at most 10,000 immigrants, who arrived in Canada until 1914 came from present-day Austria, including those who migrated via the United States.

SETTLEMENTS

In 1905, about 75,000 "Austrians" and "Hungarians," including between 55,000 and 60,000 Ukrainians and Poles, about 5,000 "Hungarians," and approximately 5,000 German-speaking people, again primarily from Galicia and Bukovina, lived in Manitoba, Saskatchewan, and Alberta. Probably fewer than 6,000 "Austrians" and "Hungarians" lived in British Columbia, that is, primarily on Vancouver Island, in Vancouver, near Kamloops, in the Revelstoke-Kootenay district and, in particular, in the coal districts near Crow's Nest Pass in Fernie and Morrissey. In Manitoba, settlements like Stuartburn, Brokenhead, Sifton, Valley River, Ethelbert, Brandon, Shoal Lake, Gimli, Snake Creek, and the city of Winnipeg had fairly large concentrations of people from Austria-Hungary. In Saskatchewan, they settled in considerable numbers in Menofield, Yorkton, Canora, Insinger, Kolin, Ebernezer, near Crescent Lake, in Rosthern, Esterhazy, Zichydorf, Mariahilf, Lemberg, Neudorf, Edenwold, and in Regina. The main settlement areas in Alberta were Lethbridge, Coleman and Frank in the Crow's Nest Pass district, near Calgary, between Red Deer and Lacombe, in Innisfail, Spruce Grove, Stony Plain, Josephburg, Vegreville, in the Edmonton area, and northwest of St. Albert.[31]

In the first decade of the twentieth century, the vast majority of the immigrants from the Austro-Hungarian Empire went to Manitoba, Saskatchewan, and Alberta. In the fiscal year 1910-11, the pattern changed, at least by intended destinations. Most Austro-Hungarians still went to Manitoba, but Quebec and Ontario ranked now second and third, respectively, followed by Saskatchewan and Alberta.[32] The largest number of post-1920 Austrians probably settled in Saskatchewan. This is based on available family histories that can definitely be identified with post-1920 Austrians. This assumption is also supported by the fact that German-speaking Catholics—the vast majority of post-1920 Austrians were Catholics—settled almost exclusively in Saskatchewan. Small numbers of post-1920 Austrians settled also in Alberta.[33] Many post-1920 Austrians came from the United States, among them numerous immigrants who had come originally from Western Hungary (Burgenland). Nonetheless, post-1920 Austrians could also be found in all parts of Canada. Some of them immigrated quite early. An example is Franz Stirsky, a Vienna-born watchmaker who had come to Halifax in 1864 at the age of 24 and who was naturalized in 1871.[34] A project (1910) of a Vienna-based group to found an Austrian colony of 1,000 (!) peasant families in Alberta, west of Calgary on the slopes of the Rocky Mountains, was never carried out.[35] The same happened to the idea to settle some fifty Tyrolean families from the higher valleys of the Zillertal in British Columbia where they "might lead the life to which they have been accustomed with a good chance of remuneration." Canadian officials had suggested the Columbia Valley near Golden for this venture.[36]

MOTIVES FOR EMIGRATION

Motives for the emigration from present-day Austria differed sometimes to a large degree from those which made people from other parts of the Empire want to emigrate. Ethno-political factors—attempts by the domestic authorities to close German schools and to suppress the German language—that persuaded many German-speaking minorities from Galicia, Bukovina, and the Banat of the necessity to emigrate, of course, did not apply to the German-speaking parts of Austria which were later to make up the Austrian Republic. Overpopulation caused by a high birth rate accompanied by a dropping death rate, poor economic conditions, political unrest, and compulsory military service led to the emigration of about four million people from Austria-Hungary; many thousands of them were bound for Canada. The lack of new land by the end of the nineteenth century, in particular in regions where large landholdings predominated, provided a growing number of younger landless workers that a retarded Austrian and Hungarian industrialization process was not able to absorb. For instance, the general standard of living of the agrarian population in Galicia, where 81 percent of the landholdings were below the five hectares deemed necessary for sustenance, was very low. The owners of the smallest holdings also had to work as wage earners. "These and unpropertied farm labourers could only partly find work as harvesters at larger landed property for an extremely low pay."[37] Young people who were growing up in large families in rural regions faced only extremely limited opportunities. However, not only those who were looking for a chance to escape poverty saw an alternative in emigration, but also people who could not expect to retain the social and economic standing of their parents.[38]

The "push factors" for emigration cannot be seen separated from the "pull factors." The main attraction for potential immigrants from Austria-Hungary to Canada was the prospect of free homesteads, namely 160 acres for a fee of $10, as well as 50 to 100 percent higher wages and incomes.[39] Homesteads—the first one was granted in Canada in 1872[40] —could be acquired by every male settler over 18 years of age and by every female head of family. Homesteaders were obliged to cultivate a portion of the land for three years, to live at least six months per year on it, and to become naturalized before sole ownership was issued. The wage level for labourers depended on the kind of work and the region. Farm labourers in Manitoba, who received wages on a monthly basis, earned—depending on the economic development of the district—$10 to $18 during the winter and on the average $25 in the summer; during the time of harvest, they could receive $30 to $40 or even $50. Day-labourers in Winnipeg, Manitoba (railway) and in Regina, Saskatchewan (sewage and water plants, and railway) earned between $1.50 and $1.75 per day. A day labourer in Edmonton, Alberta could receive $1.75 to two dollars, and miners of the Alberta Railway & Coal Company $60 to $70 per month. Someone working in the smelting works of British Columbia earned $3 per day in 1905.[41]

For immigrants from area of present-day Austria, economic reasons for emigration were usually less important than others. For them, what counted was the prospect to achieve more abroad than was possible at home. The opportunity to become a farmer in North America provided with enough land or subsistence was primarily important for emigrants from Burgenland (then Western Hungary), where small landholdings were parcelled out to the offspring, which frequently made it impossible to eke out a living from farming. Natural disasters increased the pressure to emigrate. Apart from economic reasons or the desire to avoid service in the army, there was a host of other, internal factors which were decisive for emigration: an adventurous spirit, a positive attitude towards change, and in particular, towards emigration, and the example of relatives or friends who had emigrated earlier.

For many Austrian immigrants, Canada was not the land of first choice. At first, they emigrated to the United States, probably because it was much talked about with respect to immigration. Actually, 95 percent of all Austro-Hungarian immigrants to North America and 83 percent of all Austro-Hungarian emigrants overseas went to the United States.[42] Therefore, many more prospective Austrian immigrants had relatives there than in Canada. Relatives had always been an important factor in luring people to other countries, or at least the knowledge of well-meaning relatives made the decision to emigrate easier. Another factor in favor of America was that some Austrians had left their homeland before the Canadian West was wide open for homesteading. They migrated predominantly to the American Midwest. Many worked in a trade before they took up a homestead. Some of these Austrian settlers moved on to Canada because it had also become more difficult for farmers with large families in the United States to establish their sons on farms,[43] and the homestead policy of the Canadian government lured them to Canada. To resettle was not only common among those Austrians who came from the United States, but also for Austrians who went to Canada in the first place. One family who emigrated to the U.S. moved from Wisconsin to Minnesota, then to South Dakota, and finally decided to resettle in Alberta, and after seven years moved on to Humboldt in Saskatchewan.[44]

EXPERIENCES AND LIFE STORIES

During economic crises and times of extremely large immigration, those immigrants from Austria-Hungary who were unemployed in the larger cities faced the most difficult situations. Many of them were newcomers. In 1908, according to a report from the Austro-Hungarian Consulate General in Montreal, on a single day, more than 500 "Austrians" and "Hungarians" asked for work at the Consulate; it intervened, yet only 90 men could obtain employment with the Canadian Pacific Railway. Since many shipping and railway companies were involved in the recruitment of people from Austria-Hungary, many of the unemployed blamed those agencies for their fate.[45]

To homestead was a tremendously difficult task, especially for those who had not been farmers back home. This, of course, was true not only for those from the area of modern Austria, among them numerous Burgenländer who had come from the United States,[46] but for all other immigrants as well. The settlers had to use their own resources, which were almost non-existent, to build up everything. They had to build a log house for living and barns with sod roofs. The immigrants broke land but also had to work elsewhere, in particular during the winter months, over two or three years. They worked on the railway leaving most of the farming during the summer to the rest of the family. When they had cleared enough land, the proceeds of the harvest helped them to get ahead. Food and other supplies had to be brought from the nearest town. This often meant a three days' trip with oxen. Settling on virgin land always involved considerable privation. The primitive transportation system and the distances were horrible compared with those anywhere in Austria.[47] The troublesome and time-consuming journey through a district which had just been opened up a few years earlier is described in a report from the Austro-Hungarian Consulate General in Montreal in 1905: "One had to get through dense brush and marshy land in which horses threatened to vanish forever, and, finally one had to stop at a river and return because its high water level had swept the primitive bridge away and made a passage impossible."[48]

After several years, the settlers built better houses or they gave up the homesteads in favour of a second or even a third one to improve their standard of living. The women raised chickens, geese, and ducks. They took care of a garden, made soap, knitted socks, baked bread and much more.[49] For a widow, life on a homestead could be extremely hard as in the case of Elisabeth Egger who had come from Upper Austria and lived in the area of Pilger, Saskatchewan. "The people who bought our land never could pay for it," she wrote, "so I lost the money, and had to go through all this with seven children, with only two cows and hens for two years."[50] Despite years full of privation and hard work, despite the inclemency of the weather and despite having to face a life of isolation, most Austrian homesteaders were quite satisfied in the end. In 1919 Elisabeth Egger wrote: "The way of living was and is much better than in Austria."[51] However, to those who had not been farmers in Austria, work and life on a homestead often appeared to be hard and unprofitable.

Most Austrian immigrants, in particular those who homesteaded, were strongly involved in parish activities; for instance, being a member of the church choir was a most welcome diversion. In Winnipeg, there was the "Austrian Hungarian Society" which had 200 members in 1912.[52] The Society was originally incorporated as "The Austrian German Society *Gemütlichkeit* of Winnipeg" in 1907.[53] But only a minority of the members, if any, were immigrants from the area of present-day Austria.

Other Austrians, many of them coming directly from Austria, arrived in Canada not to homestead but to work as craftsmen or to establish a business. The latter were usually prosperous from the beginning. Some of them expanded their businesses continuously or operated more than one business at a time.[54] Austrians who came to Canada as very young men sometimes led a quite exciting life. For instance, Louis Schober, a blacksmith from Greifenburg in Carinthia, joined the Canadian Navy after some time spent in Montreal and Vancouver and served on a gunboat patrolling the Pacific coastline up to Alaska before he worked for the merchant marine, travelling to the South Sea, Australia and New Zealand. Then he moved to Saskatchewan, returned to his trade and had his own shop.[55] Other Austrians served on different boards. For example, Jacob Platzer, who was born in Klagenfurt, Carinthia, "served four years as a member of the Separate School Board and nine years as a councillor of the Town of Humboldt."[56] Rudolf Kiene, who was born in Bregenz, Vorarlberg, "was involved in organizing a school for their district" (Vibank, Saskatchewan). "Over the years he served as a board member and chairperson."[57]

THE JOHN PITZL STORY[58]

John Pitzl emigrated to America from Apetlon in the Neusiedler See area in Burgenland (then Western Hungary) in 1875. He was encouraged by his mother to leave when coming of conscription age. His mother's words were: "I sooner not see you again knowing you are alive than not see you because you have been killed in battle." However, the "most significant motivation for the emigration from the area was due to extreme hardship which the people endured in those years." Crops were destroyed by a rodent infestation in 1873 and two years later 3,000 hectares of land were flooded—"the distress was of the greatest magnitude." By 1881 the whole Pitzl family—with the exception of the mother who had died in 1876— including two brothers and three sisters and their spouses and John's father, moved on to Minnesota. When land become scarce in St. Joseph, a Roman Catholic colony, where he lived then, John Pitzl resettled in 1906 to the St. Peter's Colony at Muenster in Saskatchewan. This colony was founded in 1902 as the result of the initiatives of Benedictine monks from Minnesota and Illinois.[59] One of John Pitzl's brothers also relocated to Canada where he had a butcher shop business. John Pitzl remained a farmer. His wife was the midwife and mortician in her community of Pilger. And so it turned out that almost all immigrants from post-1920 Austria, regardless of initial hardships, whether they were farmers, craftsmen or businessmen, eventually did become comfortable and prosperous.

ENDNOTES

1.   Jean R. Burnet and Howard Palmer, *Coming Canadians: An Introduction to a History of Canada's Peoples* (Toronto, 1988), p. 14.

2.   Hans Chmelar, *Höhepunkte der österreichischen Auswanderung: Die Auswanderung aus den im Reichsrat vertretenen Königreichen und Ländern in den Jahren 1905-1914* (Vienna, 1974), pp. 143, 159; Michael John, "Push and Pull Factors for Overseas Migrants from Austria-Hungary in the 19th and 20th Centuries," in Franz A.J. Szabo, ed., *Austrian Immigration to Canada: Selected Essays* (Ottawa, 1996), pp. 55-81.

3. Mabel F. Timlin, "Canada's Immigration Policy, 1896-1910," *Canadian Journal of Economics and Political Science* 16 (1960), 517.

4. Freda Hawkins, *Critical Years in Immigration: Canada and Australia Compared* (Kingston, 1989), p. 5.

5. Donald Avery, *Dangerous Foreigners: European Immigrant Workers and Labour Radicalism in Canada, 1896-1932* (Toronto, 1979), p. 20.

6. Public Archives of Canada (PAC), Record Group (RG) 19, Vol. 3227, file 13634, W.S. Fielding to Count Bylandt Rheidt, 20 January 1905.

7. Hawkins, *Critical Years,* pp. 7-8.

8. Vienna, Haus-, Hof- und Staatsarchiv [hencefoth HHStA]: Administrative Registratur [henceforth Adm. Reg.], F 15/61, Canada 3, 1 (upper left corner), 30 June 1908.

9. *Ibid.,* Canada 2a, 6, 29 October 1908.

10. Hawkins, *Critical Years,* p. 8.

11. HHStA, Adm. Reg., F 15/62, Canada 1, 88, 3 December 1913. Other immigrants considered "desirable" were citizens of England, France, Belgium, Holland, Switzerland and Iceland.

12. Howard Palmer, *Patterns of Prejudice: A History of Nativism in Alberta* (Toronto, 1982), p. 56, and Hawkins, *Critical Years,* p. 8.

13. *Report of the Immigration Branch for the Fiscal Year Ending March 31, 1947* (Ottawa, 1948), Table 2, p. 247.

14. Chmelar, *Hohepunkte,* p. 24. This number is based on European port statistics.

15. Readers should keep such discrepancies in mind throughout this volume. Wherever possible, the sources of immigration data will be given.

16. Chmelar, *Höhepunkte,* p. 63.

17. *Report of the Immigration Branch,* Tables 2 and 3, pp. 147-48.

18. HHStA, Adm. Reg., F 15/62, Canada 1, 23, 30 December 1905.

19. *Ibid.,* F 15/62, Canada 1, 37, Zl. 84000/10, 1905.

20. See Chmelar, *Höhepunkte,* p. 24.

21. Michel Lefebvre and Yuri Oryschuk, eds., *Les communautés culturelles du Québec: Originaires de l'Europe centrale et de l'Europe du sud* (Montreal, 1984) I, 61.

22. HHStA, Adm. Reg., F 15/61, Canada 5, 3, 2 May 1913.

23. Leopold Caro, *Auswanderung und Auswanderungspolitik in Österreich* (Leipzig, 1909), p. 35.

24. The church affiliation of those eleven Austrians and Hungarians (children not included) who lived on Vancouver Island in 1881 is quite interesting: five Catholics, three Anglicans/Episcopalians, one Reformed/Episcopalian, and two Jews. The motives for becoming Anglican is fairly obvious. These people had probably been living on Vancouver Island or at least in North America for several years, since the male average age was 41.6 years, and they were well integrated/assimilated

into the overwhelmingly British environment. Two of them were married to women
of English origin. The only Reformed man was also married to a woman of English
background. The Danish wife of one of the Catholics was Lutheran as were their
six children. For census lists see Peter Baskerville and Eric Sager with Raymond
Frogner and George Young, *1881 Canadian Census Vancouver Island* (Victoria: Public History Group. University of Victoria, l990). The 1891 Census of Victoria
shows that ten out of thirteen Austrian and Hungarians by birth were Catholics.
The average age of both sexes was 30 years. Six out of ten Catholics were unmar-
ried, three other men were married to Catholic women who had been born in Austria-Hungary, in Ireland, and in British Columbia, respectively. This shows at least
for this early period and Vancouver Island the correlation between the denomina-
tion of the husband and the faith of the wife. See Eric Sager and Peter Baskerville
with Jennifer Molony, Darryl Green and Chris W. J. Robert, *The 1891 Canadian
Census Victoria, B.C.* (Victoria: Public History Group, University of Victoria, 1991).

25. Provincial Archives of Manitoba (PAM), P 4425, Salem United Church of Christ,
Book No. 6, Kirchenbuch der Reformierten Salems Gemeinde zu Winnipeg,
Manitoba beginnend mit dem 25. August 1907.

26. James S. Woodsworth, *Strangers Within Our Gates or Coming Canadians* (Toronto,
1972), p. 23.

27. 1901 Census of Canada, 116 Toronto Centre, a 14, Ward 3, p. 6.

28. See PAM, P 5317 f. 11, Leonard Mariash, *A History of the Bendera, Smyrski, and
Ogrodnik Families of Thalberg, Manitoba* (Winnipeg, 1992), p. 3.

29. Österreichisches Staatsarchiv [henceforth ÖStA]: Archiv der Republik [henceforth
AdR], Bundeskanzleramt/Inneres [henceforth BKA], Wanderungsamt [henceforth
WA], 8/4, c/1, Zl. 61.787-WA/1930.

30. Gertrud Neuwirth and John de Vries, "Demographic Patterns of Austrian Canadians, 1900-1991," in Szabo, ed., *Austrian Immigration* pp. 35-37, Table 1. The data
given by the authors refer to Austrian immigrants by citizenship. All immigrants
from the Austrian part of the Empire, regardless of their ethnic background, were
Austrian citizens. Therefore, these figures most probably refer to Austrians by
"nationality" in the meaning of "ethnic origin" for Austrians not specified otherwise. See also Employment and Immigration Canada, *Immigration Statistics Year
1896 to 1961* (Ottawa: n.d.), Fiscal Years 1900-1906, p. 1. Austrian immigrants
are listed by ethnic origin, which corresponds with Neuwirth and de Vries's data by
citizenship.

31. HHStA, Adm. Reg., F 15/62, Canada 1, 37, Zl. 84000/10, 1905.

32. *Ibid.*, F 15/62, Canada 1, 60, 17 March 1912.

33. Heinz Lehmann, *The German-Canadians, 1750-1937.* Introduced, edited and
translated by Gerhard P. Bassler (St. John's, Nfld., 1986), p. 240.

34. Public Archives of Nova Scotia [henceforth PANS], microfilm, reel 15672, RG 18, series "A," Vol. 1, item 2, 190, 16 May 1871.

35. *Der Auswanderer* 1/1 (August 1910), p. 9.

36. Glenbow Archives [henceforth GA], CPR, M 2269, file 2398, Warburton Pike to R. McBride, Premier of British Columbia, 19 March 1911 and J.S. Dennis, Assistant to the President CPR, to R. McBride, 9 April 1911.

37. Chmelar, *Höhepunkte*, pp. 99-100. Cf. Herbert Matis, "Die Habsburgermonarchie (Cisleithanien) 1848-1918," in: Karl Bachinger, Helga Hemetsberger-Koller and Herbert Matis, eds., *Grundriß der Österreichischen Sozial- und Wirtschaftsgeschichte von 1848 bis zur Gegenwart* (Stuttgart, 1987), p. 16.

38. John, "Push and Pull Factors," pp. 64-65.

39. *Ibid.*, p. 68.

40. Louis Hamilton, "Foreigners in the Canadian West," *Dalhousie Review* 17 (1938), 459.

41. HHStA, Adm. Reg., F 15/62, Canada 1, 37, Zl. 84000/10, 1905.

42. See Chmelar, *Höhepunkte*, pp. 25, 65.

43. See Burnet, *Coming Canadians*, p. 7.

44. Don Telfer, ed., *The Best of Humboldt* (Humboldt, Sask., 1982), Johann Ecker family, p. 277.

45. HHStA, Adm. Reg., F 15/62, Canada 1, 37, Zl. 84000/10, 1905.

46. *The Best of Humboldt*, pp. 287-88, 312, 427-28, 528-29; Grace Solomon, *A Yandel History* (Regina, 1993).

47. The Best of Humboldt, Thomas Graf Sr., p. 312; John Wegleitner, p. 528; Solomon, pp. 4-5.

48. HHStA, Adm. Reg., F 15/61, 84000/10, 1905.

49. *The Best of Humboldt*, George Fleischhacker, p. 287; and Thomas Graf Sr., p. 312.

50. Thomas Samhaber, "The History of the Egger Family of Immigrants to Canada," in Szabo, ed., *Austrian Immigration*, p. 129.

51. *Ibid.*, p. 130.

52. Lehmann, *The German-Canadians*, p. 197.

53. PAC, RG 13, A2, Vol. 215, file 1474, 28 August 1917.

54. *The Best of Humboldt*, Louis Moritzer, p. 401, and Jacob Platzer, p. 430.

55. *Ibid.*, Louis Schober, pp. 549-50.

56. *Ibid.*, Jacob Platzer, p. 430.

57. Letter from Laura M. Hanowski, Regina, to the author regarding her great-grandfather Rudolf Kiene, 15 March 1995.

58. Letter and additional information by Gerry and Lois Pitzel, Regina, to the author, 20 February 1995.

59. Lehmann, *The German-Canadians*, pp. 204-06.

Michaela C. Schober

THE ECONOMIC SITUATION IN AUSTRIA

AFTER THE END OF WORLD WAR I and the dissolution of the Austro-Hungarian Monarchy, the newly created Republic of Austria, now a minor state of 83,850 square kilometers, had to struggle with severe economic problems which were accompanied by the difficulties of adjusting to the reality of being a small state. Pessimism about its economic viability, and fear of civil disorder and political polarization within it abounded. With the loss of the Empire's former markets economic growth was interrupted, and the whole country was threatened with economic disintegration. Its growing dependence on foreign capital and on the private-enterprise interests of Austria's large-scale businesses, together with unfavourable world economic conjunctures, led to a shrinking of the national product as well as to an interruption of the industrial process. Unresolved structural problems, combined with a growth in labour supply and austerity measures to stabilize the currency, led to mass unemployment. The unemployment rate between 1923 and 1929 was on average 9.5 percent. During the worldwide economic crisis which followed this rate rose more sharply still.[1]

In the inter-war period, the years 1923-1930 were the important years of Austrian emigration to Canada. Nonetheless, the number of emigrants was rather small. According to Canadian statistics, 5,439 Austrians immigrated during this period; then the number decreased sharply. Between 1931 and 1937 only 297 Austrians entered Canada. From 1930 to 1931 the number of immigrants dropped from 663 to 67.[2] Austrian statistics report an even lower number of emigrants to Canada.

Measured by the unemployment rate, the small number of Austrians who were bound for Canada needs further explanation. The Canadian immigration regulations with regard to Austrians were rather restrictive in the 1920s and, of course, became generally much more restrictive during the Great Depression (1930-1939). This was obviously an obstacle for potential Austrian immigrants. On the other hand, regardless of immigration regulations and the severe economic problems in Austria, a foreign country itself suffering from the Depression was not attractive, and during this time numerous Austrian emigrants did indeed return to their homeland. In addition, emigration, regardless of one's personal social and economic situation, was not everybody's idea of personal improvement because it required high flexibility or at least presupposed a certain willingness to change one's life. This usually implied the necessity of total adaptation to the new environment which, of course, was never easy and often did not work. Whether a potential emigrant could afford the passage to Canada or could at least raise the money with the help of others was also a decisive limit for emigration. The motives for emigration that can be pinpointed were primarily "lack of work," "insufficient opportunities to earn money" [in Austria], and "better opportunities" in Canada.[3]

About 50 percent of the Austrian immigrants to Canada of the period came from Burgenland; about 17 percent from Styria; eleven percent from Upper Austria, that is chiefly from the districts of Rohrbach and Steyr; nine percent from Carinthia; nine percent from Lower Austria, mainly from the district of Wiener Neustadt and the environs of Vienna; four percent from Vorarlberg; and about one percent from Tyrol as well as from Salzburg.[4] The high number of Burgenländer is explained, apart from the reasons applying to all of Austria, by the special economic problems of Burgenland due to the very small landholdings which prevailed there, and the dislocations caused by the political separation from Hungary. Owners of small holdings, which had shrunk more and more in size because they were always divided up among the heirs, had usually found jobs on the side or even worked the entire year as day labourers on Hungarian landed estates, but now they were deprived of this opportunity to make a living and had to find employment in industry, which was often a hopeless task.[5]

Such economic conditions made government officials think of emigration in a whole new positive light. In 1919 an Austrian Information Bureau for Emigrants (*Österreichische Auskunftsstelle für Auswanderer*) was established which gathered and made available information about general conditions in countries of destination for potential emigrants. Renamed Migration Office (*Wanderungsamt*) and taken over directly by the Chancellor's office in 1923, it provided information on employment opportunities abroad, immigration requirements of host countries, travel costs, and the like, to Austrian citizens contemplating emigration. It was clear, in short, that the Austrian authorities now regarded emigration as an antidote to mass unemployment and even provided some financial assistance to facilitate the process.[6]

THE CANADIAN IMMIGRATION REGULATIONS AND AUSTRIA'S STRUGGLE AGAINST THE CLASSIFICATION "NON-PREFERRED COUNTRY"

The immigration of Austrians to Canada was not possible immediately after the war "because of their war time associations."[7] The Immigration Act of 1923 "opened" Canada again for Austrians *de jure,* but was rather restrictive as Austria was listed as a "non-preferred country." This classification limited Austrian immigration to certain occupations. Generally, only farmers, farm labourers, female domestic servants, and family-sponsored Austrians were admitted to Canada. Citizens of "preferred countries," which included the Scandinavian countries, Holland, Belgium, France, Switzerland, and, since 1926, Germany, could enter Canada regardless of their occupation, provided they had sufficient means for their passage and maintenance until employment was secured.[8]

Two years later, the Canadian government came to an agreement with the Canadian Pacific and the Canadian National Railways that gave them the right to bring in and find positions for "agricultural and female domestic classes, including wives and children, whether the head of the family is accompanying or is settled in Canada," from certain countries, including Austria. Both railway companies sent accredited agents to Vienna who issued "occupational certificates" to immigrants. These certificates provided reasonable assurance of employment for farm labourers and female domestics, but immigrants had to be physically and mentally suitable for farm work. The passport regulations enforced by the Canadian authorities caused some trouble for Austrians who were not resident in Austria because they were required to have a passport which was "issued in and by the Austrian government."[9] In 1927 these requirements were slightly loosened, for from then on, in addition to the admissible classes, applicants of other occupations could be admitted in exceptional circumstances. If a potential immigrant could satisfy the immigration authorities that his occupation was in demand, a "departmental letter" was issued.

Usually, relatives, future employers, or the like applied for these immigration certificates.[10]

In the same year, the Canadian government reduced the quota for immigrants from Europe, since it had not been possible to place all immigrants as farm labourers—a situation caused by a large influx of immigrants at the beginning of the year. In 1928 the immigration of Austrians was again possible, though nominations and prepaid applications could only come from persons legally resident in Canada who had to be employed in farming, and applications were restricted to the family categories, viz. father and mother, husband and wife, son or daughter, brother or sister.[11] In 1929 restrictions again came into being as railway companies had to reduce the number of immigrants from "non-preferred countries" to 30 percent of the 1928 quota by order of the Canadian government.[12] The Depression then led the Canadian government to change its immigration policy in 1930. As a result, immigration to Canada was now generally prohibited. The only admissible immigrants were farmers with enough money to start farming immediately, or wives and children under 18 of men who were residents of Canada and had the means to take care of their immediate families.[13] The "Railway Agreement" was cancelled the following year.[14]

The "admissible immigrant" classes had been an obstacle for many potential Austrian immigrants. The majority of them were industrial workers or craftsmen, but they were not granted admission unless they were willing (or at least pretended to be willing) to work in the agricultural sector or had proof of some farm experience. The latter was usually no problem. According to official Austrian statistics, 79.8 percent of Austrian immigrants to Canada had an occupational background in agriculture or forestry, 10.9 percent were dependents, seven percent were domestic servants, and only 1.4 percent were industrial workers or craftsmen.[15] An Austrian in British Columbia, who was employed in an elegant hotel in Austria during the summer but worked as a lumberjack in winter, said that "many wanted to go but unless you had the money for the ticket, there was no chance." Even he had difficulties because in summer his hands did not look like those of a farm labourer.[16]

Since these regulations were due to Austria's classification as a "non-preferred country," the Austrian government attempted to initiate negotiations with Canadian authorities in 1927 in order to achieve a modification of this status. Apart from objecting to the obvious discrimination, another main reason for the Austrian endeavour was the fact that the classification of Germany had been changed to "preferred country" at the end of 1926. However, the Canadian government was not interested in any changes of Austria's status for several reasons. In a memorandum to the Minister of Immigration and Colonization, Robert Forke, the Deputy Minister F.C. Blair wrote: "the background against which these requests are made is the unemployment situation in the various countries seeking a change. There is a good deal of feeling in Canada against the dumping on us the unemployed of the Mother Country."[17] Another argument was that other non-preferred countries would immediately exert pressure on Canada for similar concessions if Austria's request were granted, and Canada would have to apply some other restrictions. "This request, if granted, would mean that all those states, in which there are unwanted minorities or in some cases many unemployed, would be free to send their people to Canada without any limitation of occupation or number."[18] Of course, this statement has to be read against the background of the economic problems experienced by Canada at that time.

To help change Canada's mind, voluminous information on Austria and its population was sent to the Canadian government. It was pointed out that the Austrian population was culturally, ethnically, and in regard to sanitation standards, on par with the adjacent part of Germany (Bavaria). This assurance was important because Canada's immigration policy at that time was guided by racial, political, cultural as well as sanitary considerations, and many immigrants who had arrived prior to World War I from the Austro-Hungarian Empire still claimed to be Austrians regardless from which part of the Empire they had come. Because of the Austro-Hungarian past, many people in Canada—not inclined to welcome immigrants from Eastern and Southern European countries— had the false idea that the Republic of Austria was still a state of many different nationalities. Canada also feared that too many industrial workers from Austria would come into the country if Austria's status were to be changed.[19]

Austrian newspapers blamed the Migration Office for the poor progress in facilitating immigration arrangements. In 1929, the *Reichspost* emphasized that it ought to be the business of the Migration Office to make it clear to the Canadian authorities that Austria had nothing in common with the Balkans and that it was "an injustice to German Austrians to classify them as 'non-preferred' immigrants."[20] In the same year, the Migration Office used a visit by Canadian journalists and newspaper publishers to Vienna as an occasion to do public relations work on behalf of Austria, and it hoped to launch articles in Canadian newspapers.[21] Finally, the Deputy Minister of Immigration and Colonization, J. Egan, admitted that he and other leading personages in Canada knew that Austria's classification as a non-preferred country was not justified, but Canada feared that the Czechoslovak and Polish governments would claim the same advantages for their citizens if Austria were classified as a "preferred country."[22]

In the futile endeavour for preferred status, Austria went so far as to claim that Canadians would not have to fear a torrent of industrial workers from Austria, because in Austria agriculture and forestry were very important.[23] To be sure, while Canada did not need to fear an "immense" influx of industrial workers from Austria, there would be probably more than heretofore. At the same time, Austria was also in need of agricultural workers and had to employ large numbers of seasonal farm workers from Czechoslovakia. Actually, in 1929, the Austrian Ministry of Agriculture and Forestry itself turned against the Migration Office, arguing that it was a poor idea to publish opportunities for emigration in newspapers.[24] In the same year, Karl Herzmansky, the Secretary of the Migration Office in Vienna, visited western Canada, in part to interview Austrians and obtain firsthand information about settlement conditions. His principal objective, however, was to obtain a change of Austria's classification.[25] The mission was unsuccessful, but in the second half of 1930, when the new immigration regulations made future immigration more or less impossible, the term "non-preferred countries" was abandoned.[26]

CONDITIONS AND PERSONAL EXPERIENCES OF AUSTRIAN IMMIGRANTS IN CANADA

Although there were many warning voices, many immigrants imagined Canada as a land of abundance. True, almost all Austrians were admitted to Canada as agricultural workers or domestics in accordance with the immigration regulations, but many of them had a wrong notion about their future employment. First, many Austrians thought they could just stay in the cities and work in their trade or in the factories. But this was not possible for everyone since the opportunities were limited: many other immigrants had the same idea, and Canada was still predominantly an agrarian state. Secondly, most immigrants actually were not used to or even willing to do farm work. An Austrian "farm labourer" from Graz, Styria was described by his employer as useless. However, a farmer, who had helped many immigrants come to Canada by providing or arranging work for them, was quite satisfied with the immigrants.[27] Adolf Neipl, who received letters from prospective Austrian immigrants wrote: "Some ... do not have much idea about agriculture and just want to try it ... they should rather not go to Canada. There is absolutely no place for industrial workers and the like here. Only farmers and their workers should apply, and only those who work really hard."[28]

Opinions about job opportunities in Canada differed. One immigrant wrote quite realistically:

If someone arrives in Canada without any means, he has to work hard until he knows the language and if a farmer knows that the immigrant has no money, he will force down the wages.... Women are better off than men, there is always great demand, and if they speak English, it will be a very easy beginning.... The opportunities to earn money are quite good here in Canada, but it is necessary to know one's trade because one has to work hard here. More is demanded of one, but one also works with more modern machinery than we do in Europe.[29]

Another immigrant emphasized that "someone who is used to work and wants to work and is entirely healthy can easily come to Canada, because this is the land where everyone can get ahead. For sick people and enemies of work there is indeed no place."[30] As a matter of fact, many Austrians had problems with the adaptation to the new country. In the opinion of the Austrian Consul General in Montreal, Frederick Franke, many immigrants had no goals and suffered misery. Besides, he pointed out, they were spoiled by Austria where they could rely on unemployment benefits and sick-leave funds which were not available in Canada at the time.[31]

Austrians were lured to Canada by the prospect of making a better living there than in Austria, sometimes by the expectation of unrealistically high wages of up to $100 per month.[32] In fact, the officially advertised wages for a farm labourer in 1927 were $250 to $300 per year plus board,[33] and in bad economic times, the immigrant farm labourers had trouble even getting their wages. One Austrian, who worked in a furniture factory in Ontario, received a salary of $3.50 per day in 1929 and reported being satisfied with that for the time being.[34] Others reported being quite happy as a waiter in a big hotel,[35] a second cook in a hospital,[36] a farmer,[37] or as a musician and music teacher.[38] On the other hand, a mechanic in Alberta said that his trade was not needed and he therefore began to work on a farm.[39] Another Austrian was engaged in fishery and lived for some time in a log cabin on Lake Winnipeg where he supervised two native Indians who were fishing for his employer. He reported being able to make a good living.[40]

Austrians who could not find employment on a farm in the Prairies (there was a poor spring season in western Canada in 1927) or who found the wages were not sufficient, looked for employment in the cities, in particular in the East. But for most there were no opportunities there.[41] Their last resort was to return to Austria, especially during the Depression when the general economic situation was rather bad. According to an Austrian in Toronto, hundreds of unemployed men slept in railway cars, under railway bridges, in unoccupied houses, or in closed-down factories. He had travelled on freight trains to Vancouver and back, but could not find any work. The lack of available jobs led to strong pressure not to employ immigrants. It was even hard to obtain soup from a mission in Toronto because the staff did no want to feed immigrants. This man was stopped from entering the soup kitchen by the police who even kicked him.[42]

Some Austrians who had been living in Canada for some time decided to homestead during the Depression because they could not find suitable employment.[43] Unfortunately, it had become more difficult to establish oneself as a farmer during this time. Dominion public lands in Manitoba, Saskatchewan and Alberta were transferred to these provinces in 1931, and those farmers who entered Canada in 1931 and afterwards were required to have at least $2,000 to begin their farming enterprise.[44] In 1933, an Austrian wrote: "There is no more prairie land available that is worth cultivating; it is either situated in areas without any rain or too far from the railway."[45] Nevertheless, those Austrians who did remain in Canada despite all the difficulties—and these difficulties were not experienced in the same way or with the same intensity by everyone—largely seemed to prosper sooner or later.

THE OKANAGAN VALLEY EXPERIMENT

Perhaps a classic case in point, illustrating the sorts of problems that interwar Austrian emigrants could encounter in Canada, was the disastrous "Okanagan Valley Experiment." In May 1927, sixteen Burgenland families, most of them from the town of Klingenbach, arrived in Canada on a "credit system" under the auspices of the Austrian Migration Office in

Vienna and the Association of German-Canadian Catholics (AGCC) in Winnipeg. The local settlement was to be organized by the AGCC and the Canada Colonization Association (CCA) of the Canadian Pacific Railway Company. The Austrians were brought to Winnipeg where the different settlement possibilities were discussed. Nearly all immigrants had small children and little or no money, but wished to settle as close to each other as possible. With the exception of two families, who decided to leave the group and were sent to Bruno in Saskatchewan, they declared that they were fully organized and wished to work as a group under the leadership of a certain Gustav Stawitzky and a board of four of their members. These fourteen families were shown land in the vicinity of Winnipeg and in western Manitoba; however, it did not suit them. Stawitzky was then taken to the Bulman Farm in British Columbia's Okanagan Valley where he became absolutely convinced that that area was the most suitable location for their settlement.[46]

The purchase price agreed upon was $145,00 for 3,587 acres of real estate, which included orchard land, irrigated land under cultivation (alfalfa, vegetables and tobacco) and ranch land. The terms of payment were to be one-half of all returns from production. The rate of interest was 5 percent; the payment of interest and taxes to begin at the end of the first season, that is, on 1 January 1928. The farm was fully equipped, and in addition the vendor, Thomas Bulman, had to advance $900 for the purchase of provisions and for living expenses. One of the clauses of the contract stipulated that the purchasers had to farm the property according to the wishes of the seller, whose foreman acted as supervisor (this was planned for at least one year) and as an orchard expert for the time being.[47] All families signed the agreement of sale.

However, most of these Austrians left within the very same year, with the last families leaving during the winter of 1928 and becoming wage-earners in or near Kelowna. According to the bill of sale, the settlers were obliged to run the farm. By not keeping to the stipulated conditions of sale, they committed a breach of contract whatever their grievances might be. These soon made an imposing list: the high purchase price; unfair and harsh treatment by Bulman; unclear water rights; Bulman's refusal to account for the financial yield of the crop in 1927; and the sale of a part of the farm to Stawitzky in the spring of 1928. The conflict escalated when the Austrians adopted the view that the CCA had misled them when it settled them in the Okanagan Valley. Accusations started to fly back and forth, with predictable results.

What had happened? From the very beginning, failure was virtually inevitable for a number of reasons. Misunderstandings, excessive expectations, and egotism on both sides of the argument led to the disaster. Nonetheless, it was primarily the fault of the associations which should have known better and actually did know better. The problem was that the Austrians did not really understand the terms of the bill of sale and signed the contract without having any idea about the risks of such a business. They had hoped to work the land as a co-operative.[48] Unfortunately, when the immigrants took over the farm in 1927, the whole Okanagan Valley was in extremely bad shape. Land values were under pressure, and water rates were very high and subject to fluctuations. Most of the private irrigation system was bankrupt because the water charges were apparently insufficient. It was openly doubted by the majority of men who were interviewed by the CCA and Father Kierdorf of the AGCC at that time that the Austrians could "pay for their land" by hard work and frugal living at anywhere near the prices prevalent at that time. The people were equally divided between those who thought that Bulman had been crazy for selling his land on such terms, and others who believed that the Austrians had been crazy for wanting to undertake such a business. What is more, the Austrian settlers entered into the agreement with no knowledge of the special agricultural difficulties posed by the Okanagan Valley.[49]

Another reason for the farm's lack of success were internal problems. Their leader, Stawitzky, was incapable of solving them. He was deposed as leader of the group, and the AGCC sent a supervisor to provide practical assistance to them. Constantly goaded into distrusting one another, the Austrians could not agree among themselves about anything.[50] Father Kierdorf reported that the people had no esprit de corps; their narrow-mindedness and childish behaviour grew to such an extent that living together became almost impossible. One man was said to have left the farm with his family because he did not get any cider. Most of them, that is nine families, lived in the big house on the farm, cramped together, chiefly because no one wanted to move out. Finally, the smaller houses on the land were readied and five families moved in there. But even in the big farm house, one family had only one room.[51] Another settler complained that his family had to give away the last cent they had brought with them for dishes or an iron, for a comb or an elastic band.[52]

A standing quarrel between Stawitzky and Emil Benesch, who also wanted to become head of the group, divided the Austrians. They "were constantly agitated with frequent visits and free advice from certain radical elements in the Valley who spoke their language" with whom Benesch had good contacts. According to the supervising associations, "the most damaging report spread by these was to the effect that the AGCC and the CCA had bought the property for $100,000 and were selling it at a profit of approximately $50,000."[53] Bulman and others were told that "they were continually taunting the hard-working and loyal colonists for having sold themselves to benefit moneyed landowners and others interested in exploiting the uneducated."[54] Native Canadians involved in this venture described the settlers as people who had little or no agricultural experience and could not be made to co-operate.[55] However, Bulman had sold the farm upon Stawitzky's assurances that the Austrian colonists were experienced agriculturists and that both men and women "would be willing to work not less than 10 hours a day."[56] It turned out, however, that Austrian farming methods and the equipment used were different. The Austrians had an agricultural background, but almost all of them had worked in the coal works of Neufeld, Lower Austria, before they became unemployed and had only been working occasionally in agriculture during the factory off-season.[57] The CCA remarked that "during the fruit picking season, two of the women of the group became really proficient as fruit pickers, but the men of the colony were very slow to adapt themselves to any new work."[58] One day after their arrival, it had become apparent that the Austrians had no idea about the running of a larger farm. They had to be told everything. They were willing to work, but did not know where to begin. They had to be shown how everything worked; for instance, how to harness horses, to plough, to break land, and to operate machinery.[59]

The existing letters and files about this settlement are sometimes contradictory. Nonetheless, all associations and authorities involved in the establishment of the settlement admitted that the negative outcome was clearly predictable. But why was it not undertaken differently? Was it set up as a co-operative because the Austrian families wanted to live close to each other, or were other motivations decisive? After the failure of this settlement, the CCA had to put up with the criticism that the CPR had primarily carried out this kind of settlement in regions removed from any centre in order to maximize profits for the transportation of men and goods. The CCA admitted only that it had been a risky experiment from the very beginning. But in fact, there was an extremely high risk involved in the venture. It would have been much more advantageous to the

Austrians, had they been settled in the Prairie provinces. The Austrian government admitted that the Migration Office and the AGCC had originally agreed upon accommodation of the Austrian families as farm labourers with individual farmers. After a certain period, they should have been offered the opportunity to settle as independent farmers. However, according to the supervising Canadian associations it was difficult to find farm employment for a man with a large family or small children. If they had been placed in farm employment it would have been necessary to scatter them all over western Canada.[60]

In the end, the Austrians wanted to be compensated for the damage suffered from the purchase of the farm and held the AGCC and Father Kierdorf responsible for the fiasco. But Austrian officials with the Migration Office held their own emigrants liable: the settlers had to pay off their debts because the preconditions of the immigration agreement negotiated by the Migration Office and the AGCC had been fully met. Yet, despite these setbacks, the Burgenländer still seemed not only to survive but to thrive. By 1929-30, some of the settlers owned second-hand cars, most had some savings, and some had even sent money to their relatives in Burgenland. Stawitzky, for example, managed to finance a trip to Kelowna for two relatives.[61] All the difficulties notwithstanding, one of the Austrians, Lukas Sollmer (Solmer), wrote, he was well.[62] Another, Emil Benesch, wrote to Dr. Franz Rager, the Secretary of the Chamber of Workers and Employees in Vienna, that Canada was the right choice for emigration because there was enough work (at least at that time), more than in the Prairies, and that it was also better paid. He did not worry about his future.[63]

ENDNOTES

1.   Karl Bachinger, Helga Hemetsberger-Koller and Herbert Matis, eds., *Grundriß der österreichischen Sozial- und Wirtschaftsgeschichte von 1848 bis zur Gegenwart* (Vienna, Stuttgart, 1987), pp. 42, 51.

2.   Gertrud Neuwirth and John de Vries, "Demographic Patterns of Austrian Canadians, 1900-1991," in Franz A.J. Szabo, ed., *Austrian Immigration to Canada: Selected Essays* (Ottawa, 1996), pp. 35-36, Table 1.

3.   Österreichisches Staatsarchiv [henceforth cited as ÖStA), Archiv der Republik [henceforth cited as AdR], Bundeskanzleramt/Inneres, Wanderungsamt [henceforth cited as BKA/WA], 2236/176, 8/4 c/1, Z1. 56.022 WA/1928 and 2236/289, 8/4 As/2, 1924-30.

4. *Atlas* 17/14 (29 September 1927).

5. ÖStA, BKA/WA, 2236/358, 8/4, Zl. 50.080/1927.

6. Wolfgang Meixner, "Die österreichische Auswanderung von 1848 bis zur Gegenwart." (unpublished M.A. thesis, University of Vienna, 1991), p. 99.

7. Donald Avery, *Dangerous Foreigners: European Immigrant Workers and Labour Radicalism in Canada, 1896-1932* (Toronto, 1979), p. 92.

8. Freda Hawkins, *Critical Years in Immigration: Canada and Australia Compared* (Kingston, 1989), p. 27, and Public Archives of Canada [henceforth cited as PAC], microfilm, reel C-10, 652, RG 76, Vol. 576, file 816172, F.C. Blair to Robert Forke, 29 September 1928.

9. PAC, reel C-10, 652, letter to O. D. Skelton, 19 July 1928 and J. Egan to F. Franke, 2 November 1925.

10. *Ibid.*, letter to Skelton, 19 July 1928 and *Atlas* 17/14 (24 September 1927).

11. PAC, reel C-10, 652, letter to Franke, 19 July 1928 and ÖStA, BKA/WA, 2236/176, 8/4, c/l, Zl. 52.599/1928.

12. ÖStA, BKA/WA, 2236/176, 8/4, c/1, Zl. 53.185/129.

13. Österreichisches Wanderungsamt, *Wochenbericht* 8/38 (22 September 1930), 766.

14. Avery, *Dangerous Foreigners*, p. 91.

15. Bundesamt für Statistik, *Statistisches Jahrbuch für die Republik Österreich* 10 (1929), 44.

16. Elisabeth M. Mayer, "Stories about People of German Language Background in Victoria, B.C.: As They Lived Within the Framework of Canadian and German History Between 1850 and 1985." Unpublished manuscript. (Victoria, B.C., 1986), pp. 115-17.

17. PAC, reel C-10, 652, 29 September 1928.

18. *Ibid.*, 17 August 1929.

19. ÖStA, BKA/WA, 2236/176, 8/4, c/1, Zl. 55.410-WA/1929.

20. *Ibid.*, Zl. 54.614/1929.

21. *Ibid.*

22. *Ibid.*, Zl. 55.504-WA/1929.

23. *Ibid.*, Zl. 55.663-WA/1929.

24. *Ibid.*, 2236/4, 8/4, Zl. 55.231/1929.

25. *Ibid.*, 2236/261, 8/4 1, Zl. 54.397-WA/1929.

26. Österreichisches Wanderungsamt, *Wochenbericht* 8/35 (1 September 1930), 704.

27. *Übersee* 10/42 (16 October 1928), 3 and 11/25 (18 June 1929), 3.

28. *Ibid.*, 9/11 (15 March 1927), 3; Adolf Neipl, Vancouver, 27 February 1927.

29. *Ibid.*, 9/31 (2 August 1927), 4; Martin Rieger, Prince Albert, SK, 7 July 1927.

30. *Ibid.*, 12/6 (7 February 1930), 3; John Hiebl, Alberta, 12 January 1930.

31. ÖStA, BKA/WA, 2236/176, 8/4 c/1, Zl. 55.663-WA/1929.

32. Austrian Immigration to Canada Collection [henceforth cited as AICC], Interview with John (Johann) Janschitz, Calgary, 10 April 1995.

33. *Atlas* 17/14 (24 September 1927).

34. *Übersee*, 11/11 (12 March 1929), 3; Johann Grohotolsky, Preston, ON, 6 February 1929.

35. *Ibid.*, 9/9 (1 March 1927), 3; Joe Kristositz, Winnipeg, 4 February 1927.

36. *Ibid.*, 14/5 (29 January 1932), 3; R. Roider, Vancouver, 31 December 1931.

37. *Ibid.*, 10/29 (17 July 1928), 2; Franz Neumaier, 24 June 1928.

38. *Ibid.*, 9/14 (4 April 1927), 5; Karl Horatschek, Winnipeg; the musician was born in Bregenz, Vorarlberg and went to Canada in 1927 as a "farm labourer" but was able to establish himself as a music teacher. See also ÖStA, BKA/WA, 2236/384, 8/4, Passagierlisten 1926-27, Zl. 62.467/1927, May 1927, Red Star Line.

39. Stony Plain and District Historical Society, *Along the Fifth: A History of Stony Plain, Alberta* (Stony Plain, 1982), Vincent and Lydia Assinger, p. 207.

40. *Übersee* 11/33 (13 August 1929), 3; Franz Frank, 21 July 1929 and 12/12 (21 March 1930), 3; Franz Frank, 10 February 1930.

41. PAC, reel C-10, 652, F. Franke to J. Egan, 23 November 1927 and ÖStA, BKA/WA, 2236/176, 8/4 c/1, Zl. 65.025-WA/1927 and Zl. 53.235-WA/1928.

42. ÖStA, BKA/WA, 2236/289, 8/4 As/2, Zl. 60.170/1930, Joseph Weingerl (?), 20 December 1930.

43. AICC, Interviews with Peter Frieser, Edmonton, 24 April 1995 and with John (Johann) Janschitz, Calgary, 10 April 1995.

44. See Louis Hamilton, "Foreigners in the Canadian West," *Dalhousie Review* 17 (1938), 456, 459.

45. *Übersee* 15/39 (21 September 1933), 3; Johann Schaertl, 27 August 1933.

46. ÖStA, BKA/WA, 2236/358, 8/4, Bulman Farm, Zl. 59.371/1928 and Zl. 69.784/1927, 1 August 1927.

47. Glenbow Archives [henceforth cited as GA], Canadian Pacific Railway Fonds. Land Settlement and Development Series (CPR), M 2269, file 1861 and file 650, 16 February 1928.

48. ÖStA, BKA/WA, 2236/358, 8/4, Zl. 63.618/1929.

49. GA, CPR, M 2269, file 649, 17 September 1927.

50. *Ibid.*, file 1862, 25 January 1928.

51. ÖStA, BKA/WA, 2236/358, 8/4, Zl. 69.784/1927, 8 October 1927.

52. *Ibid.*, Zl. 54.229/1928.

53. GA, CPR, M 2269, file 650, 16 February 1928.

54. *Ibid.*, file 1862.

55. *Ibid.*, file 650, 16 February 1928.

56. ÖStA, BKA/WA, 2236/358, 8/4, Zl. 59.371/1928, 7 February 1928.

57. *Ibid.*, Zl. 54.229/1928.
58. *Ibid.*, Zl. 59.371/1928, 7 February 1928.
59. *Ibid.*, Zl. 69.784/1927, 8 October 1927.
60. *Ibid.*, Zl. 63.618/1929 and Zl. 202.786/1929.
61. *Ibid.*, Zl. 72.744 WA/Act/1930.
62. *Übersee* 11/13 (23 March 1929), 3; Lukas Sollmer, 23 February 1929.
63. ÖStA, BKA/WA, 2236/358, 8/4, Zl. 54.229/1928.

CHAPTER IV
AUSTRIAN REFUGEES OF WORLD WAR II

Anna Maria Pichler and Gabrielle Tyrnauer

THE *ANSCHLUSS* represented a horrific experience for those Austrians who opposed National Socialism and its ideology, those who remained loyal to the idea of an independent Austria, and those—almost all Jews or of Jewish descent—who suddenly found themselves deprived of all civil and economic rights. Opponents to the regime who did not want to yield to violent oppression and therefore had to fear for their lives and those who had to fear for their lives on "racial" grounds, were faced with the question of where to go, now that Austria was no longer a safe *Heimat.* After the War, many people in the West will often ask uncomprehendingly when faced with the appalling legacy of the Third Reich: "Well, why didn't they just *leave* the country when there was still time?" But leaving Austria was extremely difficult. Where should these Austrians go? Who would take them? How would they get there? Could they avoid being received as "Germans"?

This chapter will address these issues from two perspectives. The first addresses the question of who these refugees were and what they experienced after leaving Austria. The Jews represented the largest group of those wanting to flee Austria; therefore the main focus here will be on their lives. The second aspect of the problem concerns the attitudes of the receiving country, in this case Canada. Which policies on immigration did Canada have in place at that time, and what were their effects on potential immigrants?

THE WORLD WAR II REFUGEES:
EXPERIENCES AND IDENTITIES

Gabrielle Tyrnauer

The mass emigration which began the moment the first Austrian Republic ceased to exist was unlike any other emigration in the history of Austria. In the days and months following the *Anschluss,* well in excess of one
hundred thousand people left, fearing for their safety and lives. Of these,
by far the largest number were Jewish, and it is this population which will
provide the focus of attention here. There were others, of course: social
democrats, communists, monarchists, supporters of the previous government, as well as outspoken writers and artists for whom Hitler's regime
represented a twentieth-century barbarism. Many of these, like my father,
were also Jews, thus doubly targeted. He was arrested in his office (he
worked for an American wire service) the day of the *Anschluss* in the presence of Adolf Eichmann. Several days later, we became refugees.[1]

The Jews of Vienna were swiftly identified in accordance with the
notorious Nuremberg Laws in effect in Germany, and isolated from the sur-
rounding population. According to the Nazi census of 1939 there were then
94,530 Jews still living in Austria after the departure of some 84,000 others, who had left Austria between March 1938 and May 1939. Non-Nazi
sources give the total pre-*Anschluss* figure as being slightly over 200,000 for
Vienna, and some 220,000 for all of Austria, thus making Jews around 10
percent of the Viennese population and 3 percent of the total Austrian population.[2] The concentration in the capital city, given as 91 percent of Austrian Jews in 1934, increased after the *Anschluss.*[3] Within months, the small
communities in the provinces virtually disappeared and were absorbed into
the Vienna community, if not directly deported elsewhere. One survivor
from Graz, for example, recalled that the mayor had proudly announced
that his city was the first to be *judenrein* (Jew-cleansed).[4]

THE *ANSCHLUSS*

The *Anschluss* marked a watershed in the lives of all Austrian refugees. For
them it was personal as well as national history when their relationships
with family, friends, neighbours and the nation changed overnight. All of

our interviewees could remember in great detail what he or she was doing that day, more than half a century ago. The hitherto outlawed Nazi party symbols suddenly appeared everywhere. Butchers, bakers, housemaids, and schoolteachers appeared in SS-uniforms or with swastika armbands, or at least sporting the Nazi party lapel pin, which many had, no doubt, worn covertly for years.[5] The editor of an Austrian newspaper reported that even as Hitler's legions were approaching Vienna and Austrian Nazis were fighting pro-independence demonstrators in the streets, many policemen went home to get their forbidden swastika badges or to buy some if they did not have them. The typesetters on the newspaper *Der Telegraf* went home to change their clothes. "What does that mean?" the editor asked a colleague. "You don't know what that means?.... It means boots, brown shirts, swastika badges and rifles."[6]

Janitors compiled lists of Jews and Austrian loyalists living in their houses for the Gestapo. In some cases, formerly underground Nazis turned violently against their Jewish neighbours, pupils, clients, or employers. In other cases, they used their new elite status to protect Jewish friends and neighbours. In our oral history interviews we had examples of both. Old scores were settled by denunciation. The apartment house neighbours who objected to the Jewish children's noisiness now had a good chance of acquiring their parents' more spacious apartment. One interviewee remembered the exhilaration of a boy's nanny returning from Hitler's victory parade on March 13, 1938; another the surprise he felt to see a favourite gym teacher shifting his National Socialist party pin from underneath his lapel to its surface. This teacher used his sudden power to warn his Jewish pupil of an impending raid. Still another interviewee remembered an SS-officer in uniform arriving at the door of his house. He recognized a former schoolfriend who warned him of a deportation order that he had been sent to deliver.[7]

Within 24 hours, a process was accomplished which took five years of Nazi rule in Germany. The editor of a leading Viennese daily newspaper prophesied in 1938:

Hitler would treat the Austrian Jews very much worse than he has treated the Jews in Germany. In Germany it was two years and more before all the laws against Jews were codified and became fully effective with the framing of Nuremberg's racial legislation. The racial paragraphs could be applied in Austria overnight. The Jews would wake up one morning and find all their rights gone.[8]

The journalist's prophecy proved correct. Several thousand Jews were arrested during the first few days following the *Anschluss*. Pogroms were spontaneous as well as organized. Shops and homes were looted. Jews were rounded up to clean anti-nazi graffiti with scrub brushes, with toothbrushes, or even with their bare hands; they had been painted to persuade Austrians to vote for an independent Austria in the last-ditch plebiscite scheduled by Chancellor Schuschnigg. The plebiscite scheduled to approve the *Anschluss* gave an immediate pretext to the Nazis for their onslaught. By tapping phone lines it was discovered that the Jewish community had contributed substantially to the previous government's campaign to keep Austria independent. They were forced to give an equal amount to the Nazi side. "Managing commissars" were installed in Jewish businesses, beginning the day after the German arrival. All Jewish enterprises were branded by glaring red signs, identifying them as such. Sadistic games were devised to torment publicly Jews of all ages.[9]

Foreign observers reported the incidents faithfully and with mounting horror. The American correspondent, William Shirer, described what followed the *Anschluss*. "What one saw in Vienna was almost unbelievable .... The Viennese, usually so soft and gentle, were behaving worse than the Germans, especially towards the Jews. I have never seen such humiliating scenes ... or such Nazi sadism."[10] The correspondent of *The Times of London* described Hitler's triumphant entry into Vienna: "Few conquerors in history have had such a reception. No adjective suffices to describe the jubilation.... There are no signs of a people bowing unwillingly to a foreign yoke." A Swiss correspondent wrote that the reception given to Hitler "mocked all description."[11] Goering commented that the German occupation of the Rhineland two years earlier is "completely eclipsed by this event especially as far as the joy of the people is concerned.... The Fuehrer is deeply moved."[12] In the Nazi-controlled plebiscite of April 10, 1938 more than 99 percent of the votes were for the *Anschluss*.

A wave of suicides swept the Jewish community. During March and April 1938, between 1,500 and 2,000 were reported, mostly in Vienna. During the worst of the pogroms, April 23 and 25, one hundred per day were recorded. Obituaries of entire families were reported in the *Neue Freie Presse,* the only pre-*Anschluss* newspaper still permitted to publish in something resembling its earlier form; other dailies continued to be published under their old names, but were transformed into Nazi propaganda sheets. A furniture manufacturer and his family of six, representing three generations, "died suddenly and had been put to the rest they so longed for."[13]

DEPARTURE

Thus, only a few days after the 1938 *Anschluss,* Jewish Austrians found themselves homeless, stateless, and impoverished. There was no exit from this situation other than death, hiding or emigration. Although the new government seemed to favour emigration in its rhetoric as a means of facilitating their job of "ethnic cleansing," the borders had in fact been effectively sealed after the *Anschluss* and the bureaucratic obstacles placed before those who expressed a desire to emigrate were often overwhelming. This situation is graphically described by an eye witness, Oswald Dutch, in 1938. Whoever attempted to cross a border, he noted, was forced through:

an almost indescribable labyrinth of red tape. He had to produce twelve different certificates to prove he was not in arrears for any kind of tax. Even if he had no dog, he had to prove he was not in arrears with his dog tax.... [E]ach of these certificates meant waiting in a queue for a whole day or even longer at the respective government office. And it was liable to happen at any moment that an official would arrive and declare that "Aryans" were to be given precedence, and Jews who had been waiting for many hours would have to return home and start waiting again the next morning with possibly the same result. One might obtain all necessary certificates within three weeks, in the course of which most of the certificates will have lost their validity, being valid for not more than a fortnight. That would mean queuing again.... [A]ll Vienna consulates are virtually besieged day after day by masses of applicants for visas.... For nearly all, no length of time, no amount of trouble is too much for the chance of at last shaking the dust of Austria from their shoes.[14]

On the individual level, Stefan Zweig has poignantly described the feelings of homelessness for a whole generation: "Every right was taken away from them; every spiritual, every physical form of violence was used against them ... and then they stood on the frontier. Then they begged at the consulates, almost always in vain—for what country wants plundered beggars?"[15] They are prepared to go anywhere, though few knew where they are going or why. Zweig's observation here touches the core of this emigration: it was unplanned, unwanted and permanent. Many left with only the clothes on their backs. The editor of the *Telegraf* remembered that he had only a toothbrush rattling around in his attaché case. He and his colleagues drove to the Czech border, but it had already been closed to Austrians the day of the Anschluss. He described the scene at the Czech border:

We and the others waited silently in the office. We were dazed ... by the fate that had overtaken us so quickly. Most of those around me were staring in front of them in dull despair. Some of them had not awakened to the horror of their situation until they had reached Berg, when Czechoslovakia had so suddenly barred the way to these unhappy refugees. They had left Vienna without making any preparations and without any definite prospect of finding work or even living accommodation.[16]

The rush to consulates and embassies of every country that could issue immediate visas seemed overwhelming to the bureaucrats and diplomats of those nations, still mired in the Great Depression. They perceived this "flood" of asylum seekers with panic, and the doors even of traditional countries of immigration began to swing shut, one after the other.

THE CANADIAN RESPONSE:

CANADA AS SANCTUARY AND PRISON

No door was shut more securely than that of Canada, following the lead of its prime minister, Mackenzie King.[17] As will be shown in greater detail in the second half of this chapter, this policy predated the specific refugee crisis of 1938, for, from the first years of the Nazi regime in Germany, "Canada had the worst record among all western states in granting sanctuary to Jewish refugees from Nazi persecution."[18] However, it was the widely observed plight of the Austrian Jews who faced brutal Nazi pressure to leave their country after its absorption into Hitler's Germany, which led to the hasty convening of a conference in Evian-les-Bains on Lake Geneva, called by President Roosevelt in the summer of 1938 to survey the possibilities for sanctuary and resettlement of Jewish refugees worldwide. Canada participated reluctantly, and then only to make sure that it did not become the involuntary focus of a resettlement scheme.[19]

In the first post-war years, this restrictive policy hardly changed as the survivors of the Holocaust, now known as "Displaced Persons," remained stateless and homeless. Only after the immigration law of 1948 outlawed discrimination based on ethnic origin did the doors slowly open again. Nevertheless, a trickle of Jewish refugees from Austria and elsewhere had managed to enter Canada before then. Ironically, those first designated to enter, a thousand Jewish children from Vichy France, were doomed by the German occupation and Canadian bureaucratic delays to follow their parents to the death camps of the East. They were "the children who never came."[20] Instead, the Canadian government agreed to accept 5,000 British children evacuees. A key member of the Canadian National Committee on Refugees said bluntly: "It is not refugees whom we want to receive ... it is part of Britain's immortality ... that we take into our keeping."[21] Non-Jewish refugees from the Sudetenland were also admitted. As for the persecuted Jews of Europe, in the words of Abella and Troper, none, it seemed, was still too many for Canada.

The only group of Jewish refugees who succeeded in setting foot on Canadian soil did not come voluntarily. Again, as will be seen in the second half of this chapter, they were individuals arrested as "enemy aliens" by the British in 1940 and shipped to Canada with German prisoners of war. A large number of Austrians who had found refuge in Britain were included in this contingent. Stefan Zweig, who fled to London, spoke for all of them when he described his reactions to the news that Austrian Jewish refugees were to be arrested and treated as German nationals—as enemy aliens. Suddenly he was transformed from the stranger seeking sanctuary to the enemy. He could scarcely grasp:

the absurd situation that a human being long rejected and expelled by the very country to which the British government wanted to attach him, to a community to which he, as an Austrian, had in any case never belonged. With a single stroke of the pen his whole life has become a contradiction. While he thought and wrote in German, the content of every thought was with Germany's enemies ... every other tie, everything past was torn and shattered.[22]

Once interned in Canadian camps most internees accepted their confinement as the first step towards their liberation, despite the often harsh conditions prevailing there. The most vehement protests, including a hunger strike in Canada's "Camp N" (Isle aux Noix, Quebec)—vividly remembered by all the ex-internees we interviewed—did not complain about camp conditions, but objected strenuously to the Canadian government's original labelling of them as "prisoners of war." This was a status stipulated by the Geneva Convention, which would guarantee them certain conditions and privileges in wartime detention. But the aspersions on their self-image and identity were what mattered to them. As part of this protest, they refused to see a Red Cross representative whose duty it was to assure the treaty conditions and privileges under the Geneva Convention. They wanted only to have their sometimes despised—but, to them, honourable—identity of "refugee" restored.[23]

Though Canadian guards at these camps seemed to show little understanding of the situation, the refugees displayed a surprising lack of bitterness. Some, particularly the younger ones who were teenagers at the time, even had fond memories of their experience. But there were others who resented the whole operation. A rabbi recalled his humiliation upon landing in Halifax:

When we came off the ship, they made us go through a line of soldiers on both sides; these soldiers took away whatever they wanted: a watch, money, a pencil or pen, whatever they liked to take. It was such a feeling of helplessness. Then they made us march through the whole city, to show off the prisoners they brought in.[24]

A particularly galling memory for many was the difference in treatment between the refugees—regardless of nationality, education or other factors—and the German prisoners of war of officer rank. The latter ate with the British officers, had better rations and accommodations. Once again, the refugees' degraded state was brought home to them. In the midst of war, the enemies received better treatment than their victims.[25] These ironic twists—these ambivalent identities—became the subject of in-group humour, such as the nickname given to the transient camp near Kent, Richborough, a camp where thousands of concentration camp veterans could obtain release only with British visas. It was popularly known as "Camp Anglo-Sachsenhausen." Many of its inmates volunteered for the non-combatant companies composed of aliens, the Pioneer Corps. They facetiously called themselves "The King's Own Enemy Aliens."[26]

EMIGRATION AND IDENTITY

With all the external identity changes that most of the refugees assumed in order to survive (false names, ages, passports, etc.), it was always these involuntary internal identity changes which were the hardest to bear. The overnight transformation from a respected member of the national and municipal community to a despised and penniless outcast caused the most anguish for the Austrian Jewish refugees. Living in a foreign language among strangers, becoming estranged not only from others but from themselves and their previous identity; living with the knowledge that "you can't go home again"—not only because there is no home to which one can return, but because one no longer is who one was when leaving Austria. All of the refugees, interviewees and others, betrayed these feelings, whether they described them or not: the lawyer, raised as a Protestant, who only discovered on the day of the *Anschluss* that his ancestry and official classification was Jewish; the blonde and beautiful actress, my mother, who discovered as she was being driven out of her beloved city that neither appearance nor sentiments defined her for the new rulers of her country, for whom she is only a "Jewess." Yet, sitting in a Paris café she burst into tears when she heard the strains of "The Blue Danube" over the loudspeaker. Finally, there was the vociferously anti-Nazi refugee arrested as an "enemy alien" in his country of refuge. These experiences create ineradicable psychic scars.

Even today, the ambivalences remain. None of those we interviewed expressed a desire to return to Austria to live. None of them defined themselves as Austrians. Yet one respondent, who said he was "no Austrian," added softly: "But I will always be a Viennese." All of these former refugees have been back for visits. In a seminar discussion group for such refugees, one participant remarked: "We had about 200,000 Jews before the war. 100,000 Jews were the assimilated kind, like myself. We were Austrians first; when we said something wrong, we were told to speak proper German.... [We] were Jews. I made my Bar Mitzvah, but otherwise we were not very different from our Christian neighbours." According to this Vienna-loving refugee, his wife is "an Austrian from head to toe. If she knows that tomorrow we will drive into Vienna, she goes bananas, she has a high ... it's *the* city. She says that if we cannot walk down *Kärntnerstraße*, then Hitler won, that the city belongs to us just as much." When asked if he would consider returning there to live, he replied "No," but he visits frequently.[27]

Another participant recounted his own experiences of anti-Semitism as a student. Many of the teachers were underground Nazis. There were frequent fights in the school. "When I became aware I would have to leave, I was relieved ... a great adventure lay in front of me. I didn't know what it entailed." He joined a youth group going to Palestine, then volunteered for the RAF. "Unlike a great number of Austrian Jews who immediately returned after the war ended and were repatriated by UNRRA, [my] patriotism wasn't sufficient for me to return to Austria." He first returned to Vienna in 1953 to investigate the possibility of reparations, discovering in the course of this trip that both his parents had perished in Auschwitz. His mother was a convert to Judaism who was not forced to go to a concentration camp, but she voluntarily accompanied his father. Recently he found deportation lists in a book which included the names

of his parents. It was a "gut-wrenching experience."[28] He reflected bitterly on Austrian anti-Semitism, and yet a melancholy attachment persisted:
"I speak the Austrian dialect like every true Viennese, and I like the kind
of food they eat." Here he broke into laughter as one commented and
others echoed, "Don't we all?" An orthodox rabbi from Montreal, recol-
lected that, despite his strong Jewish identity, he had once been a proud
Austrian, "very nationalistic." He would not buy any product which was
not made in Austria. "We were proud to be Austrian citizens. We felt this
was our country. I was attracted by the culture." Anti-Semitism was severe
when he was growing up, but it did not prevent his feelings of loyalty
towards Austria. It was simply a part of the scene and was always there:
"We grew up with it, we didn't know anything else."[29]

Another, older interviewee, who had been interned in Canada, spoke
of his religious and secular upbringing: "Let me put it this way: I was not
brought up religious. I never thought much of religion. I was always
proud to be a Jew, but I was never proud to be a practising Jew. When I
was attacked as a Jew, I fought like a tiger to defend it, but in practice I
couldn't care less." Questioned about his Austrian identity, he replied:

A: I am still proud to be Viennese ... not Austrian but Viennese. Vienna was always
anti-Semitic. We were always the Jews and I was always fighting for it.
Q: But still you love Vienna?
A: Yes, I love Vienna; I don't love the people, I love Vienna.
Q: And how about going back to Vienna?
A: [With vehemence] No way, for no money in the world would I go back to Vienna,
but I go and visit. Any time. My wife and I took a trip to Europe and we spent quite a
long time in Vienna.

He met his son and daughter-in-law there and spent a week showing
them around. As he spoke his voice softened. "I remember every small
stone in Vienna." Asked, if he felt nostalgic he responded: "Not really. I
always had in the background of my mind, the Austrian, the anti-Semitism, that's why I don't care for Austrians." But his tone belied his words.
He has been to Israel several times and recalled many fond memories of
these visits. Yet asked if he ever thought of emigrating to Israel, he replied,
"No, I am quite happy being Viennese—and Canadian."[30]

The American historian George Berkley was impelled to study Jewish Vienna by the remarks of a middle-aged Viennese Jewish refugee, who
assured him that, before the war, she had lived in "a virtual paradise." This

glorification of the city from which she had been forced to flee for her life puzzled and intrigued him. He had never heard German Jewish refugees speak so ecstatically of their native cities. Vienna, Berkley reasoned, "must have been very different."[31] Indeed, every German-speaking refugee understood the ambivalence that this city evoked in the hearts of those it had driven out. And that element was at the core of this unique emigration—ambivalence combined with an often frustrated yearning to reproduce a lifestyle that they could never feel fully a part of again. And the more assimilated they were, the more it hurt. These refugees had not been marginal to the life of the "city of dreams"—they had been at the heart of it.

CANADA'S IMMIGRATION POLICIES AND AUSTRIAN REFUGEES, 1938-1945

Anna Maria Pichler

After having welcomed many thousands of immigrants from Europe around the turn of the century, the Canada of the 1930s decided to curtail its flow of immigration severely. Economic considerations played a role in that decision, although not altogether the determining one. The worldwide Depression had had dire consequences for Canada. Many businesses had gone bankrupt, and in 1933 one third of Canada's working population was unemployed.[32] Canada decided to fight the economic crisis by trying to shut herself off from the rest of the world. Measures were taken in the form of high trade barriers to keep other countries' products out, in the form of a strong isolationism in her foreign policy to keep other countries' diplomatic problems out, and in the form of a very restrictive immigration policy to keep other countries' refugees out.

Canada—as most people know it now—prides itself on being a country with a long history of welcoming refugees and dissidents. In this respect, the years between 1938 and 1945 certainly do not represent a glorious chapter in Canadian history. At a time when Nazi oppression in Europe had tens of thousands of people applying for asylum in Canada, or any other country where they might escape impending persecution or death, Canada decided to keep its doors shut. In the years from 1938 to 1945, Canada only accepted around 10,000 German and Jewish (this includes Austrian) emigrants—less than 10 percent of the total immigration for these years.[33] One cannot talk about Austrian immigration in these years without talking about Jewish immigration. Among all Austrians, the Jews had the most obvious reasons for fleeing Hitler-dominated Austria and were the biggest group to do so. The measures taken by Canada to keep Jews out were therefore also directed against many Austrian refugees. It is impossible to tell how many Austrians were among the Jews either allowed in or kept out of Canada. We encounter the same difficulty with non-Jewish Austrian emigrants whom the Canadian statistics either classified as Germans, Czechoslovaks or Hungarians, depending on their country of birth. This portion of the chapter will therefore concentrate on a more general view of Canadian immigration policy during the years under consideration and will show its effects on Austrian refugees by means of a few selected examples.

Canadian politicians and civil servants argued that the economic crisis called for stringent measures. While Canada was hit hard by the Depression, so were other countries, and they were more sympathetic to the plight of Hitler refugees. Great Britain accepted 80,000 refugees, the United States 240,000, and even less prosperous countries like Mexico or Colombia offered asylum to 20,000 refugees each.[34] But even before economic doom had descended on Canada in the late 1920s and the 1930s, the government had taken the view that:

The racial and linguistic composition of the immigration was of paramount importance.... Settlers should be of a readily assimilable type, already identified by race or language with one or other of the two great races now inhabiting this country.... This means in practice that the great bulk of the preferable settlers are those who speak the English language, those coming from the United Kingdom or the United States.

The government then went on to enumerate a list of peoples in the order in which they were perceived to be ready to assimilate. On the bottom of their list were people from Eastern Europe, whose Canadianization was what they called "a problem," and people from the Orient.[35] Another telling sign for the government's efforts to keep "less readily assimilated races" out of Canada was the fact that Jews and Negroes were kept in separate categories in the immigration statistics regardless of their nationality. This can be seen in the immigration statistics up to the 1950s.

There was also considerable anti-Semitism in the Canadian population, but it never took any physically violent form. Still, Jews could not become members of certain clubs, a number of hotels and restaurants would not accept and serve Jews, and anti-Semitism shows up in certain legal documents.[36] There were, for instance, sales contracts concerning the sale of land which contained a paragraph prohibiting the buyer to sell the land to non-Christians. This provision was directed not only, but mainly against Jews. In a latent form, anti-Semitism was widespread in the Canada of the 1930s, and in the eyes of the government, it was of such significance that the politicians thought they had to take it into consideration in shaping immigration policy, "lest it might foment an anti-Semitic problem."[37] Many historians nowadays maintain that it was the politicians' and civil servants' anti-Semitic and xenophobic attitudes that prevented Canada from adopting a generous refugee policy. Certainly, many politicians' anti-Semitic attitudes did play an important role. But the crucial question is how the personal attitudes of a few individuals could have such far-reaching and dire consequences. The reason was the vagueness of laws regarding the eligibility for immigration and the minutely detailed regulations regarding their administration.

THE IMMIGRATION ACT

Canada's immigration policy between 1938 and 1945 was based on the Immigration Act of 1927, with amendments dating from 1928, 1936, and 1937.[38] This Immigration Act set down the broad intentions for administrative procedures. It gave details on admission and deportation of immigrants, on the appointment of immigration officials, and on other administrative matters. According to the Act, an immigrant was not permitted to belong to certain prohibited classes,[39] had to have a valid passport, and had to carry with him a sum of money to be determined by the immigration official.[40] Other than that, the act did not lay down explicit rules as to who was eligible for immigration and how to handle applications for immigration. This was left to the discretion of the immigration clerks, or, in the next instance, to the Minister of Immigration.

To make sure that the act could be quickly adapted to changing circumstances, Parliament delegated legislative powers, in the form of orders-in-council, to the Cabinet.[41] This delegation of authority applied to a wide field, as can be seen in paragraph 38 of the Immigration Act:

The Governor in Council may, by proclamation or order whenever he deems it necessary or expedient,
(a) prohibit the landing in Canada or at any special port of entry in Canada of any

immigrant who has come to Canada otherwise than by continuous journey from the country of which he is a native or naturalized citizen ...

(c) prohibit or limit in number for a stated period or permanently the landing in Canada, ... of immigrants belonging to any nationality or race or of immigrants of any specified class or occupation, by reason of any economic, industrial or other condition temporarily existing in Canada or because such immigrants are deemed unsuitable having regard to the climatic, industrial, social, educational, labour or other conditions or requirements of Canada or because such immigrants are deemed undesirable owing to their peculiar customs, habits, modes of life and methods of holding property, and because of their probable inability to become readily assimilated or to assume the duties and responsibilities of Canadian citizenship within a reasonable time after their entry.[42]

It seems reasonable enough for Parliament to have authorized the Cabinet to alter the Immigration Act under certain circumstances, provided the Cabinet's decision would remain provisional until the next parliamentary session.[43] It also seems reasonable to allow the Cabinet to make regulations prohibiting the admission of people in certain occupations, depending on economic circumstances. Subsection (c), however, set down the preconditions for regulatory power in very general terms. While parliamentary debates were open so that possible shortcomings of statutory provisions could be pointed out in the full light of publicity, Cabinet sessions were secret and members of the Cabinet were sworn not to reveal anything that had been discussed in their meetings. By giving the Cabinet more or less a carte blanche for drawing up additional immigration regulations, the Canadian Parliament relinquished its legislative responsibility. At the same time, it also gained a big advantage in doing so: embarrassing discussions about whether anybody's admission to Canada could be prohibited on grounds as "peculiar customs" or "climatic conditions" did not have to be held in public.

DECISIVE ORDERS-IN-COUNCIL

In the 1930s and the 1940s, the Cabinet issued a multitude of orders-in-council. Four of them had an strong impact on Canadian immigration policy during World War II. In September 1930, Order-in-Council PC 2115 prohibited immigration of persons from the Orient.[44] Six months later, the Cabinet issued an order-in-council prohibiting the landing of immigrants of all classes and occupations, with certain exceptions. These were either citizens from Commonwealth countries and the United

States, or spouses, fiancées and children under 18 of any person resident in Canada who was "in a position to receive and care for his dependents." Only agriculturists "having sufficient means to farm in Canada" were exempt from the prohibition to immigrate to Canada."[45] In November 1938, Order-in-Council P.C. 3016 decreed that immigrants had to have a valid passport "issued by the Government of which such person is a subject or citizen."[46] This Cabinet decision made it even more difficult for Austrians to emigrate to Canada as Austria had been occupied by Germany some eight months earlier. Although refugees might have had valid Austrian passports, they were now subjects of Germany. Their immigration could now be refused easily if they were unable to obtain German passports. Finally, four days after declaring war on Germany, the Cabinet issued Order-in-Council P.C. 2653 prohibiting the landing in Canada of "enemy aliens and nationals of any country now occupied by an enemy country," which of course included Austrians.[47]

The Cabinet's direct influence on immigration regulations was not confined to prohibiting the immigration of certain groups or individuals. It could also issue orders-in-council recommending that the immigration prohibition be waived in certain cases. Almost all Austrians who were able to land in Canada between 1938 and 1945 had a special order-in-council issued, explicitly exempting them from the immigration prohibition.

ADMINISTERING THE LAW

In the Immigration Act, Parliament not only delegated power to the Cabinet; power was also given to immigration officials to apply the Act and the regulations to each individual case coming before them. Who were these officials? In the years after 1931, immigration to Canada had been reduced to a trickle. With this development in mind, the Department of Immigration was dissolved in 1936, and immigration matters had become the "backwater" of government service. They were handled by the Immigration Branch, attached to the Department of Mines and Resources, reporting to a minister who neither had time, nor likely the knowledge, to exercise great influence on immigration matters. The Branch consisted of a handful of civil servants who displayed a great fondness for regulations and were often unbending in their application.[48] Frederick C. Blair, who had spent 30 years in the Branch, was appointed Director in 1936 and held this position until 1944—a most important period for refugees. Blair's main concern was to let only those people in "who fit in our established population pattern," and he was convinced that Jews belonged to "the unassimilable groups."[49]

The immigration officers did not have to search very hard to find regulations that helped them to keep refugees out. The Immigration Act stipulated that immigrants could not belong to certain "prohibited classes." Subsection (h) ruled out immigrants "to whom money has been given or loaned by any charitable organization for the purpose of enabling them to qualify for landing in Canada under this Act, or whose passage to Canada has been paid wholly or in part by any charitable organization."[50] As many refugees had had their possessions confiscated in Austria or Germany, and as there was a law that only ten Reichsmark could be taken out of the Third Reich, this meant that the majority of the refugees could be classified as belonging to the prohibited class (h) and could thus be denied immigration to Canada. The Immigration Act also decreed that immigrants had to carry a sum of money to be determined by the immigration officer, "which amount may vary according to the nationality, race, occupation or destinations of such persons."[51] The fact that an applicant's nationality or "race" could influence the amount of money he had to carry if he wanted to immigrate provides an idea of what could happen if the immigration officer had a personal dislike of certain "races" or nationalities.

In fact, Blair used this section fairly often to keep "less assimilable groups" out. He continuously raised the minimum amount of money required for the admission of Jewish families. Between January and November 1938, the required immigration capital for Jews rose from $5,000 to $15,000. In December 1938, the Immigration Branch refused Jewish applicants who wanted to bring $20,000 to Canada. In August 1939, the director of the Jewish Immigrant Aid Society wrote to his co-workers in Europe that Jews who were willing to invest up to $170,000 in Canada had been refused by the Immigration Branch "on the grounds that their industry might compete with others."[52] Another pretext that Blair used to keep certain immigrant groups out was that refugees had not exported their immigration capital legally. In June 1938, Blair hesitated to grant immigration to two Austrian families with enough immigration capital:

The Georg von Weisl family have $17,000; Dr. Emil von Hofmannsthal has $15,000. No doubt they would be sent to an internment camp or shot for taking this money out of Austria and it is unthinkable that they should register at a German Consulate to protest citizenship in Germany. If we take them, we must run the risk of their becoming a problem in Canada.[53]

Nowadays, Blair is seen as a very controversial figure, and many historians criticize his strong anti-Semitism.[54] After all, in September 1938 Blair had boasted, "pressure on the part of Jewish people to get into Canada has never been greater than it is now, and I am glad to be able to add, after 35 years' experience here, that it was never so well controlled."[55]

Of course, Blair was a product of his time, and it should be pointed out that the rules and regulations which he applied had been set down by the Parliament and the Cabinet years before his appointment as Director of the Immigration Branch. The policy that he administered corresponded more or less to the thinking of the Canadian government. In November 1938, the Cabinet washed its hands regarding the refugee problem:

We do not want to take too many Jews, but in the present circumstances, we do not want to say so. We do not want to legitimize the Aryan mythology by introducing any formal distinction for immigration purposes between Jews and non-Jews. The practical distinction, however, has to be made and should be drawn with discretion and sympathy by the competent department, without the need to lay down a formal minute of policy.[56]

Thus, Blair and his subordinates were given a free hand to apply the regulations as they saw fit. The fact that a civil servant as inflexible and anti-Semitic as Blair was given such wide discretionary powers had tragic consequences for tens of thousands of refugees trapped in Austria and the rest of Europe.

AUSTRIAN REFUGEES IN CANADA

As indicated above, for most of the Austrian refugees the only way to immigrate to Canada was to have an order-in-council issued for them. This meant that they had to have connections to influential Canadians who could arrange for their application to be brought up in a Cabinet meeting. With an intercessor important enough, other regulations such as not having sufficient immigration capital or having job qualifications competing with Canadians could be disregarded.

The case of the Austrian Salzmann family shows how important it was to play along with the patronage game if an immigration application was to be successful. Walter Salzmann, owner of a large shoe store in Vienna, applied for immigration at the Canadian Consulate in Vienna in March 1938. He had deposited £15,000 in a British bank account in 1928 which he was willing to invest in Canada to establish himself as a

farmer (the only occupation exempt from the general immigration prohibition). He intended to set up the farm with an Austrian cousin, a certain Mr. Leopold, who owned a farm near Vienna. Mr. Leopold, at that
time, had leased his farm to someone else. The Canadian consul refused
to grant them immigration on the grounds that Canada needed people
working on farms and not leasing them to others. Knowing that they
were Jewish may or may not have influenced his decision. Two months
later, Salzmann's son Paul accompanied Canadian business partners to
Montreal without having a visa. He was interned immediately, but was
able to contact a Canadian lawyer, Norman Genser, who had excellent
connections to members of Parliament. Genser contacted M. Vien, a
Quebec member of Parliament. Through M. Vien's intercession, Paul's
case was brought to the Cabinet and he was granted immigrant status.
Suddenly the £15,000 were very welcome in Canada and Paul set up a
shoe factory in Montreal. Further financial contributions to M. Vien
helped to obtain more orders-in-council and to bring in the rest of the
Salzmann family.[57]

Eugene Stearns, formerly an engineer in Vienna, has a similar success
story to tell. Although he and his family had neither the money to pay for
their passage to Canada nor any immigration capital to invest, Stearns
had in Mr. Morton, a building contractor in Canada, an uncle with good
connections to Canadian politicians. Mr. Morton promised that he
would help his nephew set up his own business in Canada, had a politi-
cian intercede for an order-in-council, and the Stearns family could
immigrate. Although Jewish, Stearns struck up a good relationship with
Blair who seems to have been able to make exceptions to his general views
towards Jewish immigrants.[58] Anna Askenazy was another Jewish-Austri-
an immigrant with good connections to Blair. She helped Richard Redler,
an Austrian lawyer with close connections to the pre-1938 Austrian
regime, but with no money to invest, to immigrate to Canada by inter-
ceding for him with Blair. An order-in-council was promptly issued and
Richard Redler immigrated in 1941. According to Redler, she was able to
obtain orders-in-council for six other Austrian refugees.[59] On the other
hand, countless efforts were made by various Jewish Immigration Aid
Societies to help Jewish refugees immigrate to Canada by offering to help
them set up a business. These were thwarted by Blair on the grounds that
the immigrants belonged to "prohibited class (h)."[60]

Otto Habsburg, the son of the last Austrian emperor, was also able to
obtain several orders-in-council for his relatives and people close to his

political ideals. None of these people fulfilled the required regulations. They did not have the required funds, they did not farm, and they had not paid for their passage to Canada. But having an important intercessor apparently did wonders to dispel any concerns which the Immigration Branch might have had.[61]

The biggest group of Austrian refugees coming to Canada during World War II were people who had been interned in Great Britain in June 1940 and were then deported to Canada on the grounds that they represented a serious threat to security.[62] They were victims of a mass hysteria in Great Britain just as the Battle of Britain was in progress. In June 1940, Great Britain interned tens of thousands refugees from Austria and Germany out of fear they might assist a German invasion of England. The majority of them were Jews or political refugees who had come to England to escape persecution by Hitler. Now, once again, they were branded as enemies of the country in which they lived. Around 7,000 men expressly labelled by Great Britain as combatant and dangerous enemy aliens were deported to Canada by July 1940. Among them were 2,500 Austrians and Germans who had already proved to British authorities that they were victims of the National Socialist regime.[63] These civilian internees were kept in Canadian camps for years although their innocence had been established four months after their arrival in Canada. But the Canadian government put up strong resistance against having them released in Canada on the ground that they had not come to Canada via the usual way of immigration. Half of them returned to England to be released there as early as January 1941. By February 1941, Canada reluctantly agreed to have a few students among the internees temporarily released in Canada. But it took two more years to have all civilian internees in Canadian camps either released in Canada or in England. About half of the original 2,500 were eventually released in Canada.

CONDITIONS IN CANADA

Austrian refugees were classed as enemy aliens; administratively they were treated like Germans. Under the "Defence of Canada Regulations (DOCR)," issued in September 1939, they had to fulfil certain conditions to "continue to enjoy the protection of the law and ... the respect and consideration due to peaceful and law abiding citizens." The main points were that they were not supposed to serve in another army and to engage in any activity, such as spying, that would lead to the suspicion they were trying to help the enemy. They had to appear at the Registrar of Enemy Aliens regularly. Most of the time, this Registrar's office was the same as the local police station; in other cases, enemy aliens had to register at the postmaster's or the mayor's office. Enemy aliens had to obtain special permission to leave the town in which they were registered, even if they only wanted to go away for a few days. Any failure to comply with these rules would result in internment, the regulations warned.[64]

During World War II, Canada interned about 800 Germans and Austrians on the grounds that they represented a security risk, whereas almost 9,000 Germans and Austro-Hungarians had been interned between 1914 and 1918.[65] Compared to the fate of refugees in many other exile countries, however, Austrian refugees were treated with consideration in Canada. Once they had climbed over the hurdles erected by the Canadian government and immigration officials and had been admitted into Canada, their freedom was constrained after the outbreak of war, but they had more elbow room in Canada than they would have had in many other countries. But this freedom of movement did not apply to the released civilian internees who had come to Canada via deportation from England. As they were only released in Canada on a temporary basis and did not have the status of landed immigrants, their movements in Canada were closely monitored by the Canadian authorities while the war lasted.[66] Although Canada kept emphasizing that their continued release was dependent on their good behaviour, in the event, it did not re-intern any of the refugees once they had been released.

Austrian refugees who at that time had landed immigrant status in Canada have recounted that, apart from travel restrictions and the regular appearances before the Registrar of Aliens, the regulations did not impinge on their everyday life. They were allowed to work or establish their own businesses, and they could even take on jobs in a field completely different from the one which they had written down in their application for immigration.[67] In comparison, most refugees in Switzerland, for instance, were not allowed to work in their country of exile. Of course, Canada had only accepted a very small number of refugees. Not even all of them taken together, could pose any kind of threat to the Canadian working population.

Thus, the treatment of Jewish (and other) refugees from Austria appears to have been inconsistent. On the one hand, Canada showed extreme reluctance in accepting Jewish refugees; on the other, it treated those fortunate few who were able to immigrate relatively well. However, this apparently inconsistent attitude was really not contradictory at all. It is a quite common phenomenon that a society discriminating against certain minority groups selects a few prominent members of these groups and treats them far better than the rest. The "Court Jew" known in Europe since the fourteenth century is just one of many examples of this sort of reaction. Living in a restrictive Catholic society, the "Court Jew" enjoyed the trust of the ruling classes who came to him for advice and money, and they exempted him from restrictions applied to the vast majority of Jews at that time. The fact that certain Jews were treated better than the rest did not mitigate the basic anti-Semitism. On the contrary, it strengthened the belief that, if at all, only a few Jews deserved better treatment and that it was quite all right to treat the majority badly. At the same time, the people thus favoured served as an alibi to the ruling class: critics of anti-Semitism could be disarmed because one could point to the concrete example of those few who received better treatment.

The few Jewish refugees accepted in Canada between 1938 and 1945 were useful to the government in that very same sense. While Canada remained indifferent towards the fate of millions of refugees trapped in Europe—granting admission to only about 10,000 in eight years—it treated well those who were allowed in. The 10,000 refugees were a good alibi. Should there be criticism about keeping out all the other refugees, the government could point to the exclusive few allowed in and could maintain its non-racist bona fides. Considering this fact, Canada in the years between 1938 and 1945 proved to be an exclusive exile in the true sense of the word.

ENDNOTES

1. I shall use three principal sources in this portion of chapter 4: my own experience and insights derived from growing up in a world of Viennese refugees; the writings of historians and contemporaries who documented the death of the First Republic; and the tape-recorded recollections of (now Canadian) Holocaust survivors and refugees who left Austria between 1938 and 1945. Many of these interviews were conducted as part of McGill University's Living Testimonies Project, and in conjunction with the Austrian Immigration to Canada Project. All those relevant to Austrian refugees will constitute part of the Austrian Immigration to Canada Collection [henceforth AICC], and will be cited as such in this chapter. To preserve the privacy of the individuals involved, notes will simply refer to "oral history interviews."

2. Leo Goldhammer, *Die Juden Wiens: Eine statistische Studie* (Vienna, Leipzig, 1927), p. 9; Eugen Lennhoff, *The Last Five Hours of Austria* (New York, 1938), p. 164.

3. Boris Sapir, *American Jewish Yearbook*, 1947-48, Vol. 49 (Philadelphia, 1947), p. 375.

4. AICC, oral history interviews.

5. *Ibid.*

6. Lennhoff, pp. 196-97.

7. AICC, oral history interviews.

8. Lennhoff, pp. 164-65.

9. Oswald Dutch, *Thus Died Austria* (London, 1938), pp. 244-47.

10. Quoted in George E. Berkley, *Vienna and its Jews* (Cambridge, MA, 1988), p. 306.

11. *Ibid.*, p. 302.

12. *Ibid.*

13. *Ibid.*, pp. 248-49.

14. Dutch, *Austria*, pp. 260-63.

15. Stefan Zweig, *Die Welt von Gestern* (Frankfurt, 1953), pp. 385-86.

16. *Ibid.*

17. Irving Abella and Harold Troper, *None Is Too Many: Canada and the Jews of Europe, 1933-1948* (Toronto, 1982); see also Charles Stastny and Gabrielle Tyrnauer, "Sanctuary in Canada," in Vaughan Robinson, ed., *The International Refugee Crisis: British and Canadian Responses* (London, 1993), p. 182.

18. *Encyclopedia of the Holocaust*, Vol. 1, "Canada," p. 275.

19. *Ibid.*, pp. 275-76.

20. Abella and Troper, *None is Too Many.*

21. *Ibid.*, p. 103.

22. Zweig, *Die Welt von Gestern.*

23. AICC, oral history interviews.

24. *Ibid.*

25. *Ibid.*

26. Eric Koch, *Deemed Suspect: A Wartime Blunder* (Agincourt ON, 1980, reprinted Halifax, NS, 1985) p. 7.

27. AICC, oral history interviews.

28. *Ibid.*

29. *Ibid.*

30. *Ibid.*

31. Berkley, p. xix.

32. John H. Thompson, *Canada 1922-1939: Decades of Discord* (Toronto, 1985), pp. 267-70; see also Blair H. Neatby, "The Liberal Way, Fiscal and Monetary Policy in the 1930s," in Michel Horn, ed., *The Depression in Canada: Responses to Economic Crisis* (Toronto, 1988), pp. 257-73.

33. Between 1938 and 1945, 5,073 Jews (4.8 percent of Canada's total immigration) and 5,028 non-Jewish Germans (4.7 percent of Canada's total immigration) came to Canada. The distinction between German and Jewish immigrants was made in the Canadian statistics that classified immigrants by "race." Jews were considered a race different from the Germans and were therefore kept in an separate category. *Report of the Department of Mines and Resources for the Fiscal Year ended March 31* (Ottawa, editions 1936-1945); *Canada Year Book* (Ottawa, editions for the calendar years 1939-1946).

34. J.L. Granatstein, Irving Abella, T.W. Acheson, David Bercuson, R. Craig Brown and H. Blair Neatby, eds., *Nation: Canada since Confederation*. 3rd ed. (Toronto/Montreal, 1990), p. 368.

35. *Canada Year Book* (Ottawa, 1930), p. 165. See also the editions for the calendar years 1920-1943.

36. Paula Jean Draper, "Fragmented Loyalties: Canadian Jewry, the King Government and the Refugee Dilemma," in N. Hillmer, B. Kordan and L. Luciuk, eds., *On Guard For Thee: War, Ethnicity, and the Canadian State, 1939-1945* (Ottawa, 1988), p. 152.

37. NAC, Mackenzie King Diaries, MG 26 J13, 5 October 1935.

38. The Immigration Act and Regulations. Department of Mines and Resources, Ottawa 1937.

39. Immigration Act, para. 3, 11-14.

40. *Ibid.*, para. 37, 22.

41. *Ibid.*, paras. 37 and 38, 22-23.

42. *Ibid.*, 23.

43. David C. Corbett, *Canada's Immigration Policy: A Critique* (Toronto, 1957), p. 66ff.

44. NAC, RG 26, Vol.97, File 3-15-1, Part 1: Order-in-Council, P.C. 2115, 16 September 1930. The Immigration Act and Regulations, Ottawa 1937, 51.

45. NAC, RG 26, Vol.97, File 3-15-1, Part 1: Order-in-Council, P.C. 695, 21 March 1931. The Immigration Act and Regulations, Ottawa 1937, 50. Cf. above, p. 29.

46. NAC, RG 26, Vol. 86: Department of Mines and Resources (1938): Order-in-Council, P.C. 3016, 29 November 1938.

47. Report of the Department of Mines and Resources for the Fiscal Year ended March 31, 1944, 181: Order-in-Council P.C. 2653, 14 September 1939.

48. Granatstein et al., *Nation*, p. 369.

49. NAC, RG 26, Vol. 132, Files 3-35-2, Part 1. Population Pattern for Canada. Memorandum of the Immigration Branch to Dr. Charles Camsell, Deputy Minister, Department of Mines and Resources, April 1943.

50. Immigration Act, para. 3, 11-13.

51. *Ibid.*, para. 37, 22.

52. Abella and Troper, *None Is Too Many,* p. 55ff.

53. NAC, RG 76, Vol. 896, File 569-9-513: Memorandum of F.C. Blair to T.A. Crerar, Minister of Mines and Resources, 22 June 1938.

54. Abella and Troper, *None Is Too Many,* 8ff.; Draper, "Fragmented Loyalties," p. 164; Robert Domanski, "While Six Million Cried: Canada and the Refugee Question, 1938-44," (unpublished M.A. thesis, Carleton University, Ottawa, 1975), p. 43.

55. Abella and Troper, *None Is Too Many,* p. 8.

56. Gerald Dirks, *Canada's Refugee Policy: Opportunism or Indifference?* (Montreal, 1977), p. 57.

57. Interview with Walter Salten (formerly Salzmann), Montreal, 6 February 1991. In possession of the author.

58. Interview with Eugene Stearns (formerly Sternschuß), Montreal, 6 April 1989. In possession of the author.

59. Interview with Richard Redler, Montreal, 12 June 1989. In possession of the author.

60. Extensive studies on this topic can be found in the following publications: Abella and Troper, *None Is Too Many;* Kenneth Craft, "Canada's Righteous. A History of the Canadian National Committee on Refugees and Victims of Political Persecution," (unpublished M.A. thesis, Carleton University, Ottawa, 1987); Simon Belkin, *Through Narrow Gates. A Review of Jewish Immigration, Colonization and Immigrant Aid Work in Canada (1840-1940)* (Montreal, 1966).

61. Otto von Habsburg was the unofficial head of a "Free Austrian Movement (FAM)," a legitimist organization trying to re-establish the monarchy in the Danubian basin. Former Austrian Minister Hans Rott, Wilhelm Wunsch, Franz Laizner, and the journalist Franz Klein obtained orders-in-council, as well as Otto's mother, Empress Zita, and four of her children. Vienna, Dokumentationsarchiv des österreichischen Widerstandes (DöW), Document no. 12001, Organization and Status of the Free Austrian Movement in Canada. Memorandum of the Department of the Secretary of State for External Affairs, Ottawa, 18 September 1941, photocopy. Interview with Franz Laizner, Montreal, 8 June 1989. In possession of the author.

62. For further details, see: Koch, *Deemed Suspect;* Peter und Leni Gillman, *Collar the Lot! How Britain Interned and Expelled its Wartime Refugees* (London, 1980); Michael Seyfert, "His Majesty's Most Loyal Internees: Die Internierung und Deportation deutscher und österreichischer Flüchtlinge als 'enemy aliens.' Historische, kulturelle und literarische Aspekte." In Gerhard Hirschfeld, ed., *Exil in Großbritannien: Zur Emigration aus dem nationalsozialistischen Deutschland* (Stuttgart, 1983), pp. 155-82.

63. Among the 2,500 deported refugees, approximately 850 were Austrians. This estimate was made by the author, based on documents by the United Jewish Relief

Agencies which supported the majority of the refugees in the British internment
camps in Canada. Archives of the Canadian Jewish Congress, Montreal: United
Jewish Relief Agencies [UJRA-Collection], Bb: Card Index, Box 5 und Box 6.

64. Enemy Aliens. Espionage and Acts Likely to Assist the Enemy. *Defence of Canada
Regulations* (DOCR), Ottawa 1939, 31.

65. Robert H. Keyserlingk, "Agents within the Gates: The Search for Nazi Subversives
in Canada during World War II," *Canadian Historical Review* 66 (1985), 215.

66. McGill University Archives, Montreal, Record Group 2, Box C 112, File 3027:
"Enemy Alien Internees": Memorandum of Colonel R.S.W. Fordham, Commissioner of Refugee Camps, 11 November 1942.

67. Richard Redler emigrated to Canada in 1941. On his immigration application he
wrote "ski-instructor" as intended occupation. In fact, while in Canada he worked
as a teacher, an economist, but never as a ski instructor, without ever having problems with the Canadian authorities. Interview with Richard Redler. In possession
of the author.

CHAPTER V
POST-WAR AUSTRIAN IMMIGRATION TO CANADA

Bettina S. Steinhauser

IN AN INTERVIEW BEFORE he left Austria to visit Canada and the United States in 1954, the Austrian Federal Chancellor Julius Raab said: "I owe my gratitude to Canada for the grand help ... which we have received in post-war times, and also for the fact that this country has so kindly opened its doors to approximately 30,000 refugees and Austrian citizens who have found a new home there."[1] Raab neither mentioned bilateral political issues nor did he comment on the relationship between Austria and Canada as trading partners. The reason was that these issues just did not exist. Austrian immigration to Canada was the only matter of interest that concerned Austrian and Canadian politicians and civil servants.

Why did Austrian citizens leave their home country to start a new life in Canada? At the end of the Second World War, Europe faced mass migrations caused by expulsion, hopelessness and poverty. Many people fled the countries under Soviet influence, leaving Austria with 1.5 million refugees and displaced persons who had to be absorbed or relocated. Austria itself was an occupied territory and had to struggle to survive politically and economically. Until the mid-1950s, this unstable situation induced many refugees and Austrians to emigrate to a country which had a prosperous economy and was capable of and indeed eager to absorb this labour force.

It took some time, however, before these Austrian immigrants were recognized as a distinct ethnic group. The various subtleties of ethnic identity under the larger German-language umbrella were not always clear to Canadian officials,[2] especially in the immediate post-war years, and it was not until 1953 that Austrians were classified separately from Germans in immigration statistics.[3] The Austrian State Treaty of 1955, which provided for the withdrawal of the occupation forces from Austria and which proclaimed it to be a sovereign and perpetually neutral country, certainly went a long way to affirm a separate Austrian identity. At the same time, a growing sensitivity to the multicultural heritage of many Canadians led to a refinement of such statistical reports as the Canadian census. In 1961, an amended census form, now providing for 28 separate ethnic categories,[4] also listed Austria as a "country of last residence" and "Austrians" as a distinct ethnic group of immigrants.[5] No such category had existed in the census conducted ten years earlier. By then, of course, many Austrians had already arrived in Canada, and for most these immigrants their distinct Austrian identity was never in doubt. Shortly after their arrival they began to found numerous Austrian clubs all across the country, whose objective was to keep the Austrian cultural heritage alive. By the 1960s the existence of a distinct Austrian branch in the Canadian family tree seemed beyond debate.[6]

The affirmation of this distinction notwithstanding, research on Austrian immigrants to Canada has not been very extensive. Although Canada has a long tradition as a country shaped by immigrants, Canadian historians and other social scientists have only recently begun to turn their attention in any substantive way to their country's immigration history.[7] Despite the great impact of European newcomers on post-war Canada, there is little literature which surveys the whole European immigration after the Second World War.[8] Canadian immigration and ethnic studies have tended to be very specific. While some research has been conducted on "German" immigration and on the German-speaking communities in Canada, which usually subsume Austrians within their purview,[9] no major study has dealt with the sizeable and distinct Austrian immigration wave after 1945. Similarly, Austrian historians have not done any detailed research on emigration issues in the second half of the 20th century, although a major study conducted by the Austrian Academy of Sciences on Austrian emigration is currently in progress.[10] Under the circumstances, this chapter has had to rely mostly on primary sources from Canadian and Austrian archives and on research and interviews conducted as part of the Austrian Immigration to Canada research project. As much of the primary material, such as Canadian government departmental files and letters, has only been made public for the period up to the late 1960s, this evaluation will concentrate on that time period. There is also an emphasis on the immigrants of the 1950s because most Austrian emigrants came to Canada then,[11] and most of those interviewed by the research project were members of that cohort. This chapter can thus pretend to be little more than an initial "stock-taking" and a preliminary introduction to the problem, concentrating on Canadian and Austrian government policies towards the migrants and on some of the reasons why Austrian citizens have emigrated to Canada.

Though the territories that constitute the present day Republic of Austria did not experience the massive emigrations that other parts of the Austro-Hungarian Empire did in the late nineteenth and early twentieth centuries,[12] post-World-War II emigration of Austrians was very strong. Even at the beginning of the 1990s, as the only major Austrian study on emigration has pointed out, approximately 6.4 percent of Austrian citizens lived abroad.[13] Unfortunately, accurate data are not available as the Austrian government did not keep track of the number of Austrian citizens who emigrated.[14] Data about emigration figures can only be obtained from the statistics kept by the receiving countries.[15] It seems clear, however, that the majority of Austrian emigrants did not move far afield, and most migrated to other countries in Europe. In particular, labour migration to neighbouring German-speaking countries, Germany and Switzerland, was obviously the most prominent form of migration after 1945.[16]

Nevertheless, emigration overseas was also very popular in the 1950s. The United States and Commonwealth countries, especially Canada and Australia, appeared to be an attractive destination for a new beginning.[17] With the help of international organizations, these countries offered displaced persons and refugees new homes.[18] Many Austrians citizens and their families, who were tempted "to start life all over again," left Austria permanently to begin a new life in these countries. It is commonly thought that the United States was the primary destination for Austrian emigrants, but surprisingly, "a comparison between the U.S. and the Canadian statistics reveals that since 1945 more Austrians have emigrated to Canada than to the United States."[19] This was likely due to the fact that American immigration policy returned to a strict quota system in 1952, which convinced many Austrians to choose Canada[20] as their new home. Yet, despite this, the number of Austrians in Canada was never very large: though some 106,000 Canadians claimed Austrian "ethnic origin" in the census of 1971, the most reliable estimates yield a much more conservative figure of about half that number.[21]

FROM "ENEMY ALIEN" TO WELCOME MIGRANT

How readily Austrians could find a new home in Canada in the post-war period depended in the first instance on the policies of the host country. Here there were a number of impediments. To begin with, policy-making by the Canadian Immigration Branch, part of the Department of Mines and Resources until 1950, was dependent on other departments, such as Labour and External Affairs, and decision-making was therefore extremely difficult. The Canadian Immigration Branch was also still quite small and lacked adequate personnel abroad to process potential immigrants. Finally, the prohibitive immigration category of "enemy aliens" remained in place for some years after the war, and restrictions only began to be loosened after 1948.[22] Though Austria had been reestablished as a state separate from Germany in 1945, the precise status of its citizens remained in a kind of limbo for some time.

In March 1946, however, some loosening of the restrictions for Austrians seemed to be signaled when the Department of External Affairs informed the Immigration Branch that "Austria is now an independent state once more and ... persons arriving in this country from territories under the jurisdiction of the Austrian Government may be regarded as having Austrian nationality."[23] A country's international status was of crucial importance for the processing of its citizens' immigration applications by Canadian authorities, and Austria's political situation was a significant criterion for the admission of prospective immigrants. A specific diplomatic incident in August 1947 then convinced Canadian officials of the need to clarify the policy for processing Austrian immigrants in particular. A circular memorandum, drafted by the Department of External Affairs, revealed that "a somewhat embarrassing situation arose recently when an Austrian national, named Gertz, who had been asked by the Department to come to Ottawa from the United States for discussions of post-UNRRA[24] relief, was taken off the train at the border by the immigration officials."[25] As a consequence of this incident, the Canadian government officially declared that "Austria is now recognized as an autonomous state, liberated from German occupation, [and] citizens of Austria are no longer classified as enemy aliens ... [since] November 1947."[26]

Though this ruling meant that Austrians were now at least legally eligible to enter Canada, few applications were in fact processed.[27] This was primarily due to the fact the processing of Austrian applications for immigration seemed to be nobody's particular responsibility, and that the

Canadian Immigration Branch did not have any offices in Austria. Canadian officers stationed in Germany had previously travelled to Austria to supervise the processing of Displaced Persons, but the transmission of information to their headquarters in Germany was difficult because the mail was often delayed and telephone communication unreliable.[28] Furthermore, Austrian citizens were not processed by the Canadian officers in Germany, so that applications of Austrian nationals were held in abeyance even after Austrians were legally eligible to enter Canada.[29] The need for a specific immigration office in Austria proper thus became increasingly apparent. As Laval Fortier, the Associate Commissioner of the Immigration Branch, noted early in 1949:

In my opinion, the time has arrived for the opening of an immigration office in Austria, and this could be done without waiting for a final decision as to whether or not we should close our headquarters in Germany and establish offices in the British and American zones. If such an office were opened in Salzburg, our officers could deal with Austrian nationals and at the same time deal with displaced persons; that would be of service to the Austrian nationals without affecting the processing of the displaced persons in Austria.[30]

Shortly thereafter, in April 1949, a Canadian Immigration Office was opened in Salzburg. It was moved to Linz three years later and finally opened in Vienna once allied agreement was reached to terminate the occupation of Austria in 1955.[31]

The new Immigration Office was a processing office pure and simple and did not have any semblance of consular status. As Fortier pointed out at the time, in "late fall it was suggested that we establish three separate offices in the occupied territory of Europe. In view of the difference of opinion between our Department and the Department of Labour, so far a final decision has not yet been reached.... For international political reasons we were informed that it would be preferable not to open a Consulate in Austria but to have a Canadian Government office for resettlement and immigration."[32] The Canadian government, hesitant to establish diplomatic relations for reasons discussed in chapter 1,[33] was nevertheless anxious to regulate and supervise the flow of prospective immigrants from Austria without making an official declaration about Austrian-Canadian foreign relations. Soon this processing of applicants would turn into outright recruitment, but from the Canadian point of view this still did not necessarily require any establishment of diplomatic relations.

THE BOOMING 1950S:
CANADIAN INCENTIVES AND AUSTRIAN CONCERNS

While the Canadian government thus increasingly warmed to accepting Austrian immigrants and remained cool to the establishment of formal diplomatic relations with their country of origin, Austria, ironically, was anxious to establish diplomatic relations while remaining cool to the emigration of its own citizens. The fact that Canadian immigration authorities now had an office in Salzburg through which "all Austrian nationals" could be processed from the spring of 1949 on, pleased the Austrian government. But it did so less because it made the processing of Austrian citizens possible and more because it also facilitated the emigration of Displaced Persons still living in Austria. When the Salzburg office was opened, International Relief Organizations were also requested by Canadian authorities "to present all Displaced Persons in the U.S. Zone of Austria to that office for examination."[34] The reaction of the Austrian Ministry of the Interior (*Innenministerium*), responsible for migration matters, is instructive. It expressed considerable enthusiasm about how the new Canadian office contributed concretely to the resolution of the refugee problem, but none at all about the emigration of Austrian citizens. In a response to a letter from Canadian immigration authorities, it welcomed the former, but, in sharp contrast, only "acknowledged" the subtle inducement that, from now on, Austrian citizens applying for immigration to Canada were exempted from paying visa fees.[35]

Prospective Austrian migrants profited from a further factor: Canadian immigration prejudices. Until the early 1960s, Canada preferred the immigration of people of certain races und cultural backgrounds in order to maintain the traditional cultural character of the country, namely the dominant Anglo-Saxon tradition.[36] Therefore, as one historian has put it, "Canada was prepared to accept only one kind of immigrant from the Eastern Hemisphere, the European immigrant."[37] Newcomers from countries like Britain, France, the United States and many former (white) British dominions were given first preference. The second-best "quality" of immigrants included all Western Europeans, which included Austrians.[38] The third group were immigrants from Egypt, Israel, Lebanon, Turkey and Eastern Europe, and Central and South Americans, and the last group were immigrants of Asian origin. In the words of one analyst of the 1950s: "We can infer from that, in the government's judgement, Canadians in general rank the peoples of the world in roughly this order when it is a question of admitting them to Canada and having them as fellow citizens."[39] This preferential ranking was formally introduced by the newly established Department of Citizenship and Immigration in 1952 and not abandoned until 1962.[40] One can deduce that similar prejudices had lent the tone to the Salzburg Office since its establishment, and certainly throughout the 1950s the detailed instructions passed on to Canadian immigration officers abroad did not deviate from this policy.

The Canadian Department of Labour also had a significant influence on immigration. A joint Immigration-Labour Committee had introduced Bulk Labour Programmes, which were to be open not only to Displaced Persons,[41] but were expected to recruit a suitable work force for the Canadian labour market. From time to time, the Canadian government offered bulk labour schemes, as for example for miners and woodworkers in the summer of 1951.[42] In addition, the immigration offices abroad kept lists of jobs in occupations that were available in Canada.[43] The existence of job opportunities in Canada, was, of course, a major incentive for prospective immigrants, and in a demand market the Department of Labour saw immigration as the key to an increasing and profitable labour force. The fact that several government offices were involved in making policy for migrants did not always facilitate the processing of immigrants—on the contrary, sometimes the bureaucracy caused backlogs and unnecessary delay—but on the whole, the Canadian demand for skilled Austrian immigrants rose rapidly. All these factors produced results that were immediately apparent: in 1950 approximately 400 Austrians emigrated to Canada while more than 3,500 Austrians left for Canada in 1951. The subsequent years were to prove to be the peak years of the Austrian immigration wave.[44]

This increasing rate of emigration in the early 1950s greatly disturbed Austrian officials, and the question of which authority was competent to restrict emigration to Canada soon arose. The Migration Office (*Wanderungsamt*) of the inter-war years, which was responsible for any question concerning Austrian immigration and emigration, had been revived in the second Republic as Department 12 of the Ministry of the Interior. As was seen previously, the department had to provide information for all prospective emigrants about immigration laws, living conditions in the immigration countries, and so on. But while the Migration Office was thus constitutionally responsible for negotiating migration agreements, employment exchanges with foreign countries were supervised by the Austrian Ministry for Social Administration (*Ministerium für Soziale*

Verwaltung).[45] In addition, the Austrian Ministry of Labour was more than casually interested in being informed about the kind and the number of labourers, skilled workers, or professionals who emigrated since it was obviously as interested as Canada's Department of Labour in establishing and maintaining a stable and healthy labour market. Thus in Austria, like in Canada, several ministries were involved in making policy for migrants. Though these overlaps could lead to as much—if not more—bureaucratic inefficiency in Austria as in Canada, emigration was booming, and the Austrian government desperately tried to find ways to reduce the exodus of its citizens. In the early 1950s, several other European countries negotiated migration regulations with overseas countries. When Austria learned about such a migration agreement between Holland and New Zealand,[46] it immediately launched plans to negotiate a similar accord with Canada.

In August 1951, representatives of the Austrian government met with the Canadian officer in charge of the Salzburg Immigration Office, St. Vincent, in order to regulate Austrian emigration to Canada.[47] After explaining that industrial concerns in Austria had complained about the loss of their workers who had emigrated to Canada, officials from the Austrian Ministry for Social Administration attempted to persuade St. Vincent that henceforth only the local Austrian provincial labour offices should be authorized to provide Austrian citizens with Canadian immigration forms. They also requested that labour exchange schemes should be operated in co-operation with the Austrian authorities.[48] A preliminary draft of a prospective agreement to this effect was produced by the Austrians,[49] but it met with a very frosty response. In their assessment, Canadians observed that "in this agreement it is significant to note that Article 11 states that prospective immigrants should if possible be: (a) persons on the dole; (b) persons of the D.P. status; (c) ethnic Germans. Other clauses related to the welfare of Austrian immigrants in Canada, the care of dependents of immigrants left in Austria, financial assistance, transportation, etc."[50] As a result, the proposed Austrian emigration restrictions were rejected and no agreement was ever signed. The Canadian Officer-in-Charge in Karlsruhe commented: "I see no reason for binding ourselves to a definite agreement in view of the uncertainty of the situation and especially considering that we can obtain a substantial number of immigrants from Austria without such an agreement which might restrict us in the occupational type of immigrants we could send to Canada."[51]

The Austrian attempt to reduce the outflow of its citizens to Canada in the early 1950s reflected Austrian resentment towards emigration to Canada, which continued until the mid-1960s. In 1955, the Canadian legation in Vienna reported:

The official government-owned newspaper *Wiener Zeitung* published a message today under the prominent headline "A Warning to Immigrants" on behalf of the Federal Ministry of the Interior. [The] warning states that recently published reports on Canada might lead immigrants to wrong ideas and advises that prospective immigrants who have no relatives or friends in Canada in a position to offer accommodation and assistance will only find it possible to establish themselves in Canada after a very long time and after overcoming great hardships and difficulties, unless immigrants obtain a long-term working contract in advance.[52]

Despite such negative publicity, ever more Austrian citizens applied for immigration to Canada. As Austria struggled to re-establish a prosperous economy during its years of post-war reconstruction, Austrian authorities feared that if more skilled workers and members of the professions left Austria the welfare of the whole nation would be in jeopardy. As Laval Fortier, Canadian Deputy Minister for Immigration, reported during his trip to Europe: "Austria, after the Netherlands, was possibly the place where I met the strongest opposition to the Canadian [immigration] programme."[53]

After 1955 Austrian officials therefore increased pressure on Canada to curtail her immigration programme in Austria. In particular, Austria wished "to restrict the granting of immigration visas to unskilled labourers and domestics and to eliminate all publicity and assisted passage arrangements."[54] At the same time, the Austrian government set up a policy that enabled it to manage and to some extent restrict emigration to Canada. A scheme, already considered five years before, was devised to prevent Austrians who had applied for Canadian Assisted Passage Loans from leaving the country.[55] The Assisted Passage Loan scheme had been introduced by the Canadians in 1951 to serve as an incentive for immigrants who could not afford the costs for the passage overseas immediately.[56] From 1956 on, an Austrian citizen who requested this financial support had to sign a form which was then checked by officials at the Austrian Ministry of Labour in order to determine whether "the departure of the person concerned would be detrimental to the Austrian economy."[57] However, the number of emigrants who had to go through this kind of processing was apparently small.[58] Canada, in any case, indicated a will-ingness to co-operate with the Austrian policy. According to the Canadi-an immigration officers, not many Austrians were actually prevented from taking advantage of the Canadian Assisted Passage Loan, though those same officials admitted that "restrictions against recruitment" did have at least some impact on the reduction of Austrian emigration from 1957 on.[59] In short, the Austrian government tried to ensure that it had some control over both the quantity and quality of applicants emigrating to Canada. It was very cautious about what kind of restrictive means it used in order to discourage the increasing flow of emigration, as the Austrian constitution guaranteed every Austrian citizen the right to emigrate.[60] But certainly the intervening mechanisms put in place to decide whether an Assisted Passage Loan would be granted or not was an explicit tactic to ebb the flow of skilled workers abroad.

EBBING OF THE TIDE

In 1957, over-all immigration to Canada was at its peak. "Despite a downturn in the Canadian economy, immigration to Canada in 1957 was higher than ever since 1913-14."[61] Approximately 280,000 persons entered the country during that year. The Hungarian Revolution and the Suez Crisis caused many Hungarians[62] and some British citizens to leave their countries. In addition, sponsored immigration was booming, accounting for a third of the total number of immigrants.[63] In the fol-lowing year, however, immigration began to decrease, and over the next five years immigration continued to drop[64] because of the economic reces-sion in Canada. Canada's immigration policy had to be amended as "the evident inadequacy of the Immigration Act and the need to revise admis-sion policy in the light of Canada's increasing need for skilled manpower, and widespread criticism of her present discrimination against non-Euro-pean immigration"[65] had to be considered. "When the new regulations were implemented on 1 February 1962, Canada became the first of the three large receiving countries in international migration—the others being the United States and Australia—to dismantle her discriminatory immigration policy."[66]

As a result of these factors, Austrian immigration to Canada dimin-ished throughout the 1960s. Approximately 7,400 Austrians emigrated to Canada from 1960 to 1969, compared to 25,300 in the 1950s.[67] But there were also two developments in Austria which reduced the number of emigrants. First, the prospering economy, the ready availability of housing and jobs, and the stable political situation made it more attractive for Austrians to stay at home. Second, the Austrian government itself began to encourage immigration as the Austrian labour market could absorb guest workers from abroad. The Canadian Visa Office in Vienna pointed out in August 1962 that "there is still an acute shortage of manpower in Austria. After mildly successful attempts at recruiting workers in Italy, Greece and Yugoslavia, the Austrian Government is attempting to negotiate the importation of manpower from Spain and even from Turkey."[68]

A report by the Canadian Department of External Affairs in 1968 pointed out that the immigration of Austrian citizens was minor in size compared to other nationals who emigrated from Austria: "The main bulk of Canadian immigration operations in Austria has for some time centered on processing Eastern European refugees and various special movements of migrants. In 1967, only 24.4 percent of immigrants to Canada from Austria were Austrian nationals. Austria then was a staging post by most Eastern European refugees who, after short stays, tended to migrate overseas."[69] Within a decade, therefore, the actual Austrian component of "Austrian Immigration" to Canada was reduced to a trickle. Most were refugees from countries behind the Iron Curtain. For example, in 1956 many Hungarians came to Canada via Vienna, and in 1968 many Czechs emigrated from Austria to Canada. This large share of nationals other than Austrians has to be kept in mind when examining the statistics provided by Canadian officials. Canadian civil servants often asked only for the last country of residence and not for the ethnic origin of the newcomers. Furthermore, the processing of a large number of Eastern Europeans through Austria, initiated in the early 1960s, was enhanced when the Canadian Immigration Office in Vienna was made responsible "not only for Austria but also (since last fall) for unsponsored migrants from eight countries in the Middle East, including Turkey, Lebanon, Syria, etc."[70]

In any case, the number of Austrian citizens immigrating to Canada was in steep decline. Negative publicity could still be heard in the early 1960s and might have been an additional reason for the decreasing emigration. The Visa Office in Vienna, for example, reported a notorious case of negative publicity which received prominent play on Austrian television. In an interview, a young man who had returned to Austria from Canada in the fall of 1963 asserted:

1. Unemployment in Canada is such that it is nearly impossible, particularly for an immigrant, to find work.

2. Immigrants are not accepted socially in Canada and are not treated like other Canadians.

3. Young people in Austria should not be lured by false accounts of prosperity in Canada.

4. The "real" story of what goes on in Canada should be told to everyone in Austria.[71]

The story of this young Austrian's negative experiences in Canada was reprinted in several newspapers, and enthusiasm about emigration to Canada seemed to be dampened considerably by it.[72] Indeed, the Canadian Ambassador to Austria, Margaret Meagher, inquired whether the Austrian Foreign Office could issue instructions that positive statements about Canadian immigration policy be broadcast as well. Only a few months later, the Austrian Ambassador to Canada, Franz Leitner, was invited to the same television show in order to refurbish Canada's reputation.[73]

By all appearances, Canada was disappointed by this decrease in the number of immigrants from Austria. Other Commonwealth countries, especially Australia, still seemed to be attracting a larger number of Austrians, and this was greeted with great alarm by the Vienna Immigration Office: "It is becoming increasingly important," it urged in August 1965, "that we at least open an office in Salzburg this year. In the first six months of this year, 425 Austrians emigrated to Australia (351 to Canada) and much of their success in recruiting immigrants is attributed to their four sub-offices in Austria."[74] Ottawa responded positively to this suggestion, and an additional information office was opened in Salzburg in 1966. However, this office was closed again two years later because it clearly no longer warranted the expense. The kinds of immigrants that had come in the 1950s were simply no longer to be had. As for unskilled, marginal labourers, of whom Austria had in any case very few, new Canadian immigration regulations made it more difficult for such Austrians to come to Canada, as national preferences were dropped and occupational skills as well as probable absorption into the Canadian economy became major priorities.

REASONS FOR EMIGRATION TO CANADA:
WHY DID THE AUSTRIANS LEAVE?

Despite the many reservations historians and other social scientists have expressed about a "push and pull" model of immigration in recent years, it would appear that this model still provides the most persuasive explanation for the post-war bulge in Austrian immigration to Canada. "Social network" and similar dynamic new migration models seem to offer relatively few keys in explaining the motivations of the particular wave of migrants of the 1950s. What is more, in the Austrian case, pessimism about prospects at home ("push factors") clearly preceded any assessment that Canada provided the best opportunity for an amelioration of circumstances ("pull factors"). Canada frequently represented only one of a number of potentially desirable destinations, and the initial emigration impulse was in most cases dictated by the discontent and despair prevalent in postwar central Europe. Some of these discontents hinged on traditional social factors: the conservative, hide-bound, hierarchical immobility of Austrian society. But such reports are frequently the result of comparisons made with subsequent life in Canada, and therefore must be treated with some skepticism as primary emigration motives.[75]

Many immigrants, however, do claim that one of the most crucial "push factors" in the period before 1955, was the fact that the Austrian State Treaty had not yet been in existence. The unstable political situation at the height of the Cold War, which frequently induced anxiety that war might yet return to Europe, and the unclear fate of Austria's international status, caused by the fact that the country was occupied by the four victorious allies, were decisive in making Austrians want to leave the country. As Austria was an occupied territory, the Austrian government was hindered in many respects from shaping the country's fate independently. In particular, the fear of the Russian army[76] that always seemed to threaten the successful signing of a peace settlement encouraged many young Austrians to apply for immigration to Canada.[77]

In interviews and questionnaires, Austrians who left for Canada also reported, above all, that the state of the Austrian economy was crucial for their decision to emigrate. A newspaper article published in 1951 summarized the statements that Austrian emigrants frequently made:

A mechanic, 24 years old, says: "I emigrate because I can't buy what I want for the money I earn, and I don't want to work so that our ministers can afford to buy luxurious cars."... A driver and his fiancée, a hairdresser, in their early twenties, say that it is hard to get married in Austria because, for one, you can't find a place to live, and then you can't afford to buy the furniture anyway.[78]

Unemployment and a limited labour market encouraged the emigration of members of every occupation. Besides skilled and semi-skilled workers, many intellectuals, musicians, artists, and professionals left Austria.

Despite the fact that many Austrian migrants in due course became fervent enthusiasts about the particular charms of the "Canadian cultural mosaic" and about the quality of life in their adopted home in general, the prime attraction of Canada as a destination seemed in the first instance also to be economic. Canada seemed to need an unrestricted number of people who could then find a job immediately in Canada's expanding economy. The prospect of having a good job and getting a better salary in Canada than in Austria was tempting indeed.[79] For example, in 1956 an Austrian local newspaper reported on the social advancement of an Austrian family which had emigrated: they could afford to buy a stylish Pontiac and to live in a modern, spacious apartment with a huge television set, a sewing machine, a washing machine and a huge refrigerator after only five years in Canada. In addition, they could save 40 percent of the husband's salary.[80] Such stories of spectacularly swift economic success, even if only measured in the modest indices of household consumer items, went a long way to confirm the impression of Canada as the "land of a million possibilities."[81]

For most Austrians integration into Canadian society did not seem to be fraught with undue difficulties. The main initial problem, besides the frequently reported and probably predictable homesickness in the beginning, was language acquisition. As Friedrich Riedenstein observed after his return from his post as Austrian Consul General in Ottawa: "The Canadian economy needs skilled workers, but employment for qualified jobs is only possible if the person knows English or French."[82] If the immigrant did not have any knowledge of either one of these languages, a long and difficult period of adaptation was sure to follow.

Canadian officials, such as Laval Fortier, gave assurances, however, that Austrians enjoyed the same rights and opportunities as everyone else: "Immigrants of Austria are, of course, given the same service and consideration as that accorded immigrants from other countries. Their employment is on an equal basis with other immigrants coming to Canada and they work under the same conditions as Canadians in the same types of employment."[83] In interviews with them, Austrian immigrants did agree with this statement, but commented that they were given the same chances only when they had sufficient language skills. This was, of course, true for everyone, as Fortier noted:

Immigrants who have no knowledge of the English or French language on arrival present a problem in some types of employment during the first months after their arrival.

Their services are of less value than an experienced Canadian and those who are unable to understand instructions and directions are generally paid slightly less than the highest going wages until they acquire a working knowledge of the necessary language and have demonstrated their abilities.[84]

On the whole, however, the requisite language acquisition seemed to pose few problems for most Austrians, and, indeed, the rush to English and, less frequently, French, was accelerated by popular prejudice against the German language prevalent in the host society in the aftermath of World War II. By the second generation almost half no longer spoke any German at all.[85]

The decline in the Austrian immigration beginning in the 1960s and lasting to the present is further evidence of the strength of the "push factors" of the 1950s. The Austrian economy now offered sufficient jobs and living conditions had improved. The Austrian labour market could even afford to recruit guest workers from foreign countries because unemployment figures were so low. Austrians now emigrated mainly for the sake of change. Some came to experience a new culture or to start a new life,[86] others to improve and expand their professional experiences and market their skills in the wider world,[87] and still others to improve their language skills.[88] At any rate, a spirit of adventure seems to be the most important trait that Austrian immigrants in the 1960s and since then have had in common.[89]

ENDNOTES

1. Ottawa, National Archives of Canada [henceforth NAC], Department of External Affairs (RG 25), V.6504, f. 8447-40, pt.2.1., Canadian Legation to Secretary of State for External Affairs (SSEA), 24 November 1954.

2. On these intricacies see Dirk Hoerder, "German-Speaking Immigrants of Many Backgrounds and the 1990s Canadian Identity," in Franz A.J. Szabo, ed., *Austrian Immigration to Canada: Selected Essays* (Ottawa, 1996), pp. 11-31, and the introduction to this volume.

3. NAC, Records of the Immigration Branch (RG 76), V. 818, f. 552-1-552, Statement on Immigration from Austria, 30 June 1957, "Statistics respecting immigration from Austria were not kept separate from those of German immigration until 1953."

4. On "ethnic origin" in the censuses between 1901 and 1991, see Gertrud Neuwirth and John de Vries, "Demographic patterns of Austrian Canadians, 1900-1991," in Szabo, *Austrian Immigration*, pp. 42-50.

5. Vienna, Österreichisches Staatsarchiv – Archiv der Republik (henceforth ÖStA/AdR), Bundesministerium für Auswärtige Angelegenheiten – Ministry of Foreign Affairs (henceforth BMAA), Pol.II, Ottawa 1961, Ambassador Buresch to Minister of Foreign Affairs, 23 January 1961.

6. Austrians began to receive a separate chapter in successive editions of the Canadian Department of Citizenship and Immigration's *Notes on the Canadian Family Tree* (Ottawa, 1960 et seq.).

7. Ethnic history which is closely linked to the study of immigration policy is best evaluated and criticized by Dirk Hoerder, "Ethnic Studies in Canada from the 1880s to 1962: A Historiographical Perspective and Critique," *Canadian Ethnic Studies* 26 (1994), 1-19. The literature on Canadian post-war immigration policy is not very extensive. The most prominent and comprehensive studies are Freda Hawkins, *Canada and Immigration: Public Opinion and Public Concern* (Toronto, 1972); Jean R. Burnet and Howard Palmer, *Coming Canadians: An Introduction to a History of Canada's Peoples* (Toronto, 1988); David C. Corbett, *Canada's Immigration Policy: A Critique* (Toronto, 1957); Gerald E. Dirks, *Canada's Refugee Policy: Indifference and Opportunism?* (Montreal, 1977); Richmond Anthony, *Canada's Immigration Policy* (Toronto, 1957); Reg Whitaker, *Canadian Immigration Policy since Confederation* (Ottawa, 1991).

8. Studies on certain ethnic groups do exist, but they all deal with very specific time periods and certain regional phenomena. One representative example is Gerald Tulchinsky's edition of a well-selected collection of articles on certain immigrant groups, united either by nationality or religion, from the 18th century to the present. Gerald Tulchinsky, *Immigration in Canada: Historical Perspectives* (Toronto, 1994).

9. Gerhard P. Bassler, *The German-Canadian Mosaic Today and Yesterday: Identities, Roots, and Heritage* (Ottawa, 1991); Wolfgang G. Friedmann, *German Immigration into Canada* (Toronto, 1952); Angelika Sauer, "A Matter of Domestic Policy? Canadian Immigration Policy and the Admission of Germans, 1945-50," *Canadian Historical Review* 74 (1993), 260-63; Robert H. Keyserlingk, "The Canadian Government's Attitude Towards Germans and German-Canadians in World War II," *Canadian Ethnic Studies* 16 (1984), 16-28.

10. Traude Horvath and Gerda Neyer, "Austrians Abroad: Austrian Emigration after 1945," in Szabo, *Austrian Immigration*, pp. 83-92. This paper highlights some of the major findings of a larger study carried out by the Austrian Academy of Sciences, to be published in 1996.

11. Neuwirth and de Vries, "Demographic Patterns," *Ibid.*, p. 36, Table 1. Roughly 26,000 Austrians came during the 1950s.

12. Michael John, "Push and Pull Factors for Overseas Migrants from Austria-Hungary in the 19th and 20th Centuries," in *ibid.*, pp. 55-81.

13. Horvath and Neyer, in "Austrians Abroad," *ibid.*, p. 85.

14. *Ibid.*, 6: "Unlike before 1938, post-war Austria has not kept migration statistics." The files of the *Wanderungsamt* for the post-war period are either restricted or lost. The records of the Ministry for Social Administration, however, show that the Austrian government did receive immigration statistics from international organizations like the Intergovernmental Committee of European Migration (ICEM). But these reports were sent irregularly and are not complete. ÖStA/AdR, Bundesministerium für Soziale Verwaltung/Sozialpolitik (henceforth BMfSV/SP), SA 11, Box 678, 5910/56, ICEM to BMfSV, September 22, 1956.

15. Neuwirth and de Vries, "Demographic patterns," *Austrian Immigration*, pp. 33-54.

16. Horvath and Neyer, "Austrians Abroad," *Ibid.*, p. 91, show that in 1950 46,683 Austrians lived in Germany, compared to 183,161 in the 1990s.

17. W.G. Friedmann, *German Immigration*, p. 20. In the 1950s, Germans were mostly attracted to the United States (about 47 percent), then Canada (20 percent), and Australia (10 percent).

18. Several organizations, either founded during the war or shortly after the war, aided millions of expelled and Displaced Persons in finding new homes in overseas countries. UNHCR (United Nations High Commissioner for Refugees) and ICEM (Intergovernmental Committee for European Migration), both founded in 1951, supported the transportation and processing of millions of refugees in Europe. Private organizations, in particular those set up and administered by the churches, assisted these international institutions to provide moral and psychological support for those homeless and expelled people.

19. Horvath and Neyer, "Austrians Abroad," *Austrian Immigration*, p. 88.

20. AICC, Interview with Karl Bruckner, Toronto, Ontario, April 1995: He decided to emigrate to Canada because he thought it more likely to be admitted there than elsewhere. AICC, Interview with Werner Schlechtleitner, Vancouver, British Columbia, April 1995: He was told that he would have to wait five years until he could have emigrated to the U.S.; therefore, he decided to emigrate to Canada. The United States had passed an Immigration and Nationality Act which tried to preserve the national origins quota system. Hawkins, *Canada and Immigration*, p. 6.

21. Neuwirth and de Vries have estimated the number of Austrian immigrants by citizenship to the present day to be only 38,000. See Neuwirth and de Vries, "Demographic patterns," *Austrian Immigration*, pp. 35-37.

22. "After 1948 former enemy aliens in those countries with whom peace treaties had been concluded ceased to be completely ineligible for entry to Canada and could immigrate to the country if they had requisite qualifications. This meant that sponsored immigration from Italy was possible from 1948 onwards, although it remained on a small scale until 1950. The first really large movement from

Germany did not occur until 1951." Anthony Richmond, *Post-War Immigrants in Canada* (Toronto, 1967), p. 9. Richmond's statement is not quite correct. Germany had not signed a peace treaty with the Allied Powers in 1950, but the Federal Republic of Germany had been established. Canada had different policies toward countries which had been enemies during the war.

23. NAC, RG 25, V. 6285, f. 8447-40, Hume Wrong to the Immigration Branch, 13 March 1946.

24. The United Nations Relief and Rehabilitation Administration (UNRRA) was founded in 1943, the first international agency which was established to work on postwar reconstruction. UNRRA aided the repatriation of displaced and stateless persons of the wartime period with financial subsidies and rehabilitation programs. G. Dirks, *Canada's Refugee Policy*, p. 102.

25. NAC, RG 25, V.6285, f. 8447-40, Leslie Chance to the heads of divisions, 11 August 1947.

26. NAC, Records of the Immigration Branch (RG 76), V. 818, f. 552-1-513, Department of Mines and Resources to Immigration Inspectors, Eastern Districts, 12 March 1948; *ibid.*, Laval Fortier to the Tiroler Landesreisebüro; in response to an inquiry about visa regulations for Austrians Fortier stated: "In regards to the citizens of Germany I must inform you that a wartime regulation prohibiting the entry to Canada of German nationals has not yet been revoked. Under the circumstances, we can offer no encouragement in regard to their migration to this country at the present time." The enemy alien status for Germans was revoked two years later. Sauer, "A Matter of Domestic Policy?" 260-63.

27. In 1947, only 72 Austrians immigrated to Canada; the following year 151 Austrians came to Canada. Neuwirth and de Vries, "Demographic patterns," *Austrian Immigration*, p. 36, Table 1.

28. *Ibid.*

29. In early 1949, 322 applications by 783 Austrian citizens were held in abeyance. NAC, RG 76, V.818, f. 552-1-513, Laval Fortier to Jolliffe, 11 February 1949. Admissible classes at that time included: relatives of Canadian residents, agriculturalists with sufficient means to farm in Canada or assisting their relatives on farms, and fiancées and fiancées of legal residents. *Ibid.*, "Statement on Immigration from Austria," 30 June 1957.

30. NAC, RG 76, V. 818, f. 552-1-513, Laval Fortier's memo for Mr. Jolliffe, 11 February 1949.

31. Hawkins, *Canada and Immigration*, p. 380.

32. NAC, RG 76, V. 818, f. 552-1-513, Laval Fortier to Joliffe, 11 February 1949.

33. See Chapter 1, pp. 31-35 above.

34. NAC, RG 76, V. 818, f. 552-1-513, Memo for Mr. Smith, Commissioner of

Immigration, 29 March 1949.

35. ÖStA/AdR, BMfSV/SP, Box 334, SA 11, 39880/51, Minister of Interior Helmer to Cormier, Canadian Immigration Office, 22 July 1949.

36. Howard Palmer, "Reluctant Hosts: Anglo-Canadian Views of Multiculturalism in the Twentieth Century," in Tulchinsky, *Immigration in Canada*, pp. 297-333. Prime Minister King's famous statement on Canada's immigration policy in 1947 saying that Canadians do not want to make a fundamental change in the character of their population is commented on by Palmer (p. 314): "While King's statement was concerned primarily with justifying the exclusion of non-whites, it is clear from his emphasis on immigrant absorption that he continued to underline the importance of 'assimilability' in immigration policy."

37. Hawkins, *Canada and Immigration*, p. 95.

38. Corbett, *Canada's Immigration Policy*, p. 46.

39. *Ibid.*

40. Valerie Knowles, *Strangers at Our Gates: Canadian Immigration and Immigration Policy, 1940-1990* (Toronto, 1992), p. 143.

41. Donald H. Avery, *Reluctant Host: Canada's Response to Immigrant Workers, 1896-1994* (Toronto, 1995), pp. 153-55.

42. ÖStA, /AdR, BMfSV/SP, Box 334, SA 11, 39688/51, St. Vincent, Canadian Government Immigration Mission, to Keller, Ministry of Social Administration, 17 August 1951; NAC, RG 76, V. 818, f. 552-1-513, Department of Citizenship and Immigration to Officer in Charge in Karlsruhe, 28 March 1952. Quotas for a program for Germany and Austria were passed on referring to workers that were needed in Canada. The majority of workers needed were agriculturalists, followed by miners, construction workers and wood workers, as well as domestics and nurses and skilled and semi-skilled trades. The estimated total movement added up to 21,000 plus 15,000 dependents, totalling 36,000 immigrants from Austria and Germany.

43. AICC, Interview with Manfred Wirth, Montreal, April 1995. Wirth emigrated in the early 1950s because the Canadian immigration office in Salzburg announced that workers for the steel industry were needed.

44. Neuwirth and de Vries, "Demographic patterns," *Austrian Immigration*, p. 36.

45. ÖStA/AdR, BMfSV/SP, Box 335, SA 11, 127778, BMfSV to Provincial Labour Office, 11 September 1951.

46. *Ibid.*, BMfSV/SP, Box 335, SA 11, 83354/51, Bundesministerium für Inneres (BMfI) to BMfSV, 8 August 1951.

47. NAC, RG 76 V. 818 file 552-1-513, St. Vincent, Officer-in-Charge at the Canadian Immigration Office in Salzburg, to the Director of Immigration in Ottawa, 15 August 1951.

48. ÖStA/AdR, BMfSV/SP, SA 11, Box 334, 39088/51, minutes of the meeting of Austrian and Canadian representatives, 6 August 1951.

49. NAC, RG. 76, V.818, f. 552-1-513, St. Vincent to Director of Immigration, 15 August 1951. Draft of the agreement on migration entered into by the Government of the Austrian Republic and the Government of Canada.

50. *Ibid.*, "Statement on Immigration to Austria," 30 June 1957.

51. *Ibid.*, Department of Citizenship and Immigration (RG 26), Vol. 818, f. 552-1-513, Canadian Officer-in-Charge at Karlsruhe to Director of the Immigration Branch, Ottawa, commenting on the provisional Austrian-Canadian migration agreement, 28 November 1951.

52. *Ibid.*, RG 26, V.124, f. 3-33-4, p.1, The Canadian legation in Vienna to Secretary of State for External Affairs, 22 December 1955.

53. *Ibid.*, RG. 76, V.818, f. 552-1-513, Laval Fortier to Smith, 14 February 1956.

54. *Ibid.*, "Statement on Immigration from Austria," 30 June 1957.

55. AICC, Interview with Albert Hammerling and Josef Ruckenthaler, Calgary, April 1995. Both emigrated in 1951 and used the Assisted Passage Loan. These two are part of the minority of Austrians who stated that they had used the Canadian Assisted Passage Loan.

56. ÖStA/AdR, BMfSV/SP, SA 11, Box 335, 64631, BMfI to BmfSV, 24 April 1951: "Austrian applicants are allowed to pay the overseas passage in Austrian currency; applicants who cannot afford to cover the costs immediately pay only AS 600—the remainder is provided through a loan from the Canadian government which has to be paid back within two years after their arrival. Wives and children older than 18 are only allowed to use this scheme if they apply for jobs that are needed in Canada. Applicants who want to take their relatives with them, but without applying for employment for these as well, can only bring them along at their own expense as soon as the applicant can afford to pay their passage (adults: US $170 or AS 4.420; children up to a year US $10-20, children US $85)."

57. NAC, RG 76, V.818, f. 552-1-513, Memo on Immigration from Austria, 1 January 1961.

58. AICC, Interviews with Austrian immigrants, May 1995. From some 150 interviews conducted in conjunction with this research project, one can conclude that most of the Austrians did pay for the passage themselves, or through loans from either relatives or friends.

59. NAC, RG. 76, V. 818, f. 552-1-513, Statement on Immigration from Austria, 1 January 1961.

60. ÖStA/AdR, BMfSV/SP, SA 11, Box 334, 39088/51, file of the Ministry: emigration of skilled workers: present situation, 3 November 1951. "The Minister for

Social Administration emphasized that for lack of suitable laws, Austrian skilled workers cannot be prevented from emigrating."

61. Knowles, *Strangers at Our Gates,* p. 134.
62. The Austrian government assisted and aided Canadian immigration officers to accelerate the emigration of expelled and escaped Hungarians from Austria.
63. Hawkins, *Canada and Immigration,* p. 9.
64. *Ibid.,* p. 123. In 1957 approximately 90,000 unsponsored immigrants came, and in the following year only 48,000.
65. *Ibid.,* p. 119.
66. Knowles, *Strangers,* p. 143.
67. Neuwirth and de Vries, "Demographic Patterns," *Austrian Immigration,* pp. 36-37, Table 1.
68. NAC, RG 76, V.818, f. 522-1-513, Canadian Visa Officer in Vienna to the Chief of Operations in Ottawa, 28 August 1962.
69. *Ibid.,* RG 25, V. 3170, f. 36-1968-3 Vol. I, Special Task Force on Europe: Country Study on Austria, November 1968, p. 17. "Even including Eastern European refugees, total immigration to Canada from Austria in 1967 represented only 3.6% of total immigration from Europe."
70. *Ibid.,* RG 76, V.818, f. 552-1-552, Visa Department in Vienna to Chief of Operations in Ottawa, 11 February 1963.
71. *Ibid.,* RG 76, V. 833, 552-11-513, Visa Office Vienna to Chief of Department of Immigration and Citizenship, 18 October 1963.
72. *Ibid.,* Canadian Embassy to the Under-Secretary of External Affairs, 10 October 1963.
73. *Ibid.,* 22 January 1964.
74. *Ibid.,* RG 76, Vol. 833, 552-11-513, Immigration Office in Vienna to Department of Citizenship in Vienna, 20 August 1965.
75. AICC, Interviews with Austrian Immigrants, May 1995, and responses to "Austrian Immigration to Canada Survey" open-ended questions. For this and other motives of Austrian Immigrants to Canada, and, in particular, for some gender variations in response, see the next chapter in this volume.
76. *Ibid.,* Interview with Resi and Franz Umlauf, Vancouver, April 1995. The couple emigrated in 1954 and said that the main reason for emigrating was the presence of the Russian army. They feared that they would never leave Austria. The Umlaufs are among the many interviewees who gave the unstable political situation as a crucial reason for their decision to emigrate.
77. *Ibid.,* Interviews with Austrian Immigrants, May 1995, and responses to "Austrian Immigration to Canada Survey" open-ended questions.
78. ÖStA/AdR, BMfSV/SP, Box 334, SA 11, 156 194, newspaper clipping "Volkswille,"

8 November 1951; Landesarbeitsamt Kärnten to BMfSV, 10 November 10 1951.

79. AICC, Interviews with Austrian Immigrants, May 1995, and responses to "Austrian Immigration to Canada Survey" open-ended questions.

80. "Heimkehr aus fernen Landen," *Rieder Volksblatt,* 26 July 1956, p. 5. Mr. and Mrs. Hasibeder, who emigrated in 1951 to Canada, kindly offered the author a copy of their memoirs and a newspaper article reporting about their life in Canada five years after they had emigrated.

81. AICC, Interviews with Austrian Immigrants, May 1995, and responses to "Austrian Immigration to Canada Survey" open-ended questions.

82. ÖStA/AdR, BMfSV/SP, SA 11, Box 334, 39088/51, BMAA to BMfI, 10 December 1951.

83. NAC, RG 26, V. 124, f. 3-33-4, Pt.1, Laval Fortier to Leslie Chance, External Affairs, 4 December 1951.

84. *Ibid.,* RG 26, V. 124, f. 3-33-4, Pt. 1, Laval Fortier to Leslie Chance, External Affairs, 4 December 1951.

85. AICC, Interviews with Austrian Immigrants, May 1995, and responses to "Austrian Immigration to Canada Survey" open-ended questions. Cf. below, pp. 123-57.

86. *Ibid.,* Interview with Helene and Peter Nemastil, Vancouver, British Columbia, April 1995.

87. *Ibid.,* Interview with Otto Heberlein, Ottawa, Ontario, May 1995.

88. *Ibid.,* Interview with Richard Weichsler, Vancouver, British Columbia, April 1995. Interview with Ernst Vittur, Calgary, Alberta, April 1995.

89. *Ibid.,* Interview with Franz Guschlbauer, April 1995. Guschlbauer, like many others, said that his desire for adventure made him leave for Canada.

CHAPTER VI
A SOCIOLOGICAL PROFILE OF AUSTRIAN-CANADIANS

Peter Suschnigg

THIS CHAPTER HOLDS up a small mirror on Austrian life in Canada today.
Previous chapters have focussed on the political and historical dimensions
of the relations between Canada and Austria since these relations ulti-
mately provide the context for the movement of people between the two
nations. Those chapters identify major historical, political, and economic
epochs in Austria's migration history. In this chapter we draw on the experiences and recollections of Austrians and their descendants as they live
their lives against this background of historical, political, and economic
change. Because of the quantity and richness of information sources, this
chapter presents a highly condensed sociological profile of Austrians in
Canada. It summarizes data from a number of sources, viz. a survey of
Austrian immigrants; Canada-wide interviews of Austrian immigrants;
personal communications from immigrants; and scholarly research conducted in conjunction with the Austrian Immigration to Canada project.
In drawing on these sources we have to caution against ready generaliza-
tion of the survey results presented below because of the difficulties in
obtaining a sound sampling frame. On some dimensions such as immigration flow, however, the survey sample appears to parallel the estimated
population of Austrian immigrants in Canada.

The discussion then turns to the problem of Austrian identity and
takes self-identification as the criterion of inclusion in the present study.
This is followed by a brief history of Austrian immigration and the order-
ing of Austrian immigrants into six distinct groups. A consideration of
demographic data like age, gender, marital status, the question of citizenship, and settlement patterns follows. The next part revisits the problem of
self-identification. Among the factors that play a part in self-identification

we consider language maintenance and acquisition; the preservation of emotional, and in some cases professional and commercial, ties through return visits to Austria; the expressed desire to return permanently to Austria; social networks; citizenship uptake; and membership in Austrian clubs. The next section briefly investigates the overall contributions of Austrian immigrants to the Canadian economy and society: the education and skills that they brought to Canada; the occupations the immigrants held on arrival and the ones they hold now; and their individual and family income levels. The penultimate part considers the immigrants' own evaluations of their hopes and expectations. We will discover that most of them are generally satisfied yet somewhat ambivalent about their Canadian experiences. Finally, we will discuss briefly the Canadian-born children of immigrants and observe that they have become Canadians, although some of them still maintain ties with the land of their ancestors.

DATA SOURCES

The sources of data for this chapter include: a survey of 1,462 Austrians living in Canada;[1] in-depth interviews with more than 150 Austrian immigrants;[2] a series of scholarly papers written expressly for this collection or its companion volume;[3] and personal communications from immigrants and their family members.

Late in 1994, questionnaires were delivered in bulk to Austrian clubs and organizations across Canada. Included with each questionnaire was a letter by Dr. Lichem, the Austrian Ambassador to Canada, which extended an invitation to participate in the survey to all who considered themselves fully or partially Austrian. Recipients were also asked to pass on copies of the questionnaire to any Austrian who might have been missed in the bulk mailing. Additional copies were distributed through community networks such as Austrian specialty food shops. The survey was conducted over a five-month period, between November 1994 and April 1995. In most instances, respondents completed the questionnaire themselves. Occasionally a family member completed the questionnaire on a respondent's behalf.

Thus conceived, our survey provided us with an opportunity to study immigrants' descendants as well as the immigrants themselves. Of the 1,462 valid questionnaires received, 1,165 were from Austrian-born immigrants, 151 from immigrants born outside the present borders of the Republic of Austria, and 140 from Canadian-born respondents. The country of birth for six respondents could not be ascertained. Our survey instrument contained 56 questions, producing 91 variables. While most of the questions were closed-ended, thirteen were open-ended in order to give respondents an opportunity to express their thoughts and opinions more fully. In terms of sampling, we had no choice but to conduct a non-random convenience sample. First, our survey population was not clearly defined because there are various interpretations regarding what it means to be Austrian. Second, since we had no way of obtaining a name and address list for all Austrians living in Canada, we had no access to a sampling frame.[4] We were understandably concerned that our non-random convenience sample would introduce bias into our survey data and make our results ungeneralizable to the population of Austrians in Canada. Our concern was somewhat allayed, however, when we compared our survey demographics to data presented by Neuwirth and de Vries.[5] Drawing on Canadian immigration statistics to measure immigration flow and census population data to count the number of Austrians resident from 1901 to

Table 1. Correlations Between Survey Data and Neuwirth and de Vries Data

	Birth	Citizenship	Residence	Survey
Annual number of immigrants classified by country of birth	1.0000 (61)			
Annual number of immigrants classified by citizenship	.9764 (61)	.0000 (61)		
Annual number of immigrants classified country of last permanent residence	.7248 (37)	.6787 (37)	1.0000 (37)	
Year of immigration as reported by survey respondents	.9463 (54)	.9580 (54)	.7201 (37)	1.000 (54)

Source: Neuwirth and de Vries.
(N): Number in cell

1991, these authors present statistics on ethnicity, country of last permanent residence, country of birth, and citizenship. As Table 1 shows, cor-
relating their data about country of birth, citizenship and Austrians resident in Canada between 1931 and 1991 with the data from the survey
yields very high coefficients.[6]

Figure 1. Austrian Immigrants, Year of Arrival, 1927-1994

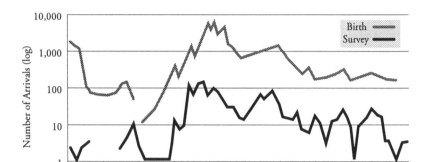

Birth: Number (log) of immigrants from Austria classified by country of birth,
1927-1994. *Source:* Neuwirth and de Vries, 1995; Table 1.
Survey: Number of immigrants as calculated from survey 1927-1991. *Source:* Survey.

To some extent then, we can be confident that our sample is representative of the population of Austrians in terms of the time of their
arrival in Canada: as Figure 1 below demonstrates, there is a close correspondence between the statistics derived by Neuwirth and de Vries[7] and
the numbers of our survey respondents who immigrated during particular years. Along other dimensions, however, we cannot be equally sure
that our sample is representative. For this reason we must be cautious
about generalizing our survey results to the population of Austrians in
Canada.

As well as on survey data, the analysis for this chapter is based on
more than 175 in-depth interviews—and numerous further incidental
conversations—that were carried out by Austrian researchers in Canada
during the spring of 1995. Approximately 30 interviews in British Columbia; 30 in Alberta; 35 in Manitoba and Saskatchewan; 40 in Ontario, and
more than 40 Austrian immigrants in Quebec. Other primary data

included in our analysis are the personal letters and curricula vitae sent by many respondents who took part in the survey. The scholarly secondary literature written expressly in conjunction with this research project was first vetted at the International Symposium "Austrian Immigration to Canada," held at Carleton University in Ottawa during May 18-21, 1995.

THE PROBLEM OF DEFINING AN AUSTRIAN IDENTITY

Anyone who attempts to research Austrians in Canada quickly realizes that it is difficult to decide who "counts" as Austrian. Even if the researcher constructs a set of criteria, those criteria will not necessarily be shared by others. This conceptual problem makes it difficult to estimate the number of Austrians living in Canada: should one use the set of criteria approach or the self-identification approach to determine numbers? Official sources of information on Austrians in Canada reflect this dilemma. Neuwirth and de Vries attempted to arrive at precise estimates of Austrian immigration into Canada by reference to the set of criteria approach but found that both census data and immigration statistics tend to inflate the true numbers. They concluded that "while the magnitude of this inflation has declined since 1961, it is not possible to state with any degree of certainty whether the most recent figures are still inflated, or whether they are telling the true story."[8]

Immigration and census data also reflect the self-identification of Austrian immigrants to Canada. This self-identification is a social construct; it is part of an immigrant's cultural identity and is not necessarily related to objective criteria such as an immigrant's country of origin or citizenship.[9] As such, an immigrant's cultural identity is subject to change—a fact which makes it even more difficult to identify and research Austrians in Canada.[10] In Canada, the official myth of two founding peoples, and the policy of multiculturalism have intriguing implications. The myth of the two founding peoples assigns secondary status to non-Caucasian and non-British and non-French groups, while the policy of multiculturalism implies equality and attenuates the urge to acculturation. In this respect, "multiculturalism" can be seen as a peculiarly Canadian manifestation of pluralism. One consequence, however, is the presumed cultural homogeneity of non-British or non-French groups to the casual outside observer, which certainly does not bear up to close scrutiny. Despite the conceptual caveats noted above, we have decided to use the self-identification criterion to determine who counts as Austrian in Canada. In doing so, we also make no distinction between Austrian sojourners and immigrants.

RECENT PERIODS OF AUSTRIAN IMMIGRATION

During most of the 19th century, emigration from Austria-Hungary was not a readily available option for most citizens of the monarchy.[11] In this century, however, the break-up of the Austro-Hungarian monarchy, the Great Depression, the rise of Nazi Germany, the *Anschluss*, World War II, and the post-war occupation provided powerful incentives for many Austrians to seek a new life elsewhere. These migration-shaping events permit us to see Austrian immigrants as belonging to one of six groups: (a) the early arrivals who came in the 1920s and 30s. The second and third groups include (b) those few who arrived before World War II, often to flee Nazi terror, and (c) those who came to Canada during the War. They were succeeded by (d) the large contingent that arrived from the mid-1950s to mid-1960s and by those (e) who came in the 1960s and 70s, and (f) who have arrived since then. Figure 2 displays the flow of immigrants who responded to the survey for each decade since 1925. The post-war immigration peak is clearly shown and the apparently small group of pre-war immigrants is a reflection of their advancing years.

Figure 2. Austrian Immigrants, Decade of Arrival, 1925-1994

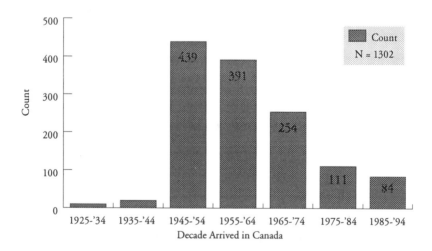

(a) The Pre-World War II Immigrants

After World War I, Canada pursued an immigration policy that differed sharply from that characterizing the pre-war era. The experience of war changed Canadian perceptions of immigrant workers' desirable characteristics. Whereas before the war economic criteria were paramount, political criteria and cultural standards predominated afterwards. However, the poor economic conditions in Canada after World War I led to a major exodus of Canadian workers to the United States. Mounting pressure from a number of Canadian industrial interests, particularly the Canadian Pacific and Canadian National Railways, soon led to a re-assessment of the post-war immigration criteria to find potential immigrants, preferably agricultural workers. Avery estimates that "more than 369,905 continental European immigrants entered the country between 1925 and 1931."[12] As a consequence of these policies, only a handful of Austrians entered Canada between 1919 and 1924.[13] Thus, the renewed search for "stalwart peasant[s] in a sheepskin coat" yielded only a relatively small number of Austrian immigrants.[14] Although we have a few questionnaires completed by descendants of these early arrivals, no living survivors of that era are included in the survey.

We were fortunate to receive questionnaires from some of the settlers who came to Canada in the late 1920s. Almost all of them were from Burgenland and arrived between 1927 and 1929. Although most of them had had farming experience, life in Canada was very difficult. One of the respondents, who arrived at the age of ten wrote that she "had to go to Saskatchewan and live on a farm (homestead) ... very difficult times." Another who had been a shoemaker in Austria recounted his "working on farms, logging and riding freight trains." And indeed, one respondent wrote that she arrived in 1929 to face unemployment. Some made good of their ordeals like the immigrant who arrived as a carpenter's apprentice, worked as a farm labourer for ten years, and eventually succeeded in buying his own farm. The worsening world economy brought about a steep drop in immigration during the 1930s. We have no accounts of any Austrian immigrants who arrived between 1930 and 1937, but we know that about 300 Austrian immigrants did arrive in Canada during that period. But the rise of National Socialism in Germany and Austria—to be followed by the disappearance of Austria from the political map of Europe—probably contributed to a crisis of identity, not only among immigrants, but also among those who stayed behind.

(b) The Political Refugees and Exiles

The small group of Austrians next to arrive in Canada was primarily composed of those who had reason to fear the Nazi tide. It is noteworthy that the majority of the very small number[15] of respondents who stated that they landed in Canada between 1938 and 1939 arrived from a country other than Austria, leading one of them to write that he was "not sure about being accepted as an Austrian as [his] roots go back to Austria-Hungary." As a group, these arrivals tended to be well-educated and in some cases highly artistic. Despite their ordeals, Canada was not an all-embracing country for most. In response to a question that asked to "tell us some of the most difficult experiences or feelings about leaving Austria" one refugee who had studied medicine wrote about "surviving the first 2 years clearing and breaking land and learning to farm and work in the bush under the most primitive conditions."

(c) Immigration during World War II

While the dissolution of Austria as a political entity exacerbates the problems of contemporary demographers and census keepers as Austrian citizenship ceased to exist, we know that some respondents to our survey did arrive during the war. Strictly speaking, this cohort is composed of two quite distinct clusters. The first is made up of those who were interned as enemy aliens, usually in the United Kingdom. The complicating factor here is the fact that most of these enemy aliens were themselves refugees and opponents of the Hitler regime and should therefore be counted with the group of exiles and refugees in (b). Indeed, some refugees arrived in Canada not from the United Kingdom but from a third country such as Portugal. The second cluster is comprised of those who came as prisoners of war. As it happened, members of all these groups were often shipped to Canada on the same vessels since the allied powers had no interest in distinguishing between them.

(d) The Post-War Immigration Peak

The peak of immigration during the 1950s reflected the poor economic outlook in Austria as well as changes in Canadian immigration policy.[16] Austria had been shattered by the war, and Canada's need for trained and qualified immigrants, particularly trades people, superseded the post-war dislike of former enemy aliens. Austrian immigration to Canada reached its peak during the 1950s. Between 1951 and 1960, approximately 25,000 Austrians sought a new life in Canada.[17] We have

718 survey responses for this period. This cohort of immigrants belongs to a generation deeply affected by the experiences of the war and immediate post-war years. Many of them had also endured the Depression and the turbulent inter-war years. The outbreak of the Korean War only heightened the sense of insecurity. These ordeals must have exerted a powerful influence. They made the search for security and a degree of physical well-being central concerns. Politics for many was forever tainted, and the apolitical character of many interviewees was striking.

When asked to give the most important reason for having come to Canada, the most frequent single reason (N=129) given was "to find financial betterment." Many members of this cohort (N=704) did not simply leave Austria because its future seemed to hold little promise—one in three in our survey either had family or friends in Canada or came with his or her parents. Another third (N=222) gave a variety of reasons for wanting to come to Canada. Many cited the scarcity of housing in Austria as a reason. Others stated that the Russian occupation made life in Austria intolerable, though not one respondent cited the occupation by one of the other three allied powers as a reason for wanting to leave Austria. A common complaint, particularly among those who came to Canada during the latter part of the decade, was the perceived need to have party-political connections if one wanted to find accommodation and decent work in Austria. A number also cited their desire to be able to live in peace as a driving motivation for wanting to emigrate. As borne out by the interviews, the stated reasons for migration to Canada differ markedly by gender. Table 2 shows that men are more likely than women to cite financial, political, or multiple reasons, while women are more likely to give familial or social and emotional reasons for their decision to emigrate. These differences are statistically significant. The decision by a majority of women to come because they had relatives, spouses, fiancées, or friends in Canada is reflected in their younger age and their apparently lower satisfaction with life in Austria.

(e) Arrivals during the Sixties

Although immigration from Austria declined somewhat during the latter part of that decade, it remained relatively high. Our survey yielded 290 valid responses for the period. During the early sixties many concerns that brought the immigrants of the 1950s to Canada still played a big part in the decision to emigrate. Lack of housing, poor economic prospects in Austria, and the Austrian-party political system persuaded ("pushed") many to leave. However, the most frequent single reason for wanting to migrate to Canada was the "pull" of family members or friends in Canada. Of the respondents in this cohort 151, or 52.1 percent, gave other or multiple reasons for their decision to emigrate. *Wanderlust,* the desire to learn another language, to further one's education, or the love of adventure began to replace gradually the old fears of destitution, political and religious persecution, and the sense of being hemmed in.

Table 2. Reason(s) given for Decision to Migrate, by Gender, 1951-1960

	Gender		
Reason(s)	Male (%)	Female (%)	Total N
Financial	21.9	12.4	129
Political	4.8	3.0	29
Familial-Social/emotional	22.8	52.6	240
Other reason	13.5	9.4	84
Multiple reasons	37.0	22.6	222
Total percent	100	100	
			704

χ^2=65.79   d.f.=4   p≤.0001

(f) From the Seventies to the Present

These years saw a steep drop in the number of Austria immigrants. As life in Austria continued to improve and the Austrian economy continued to strengthen, Canada's falling standard of living and its ailing economy offered little incentive to anyone seeking a materially better life. Our survey netted valid responses from 131 immigrants who came during that period. Although some still came to improve their material conditions, the majority now emigrated to Canada because they had friends or relatives in Canada. Some arrived because they wanted to further their education and several came because they wanted to have better business opportunities. The search for new experiences and adventure became more common.

By way of summary, it may be said that the flow of Austrian immigrants was shaped by the change in the economic and political conditions in Canada, Austria, and to some extent in Europe. As always, there were those who intended to stay only for a limited period of time and would then return. We do not know how many actually did return to Austria but there is some evidence that at least a few did return or sent their children to be educated or trained in the trades in Austria.[18] Others had no intention of staying in Canada but would have preferred to settle in a third country, typically the United States of America. About one in five (N=223 or 17.9 percent) arrived in Canada not from Austria but from a third country, most often from Germany (N=60), the United Kingdom (N=44), Switzerland (N=24), and the United States (N=22). Thus the "push-and-pull" model of reasons for migration appears to have received some support from our data, although it is difficult to specify the relative effects and quantify the processes that might have been involved.

DEMOGRAPHIC CHARACTERISTICS

(a) Age

Although most of them arrived in their twenties, Austrian immigrants in Canada are now an aging population, even compared to immigrant groups in general.[19] Their mean age was almost 57 years (N=1,460), the median age 59 years. The bulk of the age distribution appears to be fairly symmetrical, but some high age values give it a slight positive skew. The youngest respondent was 19 years at the time of the survey while the oldest was 100 years old.[20] The average age of those who were Austrian-born (N=1,163) was 59 years, the average age of those born elsewhere (N=151), generally in areas that had once been part of the Austro-Hungarian monarchy, was 61 years. A smaller number (N=140) of respondents who were born in Canada of an Austrian parent or parents was significantly younger: their average age was 34 years and seven months. If one excludes the Canadian-born from the computations, 94 percent of Austrians in Canada are above 35 years of age. Males (N=823) were on average 58 years old, females (N=637) on average 55 years and almost seven months. The age difference between males and females is statistically significant (p=.002). The lower mean age of women respondents reflects the fact that women tended to arrive later than men. One consequence is that men's median years of residence in Canada is 39 years, women's 35 years.

(b) Gender

In common with many immigrant groups, males outnumber females among Austrian immigrants. Our sample contained 669 Austrian-born males and 496 females, and 86 males and 65 females who were born neither in present-day Austria nor Canada. In the much smaller proportion of Canadian-born, however, females slightly outnumbered males. While these results may not be generalizable (among other things we do not know the proportion of male and female offspring among Austrian immigrants) it is tempting to hypothesize a somewhat stronger female attachment to Austria.

(c) Relationship status

At the time of arrival in Canada, 60.1 percent of all male immigrants (N=448) had never been married, while 38.3 percent (N=285) were married. A very small number (N=11) arrived either divorced or separated, or living with a partner. Women, however, were far less likely to arrive having never been married. 46.4 percent (N=255) were single when they came to Canada but almost as large a percentage—45.1 percent (N=248)—were married at the time of landing. Although they constituted only a small percentage of the total (5.1 percent), women were also considerably more likely than men to arrive divorced. These differences in marital status are statistically highly significant (d.f. = 5; p<.0001) and these findings are also corroborated in the summaries of interviews carried out by Austrian researchers mentioned above.

At the time of the survey, 75.4 percent (N=1,090), or about three in four immigrants were married, and 9.9 percent (N=143), or one in ten, were widowed. These statistics conceal marked differences in married status between men and women, Austrian immigrants and Canadian-born. Of immigrant men, 85.4 percent (N=637) were married while 5.4 percent (N=40) were widowed. Of immigrant women, 69.2 percent (N=385) were married and 16.9 percent (N=94), or almost one in six, were widowed. These differences in marital status are statistically highly significant (χ^2=59.27; d.f.= 5; p<.001).

Another remarkable feature, reflecting the aging population of Austrian immigrants in Canada, is the average length of their marriages. The 917 Austrian-born respondents for whom we have this information had on average lived together for 29 years and nine months, with one couple having been married for 60 years. The Canadian-born descendants of Austrian immigrants (N=78) were, of course, a much younger cohort. They had on average been married for almost ten years. Those immigrants born elsewhere (N=113) had been married, on average, for 31 years and nine months.

Although the overall proportion of the widowed out of the total is relatively small (12 percent), women were on average more than three times as likely to be widowed than men. Of women, 16.9 percent (N=94) were widowed, compared to 5.5 percent (N=45) of men, at the time of the survey. Five percent declared themselves to be divorced, and two percent were separated. We cannot be certain whether divorce and separation are rare among Austrian immigrants; however, the long average duration of marriages points in this direction. If this is indeed the case it would differ sharply from the Canadian divorce rate.[21]

Since males outnumber females by about one third, marriage or relationships with partners who are not Austrians is inevitable. Table 3 shows, however, that our older respondents demonstrated strong preferences for partners of the same national background as themselves. In fact, Austrian-born immigrants were statistically significantly more likely to have Austrian partners than the Canadian-born. Of the 954 Austrian-born immigrants in our sample, 428 or almost 45 percent had Austrian partners, and of the 82 Canadian-born, 44 or close to 54 percent had partners of other ethnic backgrounds. These differences hold when controlling for gender. The consequences of these preferences are likely to contribute to a relatively rapid absorption of Austrians into the fabric of Canadian society since a majority of the first Canadian-born generation identify themselves as Canadians rather than Austrians. The number of children per couple ranged from none to seven, with an average of two children.

Table 3. Citizenship of Immigrants' Spouses and Partners by Age Group

Spouse's Citizenship	Age Group			Total
	21-44 (%)	45-64 (%)	65-100 (%)	N
Canadian	46.8	20.5	11.6	212
Austrian	25.0	40.0	59.1	455
Other	28.2	39.5	29.4	356
Total percent	100	100	100	
				1023

χ^2=91.36   d.f.=4   p$\leq$.0005

SETTLEMENT PATTERNS

(a) Austrian Province of Origin

Almost one in three Austrian immigrants to Canada has come from Vienna; 17 percent hailed from Styria. Eight, seven, and six percent, respectively, arrived from Upper Austria, Lower Austria, and Carinthia. An interesting observation is the fact that the flow of Austrian immigrants followed an east-west pattern. Apart from those arriving from areas of "successor states," the first to arrive in the mid-1950s and earlier were immigrants from Burgenland. These were followed by those from Styria, Upper Austria, and Lower Austria in the later 1950s and early 1960s. Immigrants from Salzburg, Tyrol, and Vorarlberg tended to arrive in the mid- and late 1960s.

(b) Canadian Province of Residence

More than one-half of all Austrian immigrants now live in Ontario, almost one in five in Quebec, and more than five percent in Alberta. This seems to indicate that the earlier settlement patterns reported by the Canadian Citizenship Branch are no longer correct or that the respondents to the questionnaire are in some way atypical. Settlement patterns of Austrian immigrants within Canada mirror changing immigration policies and account for the differential age distribution of Austrians in Canada. The oldest group of Austrians lives in the Prairie provinces, Manitoba, Saskatchewan, and Alberta. At the time of the survey they were on average 61 years and one month old. Austrians in Quebec were on average almost as old (61 years), while those in the Eastern provinces (Newfoundland, Nova Scotia, and New Brunswick[22]) were on average 59 years and five months, those in British Columbia 58 years and four months, and those in Ontario 57 years and nine months.[23] The average ages of Austrians in the Prairie provinces and Quebec are statistically significantly different from those in the remainder of the country at the 5 percent level. Plainly, Austrians as a distinctive group in the Canadian mosaic are in the process of vanishing if they continue to be acculturated and no substantial numbers of new immigrants are added.

As noted above, emigration patterns from Austria are indicative of the social and economic processes at work in Austria during various periods. The oldest and largest group of Austrians in Canada hails from Vienna. Their average age is about 61 years and 11 months (N=430). Immigrants from Burgenland constituted the next oldest group. Their average age was

60 years and four months (N=83). They were followed by Austrians from Styria (59 years and nine months; N= 231), Salzburg and Lower Austria (58 years and ten months; N=94 and 101), Carinthia (58 years and two months; N=93), Upper Austria (56 years and six months; N=132), Tyrol (53 years and eleven months; N=74), and finally Vorarlberg (49 years and nine months; N=27). Thus, emigration from Austria appeared to roll from east to west while Austrian settlement in Canada proceeded from west to east.

This pattern again appears to support the "push and pull" thesis of migration. When economic and political conditions in Austria were perceived to be more difficult than the corresponding conditions in Canada, emigration became a desirable option for many. The ability to migrate was, and is, of course defined by the respective policies of the two governments. Thus immigration to Canada during the Depression and the immediate pre-war years was severely restricted by government policy although it may have been a desirable option for many. During the war, immigration was virtually nil. After the war, the economic and political conditions in Austria were the major, and somewhat related, reasons for the emigration wave of the 1950s.

The processes affecting the ebb and flow of immigration also appear to influence immigrants' decisions about questions of citizenship. Although immigrants may now obtain Canadian citizenship after a three-year residency period, Austrian immigrants tend to delay this step. Even though many factors are likely to influence the decision to become a naturalized Canadian citizen, the concurrent loss of Austrian citizenship—as revealed in both interviews and by comments written in the survey questionnaires—is keenly felt by many immigrants. One strategy to cushion the sense of loss is that only one partner of many immigrant couples seeks Canadian citizenship. The average age of those born in Austria (N=604) holding Canadian citizenship was 63 years and nine months, while the average age of the Austrian-born immigrants (N=476) still holding Austrian citizenship was 52 years and nine months. The much smaller cohort of those born in Austria (N=74) and holding either dual citizenship or citizenships other than Austrian or Canadian was on average 59 years and eight months old.

SELF-DEFINITION AS AUSTRIAN

We now return to the problem of Austrian identity. As noted above, the survey of Austrians in Canada relied on self-identification as the criterion for inclusion. Three questions in the survey instrument were designed to provide a clearer picture of the relationship between place of birth, citizenship, and national identity.

Austrian-born immigrants holding Canadian citizenship (N=603) are most likely to describe themselves as Austrian-Canadians (N=345), rather than as Canadians (N=175) or Austrians (N=78). It is possible that this designation is one preferred by the respondents in our sample as others have commented to our interviewers on many Austrians' desire "to fit in." Indeed, several of our respondents expressed impatience with Canada's multiculturalism policy. These immigrants argue that immigrants ought to immerse themselves as quickly as possible into the host society. Since the multiculturalism policy not only places no demand on immigrants to become culturally assimilated but actually encourages "hyphenated" Canadianism, the choice of Austrian-Canadian makes sense. For the smaller number of those born neither in Canada nor present-day Austria (N=79) and holding Canadian citizenship, the likelihood of describing themselves as Canadians (N=39) is somewhat larger than that of defining themselves as Austrian-Canadians (N=30). Thirty-seven of the 73 Canadian-born defined themselves as Canadians, while 31 thought of themselves as Austrian-Canadians. The relatively large proportion of Canadian-born Austrian-Canadians is more than likely a reflection of the sample peculiarities and not a generalizable finding. Three hundred and thirty-seven (71.1 percent) of the 474 respondents who had been born in Austria and retained Austrian citizenship considered themselves Austrians, while 129 (27.2 percent) described themselves as Austrian-Canadians. The number of those having been born in Canada and holding Austrian citizenship alone was too small for analysis as the anonymity of our respondents had to be assured. Thirty-six (69.2 percent) of the 52 born elsewhere considered themselves to be Austrians while ten (19.2 percent) thought of themselves as Austrian-Canadians. The remaining category of 157 respondents who held another citizenship or multiple citizenship tended to describe themselves as Austrian-Canadians. Forty-five (60 percent) of those born in Austria and 46 (69.7 percent) of those born in Canada considered themselves to be Austrian-Canadians. A small proportion of respondents (N=159) had dual citizenship or held citizenship of nations other than Austria or Canada. The great majority of these (N=126) held dual Canadian and Austrian citizenship. The most common reason for holding neither Austrian nor Canadian citizenship was the respondent's prior residence in a country other than Canada.

Many of those who were not Canadian-born still had strong emotional ties to Austria even if they had adopted Canadian citizenship. Some respondents made a point of adding that their reasons for adopting Canadian citizenship were business or employment-related. Indeed, the Austrian citizenship law was one of the most frequently cited inequities by our respondents. Many stated that they had lost their Austrian citizenship when taking up Canadian citizenship, while their Canadian-born children were able to hold dual citizenship. An additional indicator of the strong ties many felt was the frequency with which they had visited Austria since coming to Canada.

Like other immigrant groups, Austrians tend to retain certain cultural and behavioral artifacts that distinguish them from the rest of Canadian society. These artifacts may be material or non-material. Ways of furnishing and decorating homes, for instance, are material statements of cultural kinship. One interviewer, to take just one example, described a home as *gutbürgerlich*. Other immigrants strive for a sense of continuance and the familiar by decorating their homes with mementos and artifacts that they brought with them at the time of their first arrival in Canada or acquired during a subsequent trip to or sojourn in Austria. Any artifact can in this way achieve an importance that may look vastly exaggerated to contemporary Austrian observers whose links with Austrian culture have not been severed. Indeed, some interviewees dismissed the Austrian immigrants' culture as mere "souvenir culture." Other manifestations of cultural separateness relate to food and drink preferences, as well as food rituals considered as quintessentially Austrian, as for instance the *Jause*. In a foreign setting, such distinguishing characteristics acquire added meaning and importance since food and eating represent far more than means of physical survival but carry the imprint of specific cultures.

In focusing on distinguishing cultural representations many of our respondents claimed certain "Austrian" characteristics which they felt to be important. One such characteristic that they ascribed to themselves in one form or another was Austrian immigrants capacity for hard work. While there is, no doubt, some truth to this assertion it may not be a uniquely Austrian hallmark, but rather a characteristic of immigrant groups in general. Immigrants as a group, after all, have to work hard in order to make good. Our respondents clearly took pride in the skills that they and their fellow Austrians have brought to Canada. During the 1950s, when the large wave of Austrians came, trades skills were in high demand in Canada. Some will maintain that even today, Austrian trades training, from a public policy perspective, is arguably superior to its Canadian counterpart.

LANGUAGE

A major defining characteristic of many immigrant groups is their common language.[24] The overwhelming majority (98 percent) of Austrian-born immigrants claimed German as their mother tongue. A smaller majority (72 percent) of those born elsewhere and a minority of Canadian-born reported German as their mother tongue. If language can be taken as an indicator of integration (or assimilation), two factors stand out:

In the first place, about one fifth of those who had German as their mother tongue (N=1,242) still speak mainly German at home. Almost forty percent use English and German and almost 35 percent use mainly English. The remaining small percentage either speak mainly French, French and German, or another language in their homes. Table 4 demonstrates that immigrants over the age of 65 are significantly less likely to use English alone as the main language spoken at home. Indeed, the 21 to 44 year age group is more than twice as likely to use English as the main language of communication in their homes.

Table 4. Immigrants' Language Use at Home, by Age Group

Language spoken at Home	Age Group 21-44 (%)	45-64 (%)	65-100 (%)	Total N
German	14.9	16.6	27.3	260
English	55.3	38.5	23.9	470
French	1.4	.6	.9	11
German & English	22.6	40.2	45.2	508
German & French	1.4	.6	.7	10
Other	4.3	3.4	2.0	40
Total percent	100	100	100	
				1299

χ^2=83.34   d.f.=10   p$\leq$.00005

Secondly, one in five children of Austrian-born immigrants is reported to speak German fluently, while almost 12 percent speak no German at all. Almost half (46 percent) of Canadian-born respondents speak no German at all, with only 4 percent claiming fluency in the language. It is interesting to note that almost one quarter (24 percent) of the children of those born outside the present-day territory of Austria are reported to speak German fluently, and the remainder speak it quite well or a little. None are reported to have completely lost their ability to speak German. While this survey relies on subjective reporting of children's language ability, it is evident that Austrians tend not to transmit their mother tongue to their children. German language transmittal is actually declining with recency of immigration. In other words, those immigrants who have lived longest in Canada are more likely to have German-speaking children than more recent immigrants. The most important factor in language transmittal, however, is the nationality of the spouse. Three out of four immigrants with a Canadian-born spouse speak exclusively English at home with another 9 percent speaking exclusively French. A little more than half of those with Austrian-born spouses tend to speak German and English at home while a little more than 30 percent speak German. Other factors such as settlement density that might affect language transmission remain to be analyzed.

LANGUAGE ACQUISITION AND LANGUAGE LOSS

For the majority of our respondents the most frequently cited difficulty upon arrival in Canada was their inability to communicate in either English or French. After varying periods of time the need to learn one of these languages coupled with initially long absences from Austria enabled immigrants not only to "fit in" but frequently weakened their ability to communicate in German. Thus as an immigrant acquires a new language, the first language tends to recede. Among the first generation of Canadian-born, German language skills tend to be stronger among children of earlier immigrant cohorts and first-born. As stated above, however, language maintenance tends to be relatively weak among German speakers in Canada.[25] Although the data do not allow us to account for these differences with confidence, endogenous marriage patterns among early immigrants, declining nativism, and improved ethnic networks, such as club membership, may explain at least part of these variations.

RETURN VISITS TO AUSTRIA

Research by Barkan, Jones, and Samuel shows that frequent return migration and commuting reduce the likelihood of citizenship acquisition.[26] When Canadian-born and those for whom relatives or friends completed the questionnaires are excluded from the analysis (N=1,234), immigrants had returned on average almost 11 times to Austria since arriving in Canada. However, a small number of respondents had visited many more times than was generally the case. Virtually all of these frequent visitors travelled to Austria in the course of their employment. It is therefore prudent to consider the median of eight visits as more representative. Visits to Austria were in almost all cases combined with visiting relatives. What is astonishing is that more than one third of the respondents (35.1 percent) had last visited Austria in 1994. It seems therefore that a large proportion of Austrian immigrants maintains regular ties with their homeland, thus maintaining emotional ties with Austria and helping to delay Canadian citizenship acquisition. In the process many feel "torn apart on the inside" and discover no later than on their first visit home that they are now no longer at home anywhere.[27] One of the indicators of how strongly attached to Austria immigrants feel is the direction of their desire to return to live there.

RETURNING TO LIVE IN AUSTRIA

Close to 45 percent of respondents (N=1,286) consider the possibility of returning with close to 30 percent stating that they would live in Austria again, given the opportunity. While it is impossible to know to what degree economic considerations play a part in these responses, Austria's economic success compared to Canada's difficulties in recent years may affect immigrants' thoughts of returning to live in Austria. But an immigrant's age also plays a part in wanting to return. Fifty-three percent of immigrants between the ages of 21 and 44 (N=164) said that they might return. Those between the ages of 45 and 64 were slightly more likely to want to return to Austria than the younger and the older age groups. The oldest age group, those over 65 were considerably more likely to declare that they would not return to Austria, even if they had the chance to do so. These differences are statistically significant and are to some degree borne out by the responses to the interviews.

The oldest—generally those immigrants who had remained the longest in Canada—had usually raised their families in Canada. Their children, already grown and married themselves, have grown up as Canadians, or sometimes Austrian-Canadians, and have few or no ties to Austria. Their everyday language is either English or French rather than German and they are not likely to marry an Austrian. In addition, the oldest group of immigrants is now mostly retired. They have lived most of their lives in Canada and feel strongly that they have contributed substantially to the development of their adopted country. Their assets, savings, investments, and pensions are almost all in Canada and few are entitled to Austrian social benefits. Several of the interviewees who had attempted to return and recommence life in Austria stated that they found life in Austria not what they had hoped it to be. They commented on their difficulties with readjusting to Austrian bureaucracy and small-mindedness. Those who had left children in Canada found the pain of separation too great. Given the known difficulties of resettlement, and the currently unfavourable currency exchange rates for the Canadian dollar, it appears that most respondents took the question in the spirit it was asked and realized that there was little chance of such an eventuality. Of course, the voices of those who have returned and now live in Austria are missing.

SOCIAL NETWORKS

A question inquiring with whom immigrants tended to socialize most, Canadian-born, Austrian-born or non-Austrian immigrants, revealed not only a reluctance by many respondents to limit themselves to one category, but drew sharp comments from many who considered this question inappropriate. Most of these objectors wrote that they did not differentiate among their friends and acquaintances according to background. Against these assertions stand the remarks of several interviewees that suggest a degree of hostility towards more recent (and frequently non-European) immigrants. Many Austrian immigrants who have now spent several decades in Canada felt, on one extreme, that more recent immigrants enjoyed unearned privileges as, for instance, immediate access to social welfare assistance and, on the other extreme, that wealthy new arrivals raised the cost of housing for long-term residents. Austrian immigrants seem ambivalent about their place in Canadian society—on one hand, they wish to become integrated as rapidly as possible, on the other, they lay claim to distinctive characteristics that entitle them to a special place in the Canadian mosaic.

CITIZENSHIP UPTAKE

If, as Frideres and his colleagues argue,[28] "one indication of acceptance and adjustment is the extent to which arrivals become Canadian citizens," Austrians are among the most likely immigrants to eventually acquire Canadian citizenship. In our sample, 52.5 percent of all Austrians in Canada held Canadian citizenship, while 40.5 percent held Austrian citizenship, and the remaining 7 percent carried dual Austrian-Canadian citizenship or some other combination. But, as we have seen, the adoption of Canadian citizenship is often delayed. Richmond's study of post-war immigrants found considerable variation in the rate of citizenship uptake between different ethnic groups. Only 14 percent of immigrants from the United Kingdom had taken Canadian citizenship whereas 60 percent of refugees from Eastern Europe had done so.[29] Among our respondents there is also a statistically significant interaction effect between age and gender in citizenship uptake. At young ages, women are more likely than men to opt for Canadian citizenship, but are less likely than men to do so as they get older.

CLUBS

Almost one half of all respondents were members of Austrian clubs. As ethnic and "national" clubs are often thought to reaffirm ethnic and national ties, it is interesting to note that Austrian immigrants who belong to clubs are significantly less likely to hold Austrian citizenship than those who do not belong. Another role ethnic clubs are believed to fulfil is to assist new arrivals with getting settled in their new country. One aspect of this is finding a job. If this is so, one would expect those with trades or similar skills to benefit from club membership. In the case of Austrian immigrants, however, education and skill levels appear to be unrelated to club membership as such, but Austrian immigrants tend to perpetuate "old country" social class differences in their clubs.

There are some 25 Austrian clubs and associations in Canada. These are to be found in the greater Vancouver area, Calgary, Edmonton, Regina, Saskatoon, Winnipeg, the greater Toronto area, Sault-St.Marie, Windsor, Kitchener,[30] Kingston, Ottawa, and Montreal. Over the years, these clubs have eased the transition into Canadian society of many new arrivals and have helped maintain social networks for their members. Most clubs focus on cultural activities, with a few catering especially to

sports or business interests. The impact or influence of these clubs as car-
riers and disseminators of Austrian culture is still open to evaluation.
There are, however, some common denominators. While some show
signs of revival, the continued existence of most clubs is jeopardized.
Understandably, the membership of almost all Austrian clubs and societies is aging, and Canadian-born descendants are generally not interested in continuing their forebears' social and cultural pursuits. Table 5
shows this trend: the older age groups are statistically significantly more
likely to belong to a club. Some clubs have already disappeared; others
whose mandate extended beyond Austrian culture may have retained
their name but have been taken over by non-Austrians. There are notable
exceptions, as for instance "The Friends of Austria" in Winnipeg. Twenty
percent of this club's membership is made up of members "under 40 years
of age and this younger age group is growing."[31]

Table 5. Club Membership by Age Group

	Age Group			
Club	21-44 (%)	45-64 (%)	65-100 (%)	Total N
No	71.1	51.3	50.0	787
Yes	28.9	48.7	50.0	648
Total Percent	100	100	100	
				1435

χ^2=38.40   d.f.=2   p$\leq$.0001

In some cases, the Canadian-born children of immigrants learned to
speak their parents' dialect when they grew up, but encountered difficulties when they grew old enough to attend German language school as
these schools are generally conducted by Germans who attempted to
teach High German. The young people soon became disillusioned with
and disinterested in things Austrian. Another problem identified by several respondents is that the small number of Austrians in certain localities
makes it impractical to have Austrian clubs. In these cases, Austrian immigrants tend to join other German-speaking clubs, or in some other cases
other German speakers have flocked to Austrian clubs. It is difficult in
either case to maintain or foster the Austrian character of a club. Finally

there is the fundamental problem of just what is meant by Austrian culture. In a brief survey of Austrian clubs such as this, it is not possible to
more than indicate certain rift lines. Austrian culture to some is best char-
acterized by its folkloristic aspects (folk dancers, choral groups, and the
like); to others, Austrian culture is what is usually referred to as "high culture" (music, art and literature). These visions of culture are not entirely
discrete but the differences are strong enough for immigrants to align
themselves with one camp or another. In fact, these differences may be
compounded by the relative isolation from contemporary Austrian
culture and the lack of "new blood" among immigrants. Thus, the deep
status divisions of the Austria that most immigrants left behind linger on
in Canada. The majority of immigrants who came to Canada as trades
people cling to the folk vision of Austrian culture, while the much smaller but more influential group of highly educated sustains the notions of
"high culture." It is to these skill and educational characteristics of immigrants to which we now turn.

EDUCATION AND SKILLS BROUGHT TO CANADA

After the early wave of Austrians who came to Canada as agriculturists,
most Austrian immigrants tended to be skilled craftspeople or artisans on
arrival in Canada. Almost one in three arrived in Canada with a *Gesellen-*
or *Meisterbrief.* Fourteen percent had completed *Berufsschule,* and ten percent carried a doctorate or similar professional qualification. There are
considerable differences in education and skill between men and women
immigrants. As Table 6 demonstrates, women were significantly more likely than men to arrive with educational levels up to and including
Hauptschule or to have completed *Berufsschule* or *Matura.* Men were more
likely to arrive as journeymen, *Meister,* or to have had some university education, a professional degree or a doctorate. Many of the respondents
expressed obvious pride in their own and all Austrians' contributions to
what they regarded as the building of the country. But in these expressions,
too, one can detect the ambivalence of what is regarded as worthy of mention and the occasional remark about the lack of "culture" in Canada.

We know that about 64 percent (N=732) of 1,151 respondents had
been employed at the time of their migration from Austria. Another 17.3
percent (N=167) had been attending school or university. Almost 7 percent (N=91) had been in a family partnership and almost 5 percent each
had been housewives (N=65) or had been self-employed (N=65). The

small number remaining had either been unemployed, retired, or had been in receipt of a disability pension. A third of the 832 from whom we received valid responses had been manual workers (*Arbeiter*), almost 23 percent (N=300) had been office workers (*Angestellte*), and seven percent (N=93) had left their positions as civil servants (*Beamte*).

Table 6. Education and Training at Time of Immigrants' Arrival

| Education / training at arrival | Gender | | Total |
	Male (%)	Female (%)	N
No Formal Schooling	2.3	4.0	39
Elementary School	6.0	11.5	108
Some Hauptschule	1.5	4.8	37
Completed Hauptschule	1.9	6.6	50
Berufsschule	8.4	20.3	174
Gesellenbrief	37.7	16.1	369
Some Gymnasium	10.1	6.8	112
Matura	7.1	10.3	109
Meisterbrief	4.2	.7	35
Some University	8.2	7.0	99
Doctorate or professional degree	10.2	4.9	103
Other	2.5	7.0	57
Total Percent	100	100	
			1292

χ^2=175.63   d.f.=11   p≤.0001

OCCUPATIONS

Austrians arrived in Canada skilled in a great variety of occupations. Of the 742 for whom we have the data, 131 or 12.7 percent were qualified trades people. Another 99 or 9.6 percent had worked in metal working industries (*Metallerzeugung und -verarbeitung*), and another 87 had been employed in the hospitality industry (*Gastgewerbe/Fremdenverkehr*). About five percent each had been working in agriculture or forestry (N=70) and the textile industry (N=65).

On their arrival in Canada, many found employment in their chosen fields but others found that they had to change or augment their skills and education. One in five (N=252) of the 1,314 respondents for whom we have valid data have changed their occupation four or more times since they arrived in Canada. In a large proportion of cases, Austrian immigrants have succeeded materially. Going four occupations back in the immigrants' work history, the four major occupational groupings that accounted for 46.8 percent of the 252 responses fell into the 11, 61, 41, and 85 Occupational Groups as defined by Statistics Canada (that is, managerial, administrative and related positions; service occupations; clerical and related positions; and product fabricating, assembling and repairing occupations). By 1994, 48.4 percent of the current occupations of our respondents (N=753) were made up of Groups 11, 85, 87, and 21 (namely, managerial, administrative and related positions; product fabricating, assembling and repairing occupations; construction trades occupations; and occupations in natural sciences, engineering and mathematics).[32]

As before, these statistics conceal marked differences between men and women. Four occupations back in the women's work history, 60 percent (N=75) of women's occupations fell into Groups 41, 61, and 51 while 63.3 percent (N=177) of men's occupations fell into Groups 11, 85, 61, 21, 83, and 51. Women plainly not only worked in lower-status and lower-paid occupations overall than men but were concentrated in fewer. By 1994 not much had changed: 59.4 percent (N=379) of women's occupations were in Groups 41, 61, 11, and 27.[33] 60.5 percent (N= 665) of men's occupations in the same year were in Groups 11, 85, 87, and 21, while 6 percent were retired.

However, it is important to realize that individuals' occupational careers have not stood still. As Table 7 shows so clearly, Austrian immigrants, like so many other immigrant groups, have not merely brought knowledge, skills, and experience but have in most cases furthered themselves through more education and training after their arrival in Canada. This trend of steady improvement is demonstrated in Table 7. Immigrants move upward from occupation to occupation. The data show that adjoining occupational classes are positively if moderately correlated (indicating gradual upward mobility), while the relationship between occupational classifications over more than one step in occupational groups at a time is still positive but weak.[34]

Table 7. Rank Order Correlations between Successive Occupations

	SOC 1	SOC 2	SOC 3
SOC 2	.4367		
	(647)		
SOC 3	.2455	.4575	
	(401)	(393)	
SOC 4	.2281	.3377	.4294
	(227)	(224)	(224)

SOC (n): Standard Occupational Classification (Canadian Classification and Dictionary of Occupations, Statistics Canada, 1981)
(N): Number in cell

EDUCATION ACQUIRED IN CANADA

Austrian immigrants appear to have brought a love of learning with them. A little more than 43 percent of our respondents (N=1,314) furthered their formal education since coming to Canada. Of our respondents, 26.6 percent (N=568) who acquired additional educational qualifications in Canada did so by attending college or university. Fully 11.8 percent gained a doctorate (or similar professional qualification), while 11.3 percent achieved a B.A. The remaining 50.3 percent achieved other qualifications including M.A.s, college, or high school diplomas.

INCOME

Most immigrants came to achieve a better standard of living, and most appear to have attained this goal if income can be taken as an indicator.[35] The comments on many questionnaires as well as in interviews also suggest an overall material comfort beyond that of the average Canadian family. In 1993, the personal income of Austrian immigrants ranged from less than $10,000 to more than $70,000. The largest proportion, or about one in six, earned between $30,000 and $39,999, while one in ten earned more than $70,000. Almost one in five families reported combined incomes of more than $90,000. One family in five had incomes between

$30,000 and $49,000. Many wrote that they owned their own homes and a good number also owned a cottage.

Using Blishen's SES scale to map immigrants socio-economic status (Figure 3),[36] we see that the bulk of them are on the lower half of the scale, with a small group at the high end. These results conceal statistically significant differences between men's and women's incomes. These differences are most pronounced in the 45 to 64 years age group. One in four women (N=67) of the 628 respondents in this group reported incomes of less than $10,000 for 1993. On the opposite end of the scale, almost one in three men in this age group (N=111) had incomes of more than $70,000. These differences are no doubt exacerbated by the fact that many women find themselves in the housewife role, particularly if their husbands' incomes are relatively high. These differences in income are even more serious if one considers women's greater life expectancy. In the 65 years and older age group more than one half of all women (N=85) reported annual incomes of less than $20,000 for 1993. The corresponding percentage for men was 16.1 (N=41).

Figure 3. SES (Blishen) of Immigrants at Time of Survey

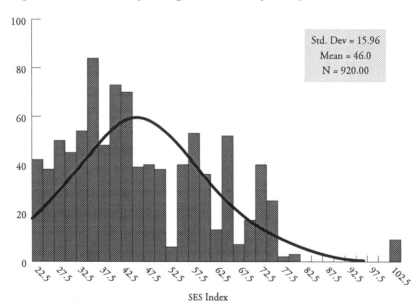

SES Index

CANADIAN-BORN AUSTRIANS

Finally, we briefly consider the descendants of Austrian immigrants. For if Austrians are to emerge as a recognizable part of the Canadian mosaic, a certain number of traits must be passed on through the generations. To rely on in-migration alone is neither feasible nor, in the long run, helpful. First-generation immigrants in virtually all instances fail to become Canadians fully. Their speech, their manners, and their attitudes set them apart. The second and following generations, on the other hand, can make a strong claim for inclusion.

We have data for a small number (N=128) of Canadian-born respondents who have strong ties to Austria.[37] The findings reported here may be indicative of the Canadian-born Austrians but must not be freely generalized to the population. About 52 percent (N=66) were from women, the remainder from men. It is not clear whether this is a reflection of a preponderance of female births among Austrian immigrants or a manifestation of women's greater interest in things Austrian. More than 52 percent (N=67) held Canadian citizenship alone, while almost 47 percent (N=60) held dual citizenship, most often Canadian and Austrian. Of the 128 respondents only a small number considered themselves to be of Austrian nationality. Almost 58 percent (N=74) defined themselves as Austrian-Canadians, and another 37.5 percent declared their nationality to be Canadian. In this respect it is interesting to note that membership in an Austrian club appears to have no bearing on Canadian-born respondents' feeling of nationality. Fifty-five percent (N=71) were married or living with a partner at the time of the survey, while almost 30 percent (N=38) had never been married. The remaining 15 percent (N=19) were either divorced, separated, or widowed. Of 71 respondents in permanent relationships, about 51 percent (N=36) were married to, or living with, partners who were non-Austrian-Canadians while only about 10 percent had Austrian spouses or partners. The rest, about 39 percent (N=57) had spouses who were neither Canadian nor Austrian, most often German, British, or Italian.

Of the 128 Canadian-born respondents only a little over one third (44) stated that their mother tongue was German; almost two-thirds (N=84) reported another language. The major proportion, nearly 86 percent (N=72), of these spoke English as their first language with the remainder divided between French and other languages. It seems therefore, that the descendants of Austrian immigrants—insofar as they feel ties to Austria—are being lost not only to the German language but also to the *francophonie*. On the other hand, 31 reported that they were conversant in German, and 26 also claimed French as an additional language. Children born to Canadian-born, however, are quite unlikely to speak or understand German. We also know that there are serious obstacles to the acquisition of German for the children of Austrian immigrants. While they may grow up speaking German at home, the German of their parents is more often than not strongly flavoured by their original dialect. The small number of Canadian-born Austrian children generally means that these children have to attend German language schools that are conducted by non-Austrian German speakers. Since children then have difficulty being understood, they often lose interest and terminate attendance. Thus, the transmission of German from generation to generation fades away rather rapidly.

Two other characteristics of second-generation may be adduced in conclusion. First, most of our Canadian-born respondents have visited Austria at least once, some more than 20 times, and others have attended school there or acquired trades qualifications. Almost one in six visited relatives while visiting Austria. A modest proportion of Canadian-born therefore appear to maintain more or less active ties with Austria. Secondly, one third of the 100 respondents for whom we have data on formal education hold a B.A., another 22 have attended or are attending college or university, and seven hold a Ph.D. or similar professional qualifications. This exceeds the overall Canadian level of formal education,[38] at least among our respondents. In sum, Canadian-born respondents, it seems, have become quite Canadianized. The overwhelming majority tend to socialize with Canadians. This is borne out by observations reported by our interviewers. It is possible, however, as witnessed at the Symposium, that there is, at least for some Canadian-born, a kind of awakening to their Austrian heritage.

It seems that Austrian immigrants have done well by most standards. When asked what they hoped to achieve in Canada, most immigrants wanted a secure future and their own home to be able to have a family and raise their children in safety. Many intended to come for a few years and save enough money to return to Austria. Although there were variations in their expectations, 63 percent of all respondents stated that their expectations had been fulfilled. Most who had stated that they wanted to return still felt that their expectations had been fulfilled. This seems to indicate that these immigrants have adjusted their expectations.

Most respondents found leaving family and friends the most difficult experience in migrating to Canada, and having arrived in Canada, many found language acquisition the most difficult adjustment. Others suffered from the extreme climate in some regions of the country and many missed familiar foods. A theme that frequently emerged from the interviews was that of immigrants' Canadianization. Generally speaking, the majority of Austrians have been at pains to blend in. But the experience of having to find one's place in a new society does not only heighten immigrants' awareness of being different but leads also to certain readjustments in life styles and world views. Thus, Austrians are generally loath to participate in politics and wish to "fit in," yet some display intolerance towards non-Caucasians. This is not a tendency unique to Austrian immigrants but one that appears to be fairly widespread.

Those Austrians who have been in Austria after having lived in Canada for some years report difficulties with readjustment. They miss the informality and relative lack of bureaucratic interference in their personal lives they have come to take for granted. Thus, despite their ambivalence about living in Canada, most respondents seem to have adjusted well to their new country and appear to be satisfied with their lives. They agree that Austrians have contributed to the development of Canada by bringing knowledge and skills, but many are concerned about Canadians' lack of knowledge about Austria. The low profile of Austrian-Canadian relations often means that Austrians are still thought of as Germans, or that Austria is being confused with Australia. However, there is almost complete agreement by Austrian immigrants that Canadians value and like their Austrian neighbours.

It is hoped that the data sources gathered for the Austrian Immigration project are not only grist for the mills of academe but mark the beginning of a better understanding of the Austrians in Canada: a better understanding by fellow Canadians, by those who have remained in Austria, and by the Austrians in Canada themselves.

ENDNOTES

1. This includes 55 questionnaires completed on behalf of family members, most often aged parents.

2. These materials form the core of the Austrian Immigration to Canada Collection (AICC) discussed in the Preface.

3. Franz A.J. Szabo, ed., *Austrian Immigration to Canada: Selected Essays*.

4. Unlike some other countries, Canada does not require residential registration; and even if it did, such a list would not necessarily render a list of Austrians in Canada. Similarly, a voters list would not have served as an adequate sampling frame because only people with Canadian citizenship are entitled to appear on federal, provincial and municipal electoral rolls; many Austrian immigrants do not have Canadian citizenship. Third, some new arrivals stay only temporarily in Canada; they are sojourners, not immigrants. Finally, while Austrian citizens may register with the nearest consulate or the embassy, not all of them do.

5. For a detailed discussion of these data see Gertrud Neuwirth and John de Vries, "Demographic Patterns of Austrian Canadians, 1900-1991," in Szabo, *Austrian Immigration,* pp. 33-54.

6. The lower coefficients for country of residence and the other variables are due to the large proportion of missing data for last country of residence.

7. The breaks in the graph lines are due to missing data for certain years. No survey responses were received from Austrians who arrived between 1931 and 1937; no immigrant giving Austria as place of birth was recorded in 1941. The apparent conflict between the two graph lines for the years prior to 1931 is due to the fact that the Neuwirth and de Vries data are based on census and immigration statistics while the survey depended on responses from immigrants, or at least responses from next-of-kin. Most of these early immigrants were too old, may have left the country, or have died and could therefore not participate in the survey.

8. Neuwirth and de Vries, "Demographic Patterns," in Szabo, *Austrian Immigration,* p. 52.

9. A number of respondents—usually people born outside the present-day boundaries of Austria—expressed concern about their eligibility to be included in our survey.

10. While some groups actively seek to maintain separate cultural identities, others strive to become acculturated in their new country. At times, immigrants who have already become acculturated are forced to undergo "secondary minority formation"—thus reversing the acculturation process. This is what happened to Canadians of Japanese descent who were interned in camps during World War II. Under certain conditions, members of particular cultural groups find it prudent or advantageous to assume different cultural identities. In the 1931 census, for example, there was a steep increase in the number of German-speaking people who claimed to be Dutch, while the rate of German-speaking people who claimed to be German declined. For a more detailed discussion see Dirk Hoerder, "German-Speaking Immigrants of Many Backgrounds and the 1990s Canadian Identity," in Szabo, *Austrian Immigration,* pp. 17-21.

11. Michael John, "Push and Pull Factors for Overseas Migrants from Austria-Hungary in the 19th and 20th Centuries," *ibid.,* pp. 55-56.

12. Donald Avery, *Dangerous Foreigners: European Immigrant Workers and Labour Radicalism in Canada, 1896-1932* (Toronto, 1979), p. 91.
13. Neuwirth and de Vries (p. 38) estimate that 229 Austrians arrived during that period.
14. Because of the difficulties in definition discussed above, Neuwirth and de Vries (pp. 35-36) give various estimates, ranging from 4,953 (immigrants born in Austria) to 2,464 (Austria as last country of residence) for the period of 1926 to 1929.
15. Canadian policies accounting for this small number are discussed in chapter 4 above, pp. 85-95.
16. These changes, as they affected Austrians, were most clearly reflected in the removal of the enemy alien designation and by the opening of the first Canadian Immigration Office in Salzburg. See above, chapter 5, pp. 104-05.
17. 21,007 by country of last residence, 26,036 by citizenship, and 26,669 by place of birth. Neuwirth and de Vries, "Demographic Patterns," in Szabo, *Austrian Immigration*, p. 36.
18. Margaret Michalowski, "Foreign-born Canadian Emigrants and Their Characteristics (1981-1986)," *International Migration Review* 25 (1991), 37, estimates that for these years "about 61 percent of the total outflow of persons from Canada consisted of immigrants."
19. Michalowski (p. 31) states that in 1986 the Canadian immigrant population was on average about 43 years of age compared to 30 years for the non-immigrant population.
20. These statistics exclude two respondents for whom we have questionnaires sent by surviving descendants.
21. In 1980 Canada's crude divorce rate stood at 2.59, up from 0.39 in 1960. *UN Demographic Yearbook,* 1976, 1981.
22. There was no respondent from Prince Edward Island.
23. No averages for Prince Edward Island and the North West Territories are given because of the small number of respondents.
24. See Hoerder (pp. 11-17) on how the notion of a "common language" in reality tends to be vitiated by differences in regional and social class speech patterns immigrants bring with them. Also Herfried Scheer, "The Largest Austrian Dialect Speech-Island in North America," in Szabo, *Austrian Immigration*, pp. 93-102.
25. For a discussion of differential language maintenance of Italian speakers in Canada and the Federal Republic of Germany see Peter Auer, "Italian in Toronto: A preliminary comparative study on language use and language maintenance," *Multilingua* 10-14 (1991), 403-40.
26. Elliot Robert Barkan, "Proximity and Commuting Immigration: An Hypothesis Explored via the Bi-Polar Ethnic Communities of French-Canadians and Mexican-Americans," in Jack Kinton, ed., *American Ethnic Revival* (Aurora IL, 1977), pp.

163-83; J.W. St. John Jones, "The Exchange of Population between the United States of America and Canada in the 1960s," *International Migration Review* 11 (1973), 32-51; T.J. Samuel, *The Migration of Canadian-Born between Canada and the United States, 1955 to 1968* (Ottawa, 1969).

27. This sentiment, expressed by Eva Wazda in "The Austrian as Emigrant," (paper read before the internatioal symposium, "Austrian Immigration to Canada," Carleton University, Ottawa, 20 May 1995) was repeated by many in the course of their interviews.

28. James S. Frideres, S. Goldenberg, J. DiSanto, and J. Horna, "Becoming Canadian: Citizen Acquisition and National Identity," *Canadian Review of Studies in Nationalism*, 14 (1987), 105-21.

29. Anthony H. Richmond, *Post-War Immigrants in Canada* (Toronto, 1967), pp. 200, 204.

30. The Austrian club in Kitchener is mainly composed of Gottscheers (a former German-language speech island from Gottschee, now Kocevje, Slovenia) and their descendants. See Sonja Kroisenbrunner-Biselli, "The Gottschee Dimension of Austrian Community in Kitchener" (paper read before the international symposium, "Austrian Immigration to Canada," Carleton University, Ottawa, 21 May 1995).

31. Juliane Schaible, "The Austrian community in Winnipeg," (paper read before the international symposium, "Austrian Immigration to Canada," Carleton University, Ottawa, 21 May 1995).

32. According to Statistics Canada's *Standard Occupational Classification: 1980* (Ottawa, 1981), these groups are: (11) Managerial, Administrative and Related Occupations; (61) Service Occupations; (41) Clerical and Related Occupations; (85) Product Fabricating, Assembling and Repairing Occupations; (87) Construction Trades Occupations; and (21) Occupations in Natural Sciences, Engineering and Mathematics.

33. *Ibid.,* (51) Sales Occupations; (61) Service Occupations; (83) Machining and Related Occupations; (27) Teaching and Related Occupations.

34. The correlation coefficients on the diagonal are clearly higher than the off-diagonal ones.

35. A few respondents took the trouble to write that they thought the questionnaire ought to ask about assets as well as income, but given even the delicate nature of income questions we refrained from appearing to pry too deeply.

36. Bernard R. Blishen, William K. Carroll, and Catherine Moore, "The 1981 Socioeconomic Index for Occupations in Canada," *Canadian Review of Sociology and Anthropology* 24 (1987), 465-88.

37. To this end we excluded questionnaires that had been completed by relatives.

38. For more information see Statistics Canada, *Education in Canada, 1991-92* (Ottawa,1993), Cat no. 81-229.

CHAPTER VII
ACHIEVEMENTS AND CONTRIBUTIONS OF
AUSTRIAN-CANADIANS

Frederick C. Engelmann and Manfred Prokop

THE FIRST RECORDED AUSTRIAN to come to what is now Canada was the Vienna-born **Hans Daigle** (possibly "Degler" or "Deger"), a soldier in the service of France, who purchased land in Charlesbourg, Québec in 1674. Sometime *courrier de bois* with Des Grosseillers and Radisson, he married Marie-Anne Perroteau in 1685. We know relatively little of his life and death, and Daigle apparently remained poor all his days. But he became the patriarchal ancestor of the enormous Daigle family of Québec, and thus can stand as a symbol for the countless unnamed and unknown Austrians who may lurk in the family trees of many Canadians.

For the two centuries after Hans Daigle appeared in what was to become Canada, there were few Austrians in a position to contribute to Canada's society, economy or culture, and few did. Since then, however, the contributions of Austrian immigrants to Canada, while in no way dominant, have grown strongly. It is not surprising that the country of Haydn, Mozart and Schubert would contribute fully and significantly to Canadian music. Art as well as the sciences and other academic disciplines and medicine also gained notably from Austrians' achievements in Canada. Possibly more surprising but important are contributions of Austrians to Canadian business. Finally, there is a slim but important strand of Austrian contributions to such fields as writing, mountaineering, photography, and even to Canada's public service.

This chapter will record, and discuss briefly, such contributions as the authors, in their best judgment, consider major. All contributions which we were able to find appear in an appendix, arranged alphabetically by the contributors' names. We are keenly aware of the limitations of such a selection which had to be made over a relatively short period of time from what turned out to be a rather large field. We beg the forgiveness of those who feel that they merit discussion rather than mere inclusion in an appendix, and equally of those who do not even appear in the appendix. The former is a matter of judgment, the latter due to the constraints of time and resources. We do, of course, also beg the indulgence of relatives and friends who feel that those no longer alive may not have been adequately recognized.

The authors are also well aware of the fact that the chapter may appear to be skewed in favour of a portrayal of Austrian scholars, artists, entrepreneurs and other "important" people. This is unfortunate but probably unavoidable in spite of the fact that literally thousands of other Austrians have left their mark on Canadian culture over the last century in virtually undocumentable ways. Who knows how many Austrian bakers, cooks, restaurant owners, tradespeople, engineers, small businessmen, journalists, and so forth have contributed to Canada's economic and social life with their unique Austrian background and training? It may well also be argued that women's contributions are therefore underrepresented in this chapter. Recognizing this fact, we can only acknowledge, with gratitude, in the most general terms the many accomplishments and achievements of these Austrian-Canadians.

MUSIC

Of those who know the difference between Austria and Australia, if asked what they relate to Austria, most would respond by mentioning music. By birth or adoption, a majority of leading composers between 1750 and the First World War were Austrian. Even today, Austria has in the Vienna State Opera one of the world's leading opera houses, in the Vienna Philharmonic one of the leading orchestras, and what is arguably the world's most renowned music festival at Salzburg. In addition, Vienna is the inspiration of the most successful waltzes and the place where many of the most successful operettas were written. Canada has received a good share of Austrian musicians who left their country for "racial" or political reasons, or who looked for opportunities abroad, either earlier or in the postwar era. Possibly, what is most important is the fact that these immigrants came close to having an impact on every last aspect of Canadian music.

Several Austrians in Canada have written music. The oldest, **Sophie-Carmen (Sonia) Eckhardt-Grammatté**, was born in Moscow in 1899 with the name of Fridman (a deceased separated husband of her mother, but not her father). She lived in Moscow, Paris and Berlin where she married the expressionist painter Walter Grammatté, whom she followed to Spain. As a child, she studied violin with Bronislav Huberman, and as a young woman, the cello with Pablo Casals. She began composing at the age of six. In 1929, after her husband's death, she moved to the United States where she befriended Leopold Stokowski and concentrated on composition. In 1934, she married the Austrian art historian Ferdinand Eckhardt. They lived in Berlin at first, but moved to Vienna in 1939 where she stayed till 1953. From 1948 to 1961 she won numerous prizes for her compositions. The Eckhardts came to Canada in 1953, when he became Director of the Winnipeg Art Gallery. While in Winnipeg, she was a prolific composer, writing among others a Duo Concertante (cello and piano), a Symphony-Concerto (piano), a piano trio, the solo violin suite "Pacific," a Concerto for Orchestra, and the Symphony No. 2, "Manitoba." The artist died during a trip in 1974 after a severe fall in Stuttgart. Her dream to have a competition of young Canadian artists playing works of contemporary composers was realized two years after her death. Ferdinand Eckhardt catalogued her compositions, which were published in Winnipeg in 23 volumes (1980-84). In 1985, Eckhardt wrote and published her biography, *Music from Within*.

The other Austrian-Canadian composers cannot match Eckhardt-Grammatté's almost unbelievable biography. One, however, has a most impressive Viennese family background. **Alfred Rosé**, born in 1902 in Vienna, is the son of a sister of Gustav Mahler and of one of Vienna's great musical figures. His father, Arnold Rosé, was first concert master of the Vienna Philharmonic from 1881 to 1938 until removed by the Nazis. He was also the founder of one of the most illustrious string quartets in Austria's musical history, which bears his name. Alfred's sister, Alma, gained sad world fame by becoming the conductor of the camp orchestra at Auschwitz. Alfred Rosé, who had studied composition with Arnold Schoenberg and others, left Vienna in 1938 and came to London, Ontario. He taught at the University of Western Ontario from 1948 to 1973. Although he did most of his composing in Vienna, an "Adagio for Cello and Orchestra" was premiered in London, Ontario in 1974. There he also pioneered in music therapy. The University of Western Ontario has his extensive collection of scores and letters.

Ernst Friedländer, even better known as a cellist, was born in 1906 in Vienna. He lived in the United States, mostly as cellist and university professor, from 1937 to 1958. In that year, he moved to Vancouver where he died in 1966. Here, he was principal cellist of the CBC Chamber Orchestra and the Symphony Orchestra. While in Vancouver, he wrote a cello sonata, a cello concerto, a "Minnelied" for cello and orchestra, a rhapsody for cello (or bassoon) and orchestra, and works for string quartet, brass sextet and chamber orchestra.

Gerhard Wuensch, born 1925 in Klosterneuburg (Lower Austria) received a doctorate in musicology in Vienna in 1950. A staff composer with the Austrian radio till 1954, he then studied and taught music in the United States. In 1964, he came to Canada where he taught at the Universities of Toronto and Calgary and has been teaching, since 1973, at the University of Western Ontario. While in Canada, he composed the cantata "Laus Sapientiae," a concerto for two pianos and orchestra, a concerto for bassoon and chamber orchestra, the cantata "Silva Domus," and an opera, "Nice People," which is his opus 100. He has also written numerous articles.

A number of Austrians have come to Canada, temporarily or permanently, to be conductors of orchestras. Haymo Taeuber (born in Graz in 1908) was conductor of the Calgary Philharmonic Orchestra from 1963 to 1968. He came to Canada after conducting in Graz, Vienna (Volksoper, Vienna Symphony and Choir Boys), Ankara and Teheran. He moved from Calgary to California where he was an active conductor for two more decades. He died in early 1995 in Pebble Beach, California. Georg Tintner (born 1917 in Vienna) went to New Zealand as a Hitler refugee, then to South Africa and Australia. From a position in Brisbane he was called to Halifax in 1987 where he conducts the Symphony Nova Scotia. Under his direction, that orchestra, although financially troubled, has established a national prominence. He has been known especially for his interpretation of Austrian classics from Mozart to Bruckner. An interesting younger Austrian conductor in Canada is Agnes Grossmann. Born in Vienna in 1944, she came to Ottawa in 1981. From 1984 to 1990, she was artistic director of the Chamber Players of Toronto—Canada's first female music director. She is with the Orchestre Métropolitain of Montreal and with the Orford Arts Centre in the Eastern Townships. Twenty-seven years after Taeuber's resignation from Calgary, and after the Calgary Philharmonic had achieved fame under Mario Bernardi, another Austrian, Hans Graf, became conductor of that orchestra. He was born in Linz in 1949 and has conducted both the Vienna Philharmonic and the Vienna Symphony, and he was principal conductor of the Mozarteum Orchestra of Salzburg. He has also conducted opera in Munich, Berlin, Venice, Florence, and Paris.

Some of the musicians already mentioned, Grossmann, Rosé and Wuensch, are also known as pianists. **Lubka Kolessa**, born in 1902 in Lviv (now in Ukraine), grew up in Vienna and was acclaimed as a pianist throughout Europe, playing under Wilhelm Furtwängler, Karl Böhm, and other famous conductors. She came to Ottawa in 1940 and taught at the Royal Conservatory in Toronto in the forties. She performed until 1954 and ended up teaching at McGill University. A remarkable Austrian-Canadian pianist, who settled in Canada in 1965, is **Anton Kuerti**. Born in 1938 in Vienna, his parents took him to the United States as an infant, but he definitely identifies with his Austrian origin. Kuerti has become an internationally renowned pianist, who records much and has performed around the world. *Musical America* wrote about him after a New York concert in the early nineties: "Not since Schnabel, or Serkin in his prime, has late Beethoven been given such intelligent and fiery performances." While in Canada, Kuerti has also been an active and versatile composer, for orchestra, string quartet, violin, cello and piano.

Canada's most prominent harpsichordist is **Greta (Grete) Kraus**, born in Vienna in 1907. Her musical career began at age seven when she sang for Sigmund Freud, not knowing that he was tone-deaf. Kraus studied at the Vienna Academy of Music from 1923 to 1930 and became a pianist and piano teacher. In 1935, the Austrian-American harpsichordist Jella Pessl asked her to take her place in a concert. Kraus had only heard an harpsichord once before and had found its sound horrible. Teaching herself the instrument within a week, she came to the conclusion that it was her instrument, playing it in concerts in Vienna and London. Half Jewish, Kraus was persuaded to emigrate after she was mobbed by Nazis. A cousin took her to Canada as his secretary in 1938, and she managed to gain landed immigrant status. Sir Ernest MacMillan soon used her for "St. Matthew's Passion" and other works requiring an harpsichord. She taught at the Royal Conservatory of Music from 1943 to 1969. She is a Member of the Order of Canada.

Like Greta Kraus, **Eli Kassner** was able to introduce an instrument to Canada—the classical guitar. Born in Vienna in 1924, Kassner began to play the guitar at the age of eight. He and a brother were the only family members to escape the Holocaust. He made it to Israel on one of the last pre-war transports, where he served in the army. In 1951, his brother was able to invite him to Canada. Kassner introduced the classical guitar to Toronto, teaching since 1953 and founding the Guitar Society of Toronto in 1956. In 1959, he was appointed to teach guitar in the music department of the University of Toronto—the first such appointment in Canada. In the same year, Andres Segovia, the world's greatest guitarist, invited him to Spain to study with him, and a Canada Council grant made this trip possible. In 1975, Kassner was the driving force in organizing an international festival, "Guitar '75," which was a great success. Kassner has succeeded, at first single-handedly, to make the classical guitar a respectable and respected member of Canada's music world. Among Kassner's many students was a young Austrian, **Norbert Kraft**. Born in 1950 in Linz, Kraft moved to Toronto with his parents as a child. After playing the electric guitar in a rock band, Kraft studied classical guitar with Carl von Feggelen and Eli Kassner, and later in England and the United States. Teaching at the Royal Conservatory since 1971 and the University of Toronto since 1978, Kraft, who has been on many Canadian and international concert tours, is now acclaimed as Canada's leading classical guitarist.

Several Austrian singers emigrated to Canada, though their singing careers had peaked in Austria and other countries. **Emmy Heim** was born in 1885 in Vienna. She learned to sing from her mother and began singing Lieder at the age of seven. During her international career, she moved to England in 1930 and made several trips to Canada. In 1946, she moved to Toronto and taught at the Royal Conservatory for the rest of her life. The celebrated Lois Marshall was among her students. Heim died in 1954. **Rita Georg**, born in Vienna in 1900, was a celebrated operetta star in Europe before the Second World War. She was known especially for her rendition of the leads in Emmerich Kálmán and Franz Lehár operettas, and as singing partner of the famous tenor Richard Tauber. She sang mostly in Vienna, Berlin, and Paris. In 1941, she accompanied her industrialist husband Karl Bloch-Bauer to Vancouver where she lived until her death in the 1980s. While in Canada, she sang only occasionally and privately. **Irene Jessner** was born in 1901 in Vienna and became an opera singer in the thirties. In 1936, she was engaged at the Metropolitan Opera of New York where she had a distinguished career. When she retired in 1952, Edward Johnson, the Met's former Canadian director, invited her to Canada. She taught first at the Royal Conservatory and then at the University of Toronto. Her most famous student was Teresa Stratas. Jessner died in Toronto in 1994. The daughter of an Austrian father and a German mother became a successful pop singer. Born in Montreal, **Solveig Angélique Nikischer** began to sing at four, had her New York debut at five, and appeared in a musical lead at twelve. The

Montreal Olympics spread her fame. She studied at McGill and Ottawa and has become known as Solveig-Angélique in Canada, the U.S., and Germany.

Four Austrians became prominent music administrators in Canada. **Luigi von Kunitz**, born in 1870 in Vienna, studied with Anton Bruckner and came to the United States in 1893. He came to Toronto in 1912 and reorganized the Toronto Symphony, which he conducted from 1923 to 1931. In 1915, he founded the *Canadian Journal of Music*. He also composed. Kunitz died in 1931. The second, **Franz Kraemer**, was born in Vienna in 1914 and came to Canada in 1940. He joined the CBC as producer in 1946 and became a pioneer of opera on television. In 1971, he became music director of the Toronto Arts Foundation (later, the Toronto Arts Productions). He did much to promote young Canadian performers and headed, from 1979 to 1985, the music section of the Canada Council. He is an Officer of the Order of Canada. The third, **Arnold Walter**, was the most important. Since he never lived in Austria within its 1919 borders, we hesitated to include him and did so only when people who knew him assured us that he definitely considered himself an Austrian-Canadian. Born in 1902 in Hannsdorf, Moravia, Walter studied law in Prague at his father's insistence, but soon turned to music in Berlin where he studied piano with Breithaupt and composition with Schreker. Since there was little need for a fledgling pianist and composer, he decided to write about music. His contributions to *Vorwärts* and *Weltbühne*, both left-wing journals, forced him to leave Berlin as a political refugee, first to Majorca, then to London. Walter came to Canada in 1937 when he accepted an offer to teach at Upper Canada College. In 1945, he joined the staff of the Royal Conservatory of Music, from where he organized the Opera Division at the University of Toronto. When Toronto reorganized its music offerings in 1952, Walter became director of its Faculty of Music, a position he held till 1968. He composed intermittently, but his stellar contribution was in the development of music education in Canada. He was made an Officer of the Order of Canada and was given many other honours. He died in Toronto in 1973. The fourth important organizer and administrator of music is **Nicholas Goldschmidt**. Born in 1908 in Moravia (Czech Republic), he received his musical education in Vienna. He came to the United States in 1937 and was director of opera at San Francisco Conservatory, Stanford University and Columbia University. In 1946, Arnold Walter called him to Toronto as music director of the Royal Conservatory Opera School in Toronto. Goldschmidt subsequently founded the opera group of the CBC, became music director of the Opera Festival Association and initiated the music festivals in Vancouver, Guelph and Sault Ste. Marie, conducting a number of operas in them. The Royal Conservatory Opera Company is now the Canadian Opera Company. Throughout his still ongoing career, he has worked with all of Canada's opera stars.

An Austrian musicologist who became a leading Canadian musicologist is **Ida Halpern**. Born Ida Ruhdörfer in Vienna, she married the music critic George R. Halpern and earned a doctorate from the University of Vienna. The Halperns left Vienna for Shanghai in 1938, and they came to Vancouver in 1939. She taught at the University of British Columbia for two decades. Halpern's most significant work was in British Columbian native ethnomusicology. She documented and preserved the music of Kwakiutl, Nootka, Haida, Bella Coola, and Coast Salish Indians in northern coastal British Columbia. She conceived and helped organize the Centennial Workshop on Ethnomusicology at the University of British Columbia (1967). A Member of the Order of Canada, she has honorary degrees from Simon Fraser and the University of Victoria. Another musicologist who is also a performing pianist is **Karl Steiner**, born in 1912 in Vienna. Until leaving for Shanghai (1939) as a Hitler refugee, he was in touch with Arnold Schoenberg, Alban Berg, Anton Webern and Egon Wellesz, and worked with their pupils. In 1949, he came to Montreal as a piano teacher. Appointed to McGill University in 1964, he lectured on the Schoenberg School (also known as the Second Viennese School). In 1988, the International Schoenberg Society invited him to give an anniversary lecture-recital at the Schoenberg-Haus in Mödling near Vienna.

THE FINE ARTS

Austrian-Canadians have made significant contributions to the fine arts in Canada. The outstanding Austrian in Canada's art world was primarily an administrator in the best sense of the word, **Ferdinand Eckhardt**. He was born in 1902 in Vienna into a family greatly interested in painting and music. He studied art history and became by far the youngest member of the Society for the Promotion of Modern Art. He then edited and wrote in the fine arts field in Augsburg and Berlin. The centre of his interest was Berlin's expressionist painter Walter Grammatté, who had died young. This interest led to Eckhardt's courting and marrying Grammatté's widow, the noted pianist and composer S.C. (Sonia) Grammatté. In 1936, Eckhardt produced an hour-long 16 mm film of the Berlin Olympics. He returned to Vienna in 1939 and became director of art education for Vienna's museums. At the end of the war, Eckhardt was one of the founders of the Austro-American Society, which put him in touch with North America and led to the offer, in 1953, of the directorship of the Winnipeg Art Gallery, which he accepted after his wife surprised him by urging him to do so. He not only revived the nearly moribund gallery, but he also attracted, in two decades, about five hundred exhibitions, many of considerable importance. His most notable activities were the awakening of the talents in many young people and the finding of many pieces of Canadian art. For two decades, the Eckhardts' house was the center of Winnipeg's art life. 1974 was a crucial date in Eckhardt's life— he retired and his wife died suddenly. While he continued his keen interest in Canadian art, his main concerns were the appreciation of Walter Grammatté's art and the cataloguing of Sonia's compositions and recordings. He was celebrated on his 80th and 90th birthdays, and on the 40th anniversary of his arrival in Winnipeg. He was given three honorary degrees and the Order of Canada. Eckhardt died in December 1953.

An early Austrian-Canadian painter was **Georg Theodore Berthon**. Born in Vienna in 1806, he came to Toronto in about 1841. As a classical European portraitist, he had a successful career painting formal portraits of members of the business and judicial establishments of Canada West and Ontario. His works can be seen in Osgoode Hall and Trinity College, Toronto, and in the Senate Chamber in Ottawa. The portrait of Chief Justice Sir John Beverley Robinson is considered to be his masterpiece. Berthon died in Toronto in 1892. **Ernestine (Erni) Tahedl-Ogilvie**, born in 1940 in Ried in der Riedmark (Upper Austria), emigrated to Canada in 1963 and became a noted Austrian-Canadian painter. Following in the footsteps of her father, Heinrich Tahedl (1907-85), she studied graphics and, from 1961 to 1963, she did stained-glass work with her father. She created the stained glass for the Canadian pavilion at Expo '67 and she exhibits frequently throughout Canada and the world.

Anne Kahane (Mrs. R. Langstadt) is a noted Austrian-Canadian sculptor. Born in 1924 in Vienna, she came to Canada when one year old, and to Montreal in 1929. She is internationally recognized for her dense, monumental three-dimensional figures carved in wood, which portray satire, humour and human foibles. In the 1960s, she carved decorative panels for the airport and the General Hospital in Winnipeg and figures for Montreal's Place des Arts. By 1978, she had abandoned wood for thin, strong sheets of aluminium which gave flexibility to figures flattened into abstraction. The sculptor **Elfriede Berger**, born in Graz, came to Winnipeg in 1953. She is a naturalistic sculptor, capturing remarkable likenesses of her subjects. She has been working in Manitoba where she did political leaders, and in Germany. She is best known for her bust of Wernher von Braun, of rocket fame.

An important Austrian-Canadian lithographer was **Ernest Lindner**. Born in Vienna in 1897, he worked for his father's wood-turning business and was influenced artistically on business travels to Italy and Switzerland. In 1926, he came to Saskatchewan as a farm labourer and illustrated a book in 1927. After working as a house painter during the Great Depression, he taught at the Saskatoon Technical College. Soon, he showed linocuts in print exhibitions and became the western representative of the Society of Canadian Painter-Etchers. He later exhibited in New York. His images are often composites of human and plant forms, overlapping and blending into each other.

The architect **Harry Seidler** did not spend much time in Canada, and was not able to enjoy some of it. Born in 1922 in Vienna, he came to England as a Hitler refugee in 1938. He was interned as an "enemy alien" for more than two years in one camp in England and two in Canada. Later, he was able to study architecture at the University of Manitoba. His success there enabled him to study at Harvard under Walter Gropius and to work in New York with Marcel Breuer, both eminent architects. In 1948, Seidler moved to Australia where he became a famous architect. When Seidler was released from the notorious Camp "N" in Sherbrooke, he was warned, under threat of re-imprisonment, never to talk or write about the camp experience. In the early eighties, in Australia, a researcher found out that Seidler had kept a diary of his camp experiences in England and Canada. He persuaded Seidler to let him translate the diary into English, and it appeared in 1986 as *Internment: The Diary of Harry Seidler.* Canada made up for his suffering in part in 1988 when the University of Manitoba conferred an honorary degree on its graduate.

An Austrian-Canadian who became prominent in metal, jewelry and enamel work is **Helga Palko**, née Jandaurek. Born in 1928 in Linz, she studied in Vienna at the University and the Academy of Fine Arts and taught at a *Realgymnasium* in Linz. She emigrated to Canada in 1954 and settled in Regina. In addition to her renowned jewelry work, she did three murals in Saskatchewan. **George Swinton**, born in 1917 in Vienna, came to Canada in 1939 and did some work with linocuts. He studied in Montreal and New York and was appointed to the staff of the University of Manitoba. He soon became enamoured with Inuit art which he studied intensively. His publications on Inuit sculptures and prints did much to impress the importance of Inuit art on Canadians. For his Inuit book he was made a Member of the Order of Canada.

An Austrian Hitler refugee, who contributed to Toronto's art life during the past generation after a career in Colombia, is **Walter Engel**. Born in 1908 in Vienna as the son of a textile manufacturer, he emigrated to Bogotá, Colombia, in 1938. While being groomed for a business career in Vienna, he also studied art and art history. In Bogotá, he combined business with art and became an art critic and a friend of the painter Fernando Botero. He moved to Toronto in 1965, became active in art criticism and founded, in 1968, the Walter Engel Gallery, together with Clara Engel, his second wife. The gallery, which he directed till his retirement at age 82, did much to introduce Latin American art to Toronto, but it also had many exhibits in Canadian art, and in prominent modern art in general.

Anna Wyman showed that Austrian dance art can succeed in Canada. Born in Graz in 1928, she studied dance and contemporary movement in various European cities and danced in Austria until 1948, when she emigrated to Vancouver. There she established the Anna Wyman School of Dance Art in 1968 and the Anna Wyman Dancers in 1970, which became the Anna Wyman Dance Theatre in 1973. **Jeanette Aster**, born in 1948 in Linz, was educated in Quebec (B. Mus., McGill, 1969). She has been a successful stage director of operas in Germany, the Netherlands, Glyndebourne, London, Vienna, Paris, and many renowned opera houses in the United States. Her "Tristan" in Florence (1990) received the Critics' Prize. Since 1988, she has been artistic director of the Opera Lyra Ottawa. Born in Austria, **Rudi Dorn** came to Canada in the early fifties with a diploma in architecture from the Academy of Fine Arts in Vienna. He was a pioneer in television design in Toronto and soon became a producer/director. In 1975, he became artistic director/designer at CBC Toronto. At the Calgary Olympics of 1988, he was production designer for the opening and closing ceremonies. He also did the design for the opening ceremonies of the Toronto Skydome.

Austria gave Canada several distinguished photographers. **Walter Curtin** was born Walter Spiegel in Vienna in 1911. After his father died in 1933, he managed the family's food business. A Jew, he emigrated to

England in 1939. He was interned and transported to Australia, but managed to return to England in 1941 where he joined the Pioneer Corps of the British Army. In 1943, he was transferred to the Royal Engineers and helped prepare bombing target maps of Germany for the RAF. In 1946, he became a photographer and, in 1952, emigrated to Toronto. He photographed for, among others, *Time, Life, Maclean's, Chatelaine, Saturday Night, Fortune, Star Weekly* and the National Film Board Still Division. In the late fifties, he went into advertising photography, taking pictures of real people in spontaneous situations. After four years in London in the sixties, he returned to Toronto, primarily to document Canada's classical music scene. **Eugen Kedl** was born in Stadtschlaining, Burgenland in 1933. In 1954, he emigrated to Quebec with a diploma in photography from Vienna. After several years as an aerial photographer, he founded, in 1961, the firm Légaré et Kedl. He did a number of photographic reports of areas in Canada and Austria. Kedl had many exhibitions in Canada, Austria, and several other European countries. **Franz Moeslinger**, born in Austria in 1939, emigrated to Canada in 1958. Living in Kingston, Ontario, he is an active and exhibiting photographer. In addition, he is an accomplished skier and mountaineer. He is a successful climber in the Rockies, having conquered Mt. Robson, Mt. Assiniboine, Mt. Athabasca and Mt. Victoria.

WRITERS

Today, most Austrians contemplating emigration have at least a working knowledge of the English language. This was often not the case during heavy periods of emigration to the United Kingdom, the United States or Canada. It is all the more remarkable that several Austrians who came to Canada mastered the English language sufficiently to become professional writers, even creative writers. **Carl Weiselberger** was born in Vienna in 1900. Because his uncle was a bank manager, he decided to work for the Bankverein, a major bank, rather than to go to university. He worked for the bank using French and Italian, but he knew no English prior to 1938. In the thirties, he wrote short stories and a novel (*Die Zeit ohne Gnade*) which was serialized in a newspaper. A Jew, he managed to get to London in 1939. In 1940, he was interned as an "enemy alien" on the Isle of Man, deported to Canada and again interned in Sherbrooke. He continued to write while interned and influenced the future career of his fellow internee, the young Henry Kreisel. Some of Weiselberger's camp experiences are reflected in the title story of his later volume *Der Rabbi mit der Axt.* Released in 1943, Weiselberger worked for the government mail censor's office as translator and interpreter. After the war, he became art critic of the *Ottawa Citizen,* a position he held until 1965. During that time, he wrote prolifically, in English, on Austria and Europe for Canadian magazines and newspapers, and he wrote reports on Canada, in German, for Austrian newspapers and magazines. In both types of reports, he attempted and succeeded in depicting Austria and Canada realistically, modifying the many prevailing myths. He moved to Victoria, B.C. in 1968, where he died in 1970. Having moved to the English-speaking world at the age of 39, he felt that there were restraints on his creative mastery of English, and that he had tragically lost *his* language.

Henry (Heini) Kreisel was born in Vienna in 1922 into a Jewish family. He emigrated to England in 1939 and worked in a factory in Leeds. Like many others who made it to Canada, he was interned in 1940 as an "enemy alien," transported to Canada and once more interned in Sherbrooke. While interned, he read widely, mostly English literature. He decided that he could and would write and, wanting to emancipate himself from the language of Hitler, that he would write in English. In wondering whether he would be able to do this, he was reinforced in his intentions when told about the success of Joseph Conrad, of Polish birth, in creating literature in his adopted language. Released in late 1941 and after a year in school, Kreisel entered the University of Toronto in 1942 to study English language and literature. In 1947 he was given a teaching appointment at the University of Alberta in Edmonton where he lived and worked for the next forty-four years. His ability, vitality, grace and elegance made him a successful and beloved head of the Department of English, a willingly accepted Vice-President (Academic), and president of his national professional association, ACUTE. In his last years as an active professor, he moved to the Department of Comparative Literature, and he continued to be a vital force at the University after retirement until he was felled by cancer in 1991. Kreisel's creative work is more outstanding in quality than quantity. Both his successful novels, *The Rich Man* (1948) and *The Betrayal* (1964), deal with the fate of European Jews. His short stories, and his internment camp diaries, were published in two collected volumes. He was made an Officer of the Order of Canada.

Charles Ulric (Karl Ulrich) Wassermann was born in 1924 in Vienna, the son of the celebrated writer Jakob Wassermann (1873-1934) and the writer and psychoanalyst Marta Karlweis (1888-1965). As a Hitler refugee, he emigrated to the Isle of Wight (England), was interned in 1940 as an "enemy alien," taken to Canada and again interned, until his mother, who had managed to get to Montreal, intervened with Mackenzie King and obtained his release. He then graduated from Lower Canada College and McGill University. During most of his short life, he worked for the CBC. He had two residences: one in Montreal and one in the Austrian resort Altaussee, where his father had entertained Schnitzler, Hofmannsthal and Thomas Mann. Wassermann went blind in 1963, two years after a serious blood poisoning, but this hardly slowed his hectic pace of creative work in print, radio and television. While his early writing was in English, he discovered, when commissioned to write on the Hungarian revolution of 1956 (which he witnessed) that he could write in German successfully. The German publisher Bertelsmann asked him to write a combined travelogue and history of Canada, *Das Land der Zukunft*, which was a great success. Later, he did a successful book, in German, on the Canadian Pacific Railway. He also wrote German detective novels. As a diabetic, he also wrote on Banting and Best, the discoverers of insulin. He died, underestimated in Canada, in 1978.

ACADEMICS

In the area of German literature, several Austrian-Canadians have made their mark. The most important of them is **Hans Eichner**, who was born of Jewish parents in Vienna in 1921. He managed to walk into Belgium through hilly terrain on Christmas Eve in 1938 and made it to England two months later. He received his education at the University of London and came to Canada in 1950. He taught at Queen's (1950-67) and the University of Toronto (1967-88) and chaired both German departments. He is a Fellow of the Royal Society of Canada and received an honorary LL.D. from Queen's, where he holds the post-retirement position of adjunct professor. Eichner has been a prolific scholar, continuing his productive academic work after retirement. He is internationally recognized, especially for his work on Thomas Mann and Friedrich Schlegel. His work is equally divided between the English and German languages as it has been throughout his career.

Helfried Seliger was born in Vienna in 1939. He went to Calgary in 1957 and has degrees from the University of Alberta and McGill University. He has taught at Victoria College (part of the University) in Toronto since 1966. From 1992 to 1994, he was president of the Canadian

Association of University Teachers of German. He has written books on Berthold Brecht, and on the concept of *Heimat* in contemporary German literature. One of Canada's leading scholars in the teaching of second languages is the Austrian-Canadian **Manfred Prokop**. Born in 1942 in Vienna, he came to the United States in 1963 as a Fulbright student. He studied at the University of Notre Dame in South Bend, Indiana, where he received an M.A. in Applied Linguistics (German) and a Ph.D. in Education (Instructional Theory). Since 1969, he has been a member of the Department of Germanic Languages at the University of Alberta; he served as its Chair from 1990 to 1995. He pursues a very active career in research in second language teaching, especially German. He was a founding member of the Association of English-German Bilingual Education and served as its president from 1978 to 1979. Among his numerous publications, the most important are two books, *Learning Strategies for Second Language Users* (1989) and *The German Language in Alberta: Maintenance and Teaching* (1990).

In the social sciences, one of the most impressive Austrian-Canadians came from a Jewish-Polish-Hungarian family and ended up teaching in the United States, the economist **Karl Polanyi**. His daughter assures us that this celebrated economist and social philosopher would have wanted to be included in this book. After his birth in Vienna in 1886, the family moved back to Budapest. While in school, he was greatly influenced by his highly intellectual mother. At university in Budapest, he became an active—but never quite orthodox—socialist. In the years before the First World War, he worked as a journalist and presided over two important intellectual groups. In the War, he served as Hungarian cavalry officer and was severely wounded. A refugee from the Horthy regime in Hungary, he lived in Vienna from 1919 to 1933 and became an Austrian citizen. He married the Austrian journalist and author Ilona Duczynska. In Vienna, he was on the editorial staff of the *Österreichische Volkswirt* (1924-33). After he left for England, a refugee from the Dollfuss dictatorship, he continued to write for this prominent economic journal until 1938. Polanyi's first North American experience was teaching at Bennington College, Vermont from 1940 to 1943, after which he returned to England. Much of his English work was extra-mural teaching for Oxford and the University of London. In 1947, when he was appointed to a professorship at Columbia University in New York, Ilona Duczynska, who had been a member of the Communist parties of Hungary and Austria and had been expelled by both, was not admitted to the United States. The Polanyis therefore settled in Pickering, Ontario, from where Polanyi commuted to New York. From his retirement (1957) to his death in 1964, Polanyi lived in Pickering where his rich intellectual life was maintained with visitors from all over the world. Polanyi was much more than an economist. He considered himself an economic anthropologist, but he was also a great social philosopher. Probably his main thesis was that the economy needs to be embedded in society. His magnum opus, *The Great Transformation,* was published in 1944 and translated into many languages. Polanyi had hoped that the lessons of the 1930s would lead to the transformation of the 19th century liberal economy, driven by greed, to some state-guided economic order. His daughter considers the book a warning to those who want to subordinate societies and cultures to the accumulation of capital on a global scale.

While not an academic in the formal sense, **Ilona Duczynska** should be discussed along with Karl Polanyi. She was born in 1897 in Maria Enzersdorf, near Vienna, to an Austrian minor nobleman of Polish descent and a Hungarian mother. She spent some time in Budapest, worked for the short-lived Hungarian Soviet Republic, and returned to Vienna in 1919. Divorced, she married Karl Polanyi in 1923. Their Viennese home was a centre of intellectual life. When Polanyi left for England in 1933, she stayed in Vienna for another three years, working for the then illegal Austrian social democrats. After Polanyi's death, she took many trips to Vienna and Budapest and wrote on the Social Democrats of Austria. Duczynska died in Pickering, Ontario in 1978.

Polanyi's and Duczynska's daughter, **Kari Polanyi(-Levitt)**, was born in 1923 in Vienna and came to Canada in 1947. She spent much of her life teaching economics, later primarily economic development, at McGill University. She continues as visiting professor at the University of the West Indies in Kingston, Jamaica. Her best known book, *Silent Surrender* (1970), deals with the Americanization of the Canadian economy through multinational corporations. She has also published an input-output study of the economy of Canada's Atlantic Provinces. In 1987, she was co-founder of the Karl Polanyi Institute at Concordia University in Montreal. In 1990, she edited *The Life and Work of Karl Polanyi.*

Another Austrian-Canadian developmental economist is **Joseph (Sepp) Richter**. Born in the Yugoslav Vojvodina in 1920, he served in the Yugoslav army and was permitted, after the region's conquest by the Germans, to study in Vienna. In 1942, he was sent to the Russian front and, by 1945, he had survived the Second World War on both sides. He then studied and worked in Austria and came to Vancouver in 1954 where he studied economics. From 1957 to 1965, he taught agricultural economics and economic theory at the University of British Columbia. During the next five years, he worked on international development for the Government of Canada, the Food and Agricultural Organization, the World Bank, and the developmental program of the United Nations. From 1970 to 1985 (retirement), he was professor of rural economy at the University of Alberta.

Karl Helleiner, born in 1902 in Vienna, received his Ph.D. in 1925 and worked in Vienna and St. Pölten, Lower Austria, where he was the archivist. As Hitler refugees, the family managed to emigrate to Canada in 1939 and settled in Toronto. Appointed to the University of Toronto in 1942, he authored several books and many articles, the best known of which is the "Population of Europe from the Black Death to the Eve of the Vital Revolution" in *The Cambridge Economic History of Europe*. Known as a humanist, he became a Fellow of the Royal Society of Canada. **Gerald Karl Helleiner**, Karl's son, was born in St. Pölten, Lower Austria, in 1936. Coming to Canada in the early fifties, he studied at Toronto and Yale. Teaching first at Yale, he has been at the University of Toronto since 1965. Like Polanyi(-Levitt) and Richter, he also concentrated on economic development. His most important work has been on the economics of Africa. A prolific publisher, he is a Fellow of the Royal Society of Canada and has an honorary degree from Dalhousie University.

Eric Waldman was born in 1914 in Vienna and studied at the University of Vienna. A Hitler refugee, he emigrated to the United States in 1938. In the U.S. Army in the Second World War, he retired as lieutenant-colonel. He finished his education in political science at George Washington University and worked, 1952-55, in the War Documentation Project at Columbia University. After teaching from 1958 to 1966, at Marquette University in Milwaukee, Wisconsin, he came to Canada in 1966 as professor of political science at the University of Calgary, retiring in 1980. Waldman's main work has been on post-war German politics, on which he published seven books, five in German and two in English. He was decorated by the Federal Republic of Germany, and he is a Maltese Knight.

Frederick C. Engelmann was born in Vienna in 1921 into an originally Jewish family. He emigrated to the United States in 1938, was a junior officer with the U.S. Army and studied political science at UCLA and Yale. After teaching in Western New York, Engelmann, possibly the only U.S. political science student ever to have four professors who were interested in Canada, was appointed to the University of Alberta (Calgary 1962, Edmonton 1965) where he taught till retirement. He was president of the Canadian Political Science Association (1985-86). Recipient of a Rockefeller grant to Austria (1959-60), Engelmann developed a lifelong interest in Austrian politics, resulting in a number of chapters in books and articles. Together with the prominent political sociologist Mildred A. Schwartz, he published what is still the only authored (not edited) volume on Canadian political parties and the party system (1966, 1975).

One of the few academics who teaches Austrian history in the Canadian post-secondary education system is **Franz Szabo**. Born in Graz in 1946 he emigrated to Canada with his parents in 1956. He studied history at Loyola College (Montreal) and the University of Alberta, where he received his Ph.D. in 1976. After a number of visiting appointments at half a dozen universities across Canada, he joined the Department of History at Carleton University in 1986. His publications deal mainly with eighteenth and nineteenth century central European history and culture. His major work, *Kaunitz and Enlightended Absolutism, 1753-1780*, published by Cambridge University Press in 1994, was awarded the "Barbara Jelavich Prize" of the American Association for the Advancement of Slavic Studies for the best book published in the English language during 1994 in the area of Habsburg studies.

The Austrian-American sociologist **Gertrud Neuwirth** was also born in Graz where she received the Dr. rer. pol. in 1953. She came to the U.S. as a Fulbright scholar and obtained a Ph.D. in sociology from the University of Minnesota (1958). From 1959 to 1963 in Germany, she worked for the DIVO Institute and taught at the University of Munich. After teaching in the U.S., she came to Ottawa in 1967 where she is Professor of Sociology at Carleton University; she is also Director of the Research Resources Division and the Centre for Immigration and Ethno-Cultural Studies. Her research work centres on the settlement and integration of refugees and Third World immigrants. The anthropologist **Gabrielle Tyrnauer**, was born in Vienna which she was forced to flee as a small child. After having immigrated to the U.S., she studied at Brooklyn College and received the Ph.D. from Cornell University. She is now Associate Professor of McGill University's Refugee Research Project and Research Associate of "Living Testimonies," a project videotaping narratives of Holocaust survivors. The main focus of her work is on the fate of gypsies during the Holocaust and their survivors. She has held Fulbright and Ford Foundation fellowships.

A number of Austrians made their mark in the pure sciences. The outstanding theoretical biologist in the Canada of his time was the Austrian **Ludwig von Bertalanffy**. Born in 1901 in Atzgersdorf, Lower Austria (now part of Vienna), he received a doctorate from the University of Vienna in 1926. He taught at the University of Vienna from 1934 to 1948. One year later, he emigrated to Canada, taught at the University of Ottawa till 1954 and became a Canadian citizen. He then spent seven years in the United States, teaching at the University of Southern California and researching in Topeka, Kansas at the institute of the famous physician Karl Menninger who had been his student in Vienna. He returned to Canada in 1961 to accept an appointment at the University of Alberta as professor of theoretical biology. Because of his many accomplishments he became, in 1968, the first person on whom that university bestowed the title of University Professor. He left Edmonton in 1969 for the State University of New York at Buffalo where he received the rare title of Distinguished Faculty Professor. He died soon after moving to Buffalo. Bertalanffy was a great theoretician, who became best known for his general systems theory. While in North America, his main contribution was the application of this theory to psychiatry. On moving to Edmonton, he wrote that he would feel at home in any one of these departments: Biology, Physiology, Biophysics, Behavioral Science, Psychology, and Philosophy. He wrote about two dozen books, in German and English (some were published in five languages), and innumerable articles. Among his most important books are *Problems of Life* and *Robots, Men and Minds*. The thesis of the latter is that men are becoming robots in a society in which the value system cannot cope with the complexity of life. A Rockefeller Fellow in his youth, Bertalanffy was a fellow (1954-55) of Stanford's world famous Center for the Advanced Study of Behavioral Sciences. In 1967, the mayor of Vienna personally invited him to be the keynote speaker of the *Europagespräch* at the Vienna Festival. He was the first Canadian elected Honorary Fellow of the American Psychiatric Association.

A prominent Austrian-Canadian biochemist is **Harry Schachter**. Born in 1933 in Vienna, he left in 1938, a Hitler refugee, for Trinidad where he stayed until 1951 and received his schooling. He arrived in Toronto in 1951 and received three degrees from the University of Toronto. In the late sixties, he was a post-doctoral fellow at Johns Hopkins University. He taught at the University of Toronto from 1964 to 1989 and headed the Division of Biochemistry Research at the Hospital for Sick

Children from 1976 to 1989. In 1989, 1990 and 1992, he was a visiting professor at the Universität für Bodenkultur in Vienna. He published numerous articles, primarily on the biochemistry of glycoproteins.

An eminent Austrian-Canadian physicist and meteorologist was **Walter Hitschfeld**. Born in Vienna in 1922, he went to England and was, though a Hitler refugee, interned as an "enemy alien," transported to Canada, and again interned at Farnham. There he did so well in a McGill program that his sponsors achieved his early release. He studied engineering physics at the University of Toronto and worked briefly at the Defence Research Board in Ottawa. He did his doctoral work at McGill, doing important work in cloud physics. He taught at McGill from 1951 on, helped develop the discipline of radar meteorology and became, in 1959, a charter member of the Department of Meteorology. He served, among other functions at McGill, as Dean of Graduate Studies and Vice-Chancellor of Research, and he became Director of the McGill International Office in 1981, cultivating relations between McGill and the Third World. He was Secretary, then President, of the International Commission on Cloud Physics from 1967 to 1984. He became a Fellow of the Royal Society of Canada. Hitschfeld died of cancer in 1986.

The noted physicist **Paul Pfalzner** was born in Vienna in 1923. Educated in Austria, England and Wales, he received advanced degrees from Toronto and McGill universities. He is a medical physicist who has worked on cancer research and radiation dosimetry. He has done important work in the Third World and has authored several books and numerous articles.

An ecological botanist from the Tyrolean Oetztal became a botany professor and church musician in Alberta. Born in Längenfeld in 1930, **Walter Moser** emigrated to Canada in 1979. He studied at the University of Innsbruck, where he earned a doctorate in botany and geology and habilitated in Alpine ecology. From 1970 to 1979, he was acting director of the University of Innsbruck's Alpine Research Institute Obergurgl, situated in Austria's highest village. There, he initiated and coordinated the UNESCO Man and Biosphere project. At the University of Alberta, he taught a wide variety of courses, ranging from introductory biology to plant ecology, mountain plant ecology, and ecophysiology. While at the University of Alberta, he presented papers in the United States, Switzerland, and Austria. Having been a church musician in Tyrol, he retired to an acreage in Tofield, east of Edmonton, where he has been an active church musician (choir and trumpet) since 1989, serving as chair of the music committee of the Catholic Archdiocese of Edmonton.

The Austrian-Canadian mathematician **Paul Mandl** was born in Vienna in 1917. As a Jewish refugee to England, he went through the usual *via dolorosa* of internment in England, transport to Canada and internment in Canada. He received his B.A., M.A. and Ph.D. degrees from the University of Toronto. Until 1967, he was a research scientist at the National Aeronautics Establishment in Ottawa. From 1967 to 1982 (retirement), he taught at Carleton University. He spent a sabbatical at the Institut für Strömungslehre and Wärmeübertragung at the Technische Universität Wien.

MEDICINE

A number of Austrian-Canadians made significant contributions to medicine. One of the truly outstanding Austrian-Canadians in any field was **Hans Selye**, born in 1907 in Vienna as the son of a Hungarian physician in the Austro-Hungarian army and an Austrian mother who was related to the famous German von Bülow family. His youth was spent first in Vienna, then in his father's home town. While he went to a Catholic Gymnasium there, that town, located on the Danube, changed from Hungarian Komarom to the Slovak Komarno. Now an (involuntary) Czechoslovak citizen, he studied medicine at the German University in Prague. He also did some work in Paris and Rome. With his Prague M.D. (1929) he returned to Vienna. A Rockefeller Foundation grant brought him to the U.S. in 1931, from where he moved in 1932, and soon permanently, to Montreal, joining the staff at McGill University in 1932. A trained endocrinologist, he became, once in Montreal, a world-famous pioneer and popularizer of research on "biological stress." From 1945 to his retirement in 1976, he was the first director of the Institute of Experimental Medicine and Surgery at the University of Montréal. In 1977, he founded the International Institute of Stress, located in his home in Montreal. Selye died in Montreal in 1982. The Selye theory about a General Adaptation Syndrome presents a model in which all stimuli are said to be "stressors," producing in all persons a general response of "stress." Selye analyzed the various stages of stress. He maintained that stress plays some role in the development of every disease and in the non-specific response of the body to any demand made on it. The phases of the syndrome are alarm, resistance, and exhaustion. Failure to cope leads to diseases of adaptation, such as high blood pressure and ulcers. Later, Selye distinguished "eustress" (curative) and "distress" (disease-producing). He eventually claimed that, if his English had not been inadequate, he would have called the syndrome "strain syndrome" and would have avoided much controversy (he was, however, fluent in English and five other languages). Selye wrote three important books, one an autobiography. He received some twenty honorary degrees. Canada bestowed on him the highest honour, the Companion of the Order of Canada.

Born in 1911, **Milo Tyndel** received an M.D. (1933) and a Ph.D. (1948) from the University of Vienna. Since his immigration to Canada in 1954, he has been active as a psychiatrist, first in Manitoba, then in Toronto. He has made significant contributions to the study of chronic drunkenness. A respected physician who became an active booster of Austria in Alberta is **Harald A. Schwarz**. Born in Austrian Silesia (now Czech Republic) in 1916, he studied in Prague. He emigrated to England in 1939 and soon after went to Alberta where he had to eke out a living by being part of an isolated community in northwestern Alberta as a lumberjack and a swamper. In 1941, he was declared a "friendly alien" and served in the army medical corps. In 1945, he was able to study medicine at the University of Alberta where he taught as clinical professor till his retirement in 1982. He was a prominent member of the medical profession in Edmonton, and he serves as president of the Johann Strauss Foundation, which awards musical scholarships to Vienna and Salzburg, an achievement for which he was decorated by Austria and Alberta.

Bernhard Cinader, born in Vienna in 1919, emigrated to England where he studied biochemistry. From 1945 to 1956, he was with the Lister Institute of Preventive Medicine in London. He came to Canada in 1958 and taught medical cell biology, medical genetics and clinical biochemistry at the University of Toronto until his retirement in 1994. He served as President of the Canadian Society for Immunology and the International Union of Immunological Sciences, and he is a Fellow of the Royal Society of Canada and an Officer of the Order of Canada. He has done much international work and has been decorated by a number of countries. His research on age-related changes and other subjects has been communicated in hundreds of articles.

Felix Bertalanffy, son of the eminent biological theorist Ludwig von Bertalanffy, was born in 1926 in Vienna. He came to Canada in 1948 and did advanced work at McGill. From 1955 to 1991 (retirement) he was professor of anatomy at the University of Manitoba. In addition to numerous publications on cell kinetics, he became a publishing expert on Japanese philately and postal history. An Austrian-Canadian physician who is a specialist in reconstructive techniques at the Ottawa General Hospital, **Robert Feibel** came with his parents from Moschendorf near Güssing, Burgenland, to Canada in 1957. He has become known for using two techniques: the Ilizarow bone reconstruction technique, developed in Siberia, and a soft tissue transplant technique developed in the treatment of farmworkers in southern California. **Frederick H. Lowy**, born in 1933 in Grosspetersdorf, Burgenland, became a Jewish refugee in 1938 and was able to settle in Canada in 1944. He graduated from the Faculty of Medicine at McGill in 1959. He has taught at the Department of Psychiatry of the University of Toronto since 1974 and was its Dean of Medicine from 1980 to 1987. He has served on many bodies and agencies, including the board of the National Ballet of Canada. He is a very active researcher and publisher.

Harald O. Stolberg, born in 1925 in Graz, became a prominent Canadian radiologist. He was educated in Graz and Vienna and emigrated to Canada in 1953. After postgraduate work in Toronto, he became a staff member at McMaster University in 1967. He is a very active researcher and publisher in the field of radiology. A noted Austrian-Canadian psychologist is **Ernest G. Poser**. Born in Vienna in 1921, he emigrated to Canada in 1942 and studied at Queen's and the University of London. Poser taught at McGill University until 1983, when he became clinical professor of psychology and psychiatry at the University of British Columbia. He wrote books on adaptive learning and behaviour therapy.

BUSINESS

Austria's business pioneer in Canada, following Hans Daigle by more than a century, was **Nikolaus Klingenbrunner.** He was born in Vienna and served Great Britain in the American War of Independence. Having served in the Brunswick regiment of Lieutenant Colonel Breymann, he was discharged honourably in Québec in 1783 and settled in York (Toronto). There he opened the first tailor shop in 1795. His descendants, who excelled in silversmithing, watchmaking and agriculture, changed the family name to Clinkenbroomer.

There are two Austrian-Canadians who were would-be pioneers, but about whom little seems to be known. **Adolph Grohmann**, early in the 20th century, had an idea for a network of canals in Western Canada, but they were never constructed. **Alfred von Hammerstein**, also early in the 20th century, made an unsuccessful attempt to produce oil from the Athabasca tar sands in Alberta—a project which became reality in the 1970s.

Easily the most flamboyant and probably the most well-known Austrian entrepreneur in Canada is **Frank Stronach**, whose "rags to riches" story is quite rare in the second half of the 20th century. Stronach was born in 1934 in the village of Kleinsemmering near Weiz, deep in rural Styria. When he arrived in Canada in 1954, he had some experience in tool and machine engineering. He started work as a tool and die maker in Kitchener and soon moved to a similar job in Toronto. In 1957, he went into business for himself, founding the tool and die firm of Multimatic Investments Ltd. Before long, Multimatic expanded into the production of stamped automotive components. He began the move toward becoming Canada's largest automotive parts manufacturer by sharing ownership and profits with energetic managers. In 1969 came the merger of Multimatic with Magna Electronic Company Ltd., with Stronach in firm control. Two years later, he extended the principle of equity participation to include every Magna employee. He called this business philosophy "Fair Enterprise," based on a business Charter of Rights, predetermining the annual percentage of profits shared between employees, management and investors and making every employee a shareholder in the company. From then on, there was no stopping Stronach. Magna grew at a remarkable annual rate of 30 percent. The year 1973 brought the consolidation of Magna into Magna International, Inc., with Stronach as chairman and CEO. The firm has become one of the world's largest and most diversified automotive systems suppliers in the world. In 1993-94, Stronach's income was reportedly not only the largest in Canada, but he received a raise of 416 percent, to $40,700,000.00, quite a feat for someone who came to Canada as a 22-year-old immigrant from a small Styrian village. But despite the size of his income, Stronach wanted more than money. With the slogan "Let's be Frank!" he attempted, in 1988, to be elected to Parliament as a Liberal. He failed in his effort to help determine the shape of Canadian politics, but Stronach's leading impact on Canadian industry continues.

Rather different is the story of the Bentley/Bloch-Bauer and Prentice/Pick families in British Columbia. They were Hitler refugees, managing to come to Canada not as the very rich people they had been in Austria, but yet with a fair amount of funds to invest. It all began when young **Leopold Bloch-Bauer (Bentley)**, a passionate hunter, went on a hunting and hiking trip to the Canadian Rockies in 1937. The favourable impression which Western Canada and its people made on him led to the determination to immigrate to Canada as soon as Hitler took Austria in 1938. Leopold (Poldi) Bloch-Bauer was born in Vienna in 1905. His father was an industrialist, refining sugar and engaging in agricultural operations. His mother's sister (two sisters married two brothers) was Adele Bloch-Bauer who is depicted in one of Gustav Klimt's most celebrated paintings. He studied at the University of Vienna, and textile engineering in Germany, and was one of Austria's first private pilots. He worked for his father-in-law (Pick) when Hitler invaded. He immediately sent his wife and his son Peter to London, met them and the family of his brother-in-law, Hans Pick, in London three months later, and they all arrived in Vancouver in August 1938. Soon after arrival, he changed his name to Bentley; Pick changed his to John Prentice.

Bentley and Prentice had been in the textile business, which they did not consider profitable in British Columbia. Together with a Hungarian veneer manufacturer, John Bene, they founded the Pacific Veneer and Plywood Company, which began production in 1939. The time could not have been more propitious. The Royal Air Force found itself cut off from its Scandinavian plywood supply, and Pacific Veneer became the largest supplier of plywood for the RAF. The firm grew during the war, and in 1945, it began producing Douglas fir plywood for British reconstruction. In 1947, the company, now run only by Bentley and Prentice, reorganized as Canadian Forest Product, Ltd. (Canfor). In the early sixties, the firm also went into pulp and paper production in the interior of British Columbia. In 1975, Leopold's son Peter succeeded him as president and CEO of Canfor. Leopold Bentley died in Vancouver in 1986. His brothers, **Karl Bloch-Bauer** and **Robert Bentley**, had also been connected with the firm. Karl was a member of the original board of governors of Simon Fraser University. He was the husband of the famed soubrette Rita Georg. **Peter Bentley**, Leopold Bentley's son, was born in 1930 in Vienna. He was educated at the University of British Columbia and the Banff School of Advanced Management. Chairman and CEO of Canfor Corporation, he is a director of, among others, the Bank of Montreal and Shell Canada. He is an Officer of the Order of Canada. **John Prentice (Hans Pick)** was born in Vienna in 1907 and from the thirties was closely associated with his brother-in-law, Leopold Bentley. Along with Bentley, he held the highest executive positions in Canfor. He was also prominent in the international world of chess. He served as director of the CBC and, a prominent patron of the arts, he was chairman of the Canada Council from 1969 to 1974. He became an Officer of the Order of Canada. Prentice died in Vancouver in 1986.

It should not surprise anyone that Canadian winters and mountains would attract Austrian immigrants as ski entrepreneurs. A prominent Austrian-Canadian mountain guide who pioneered in mountain climbing, skiing and snowshoeing, was **Konrad Kain**. Born in Nasswald in the mountainous part of Lower Austria, in 1883, he spent four seasons climbing in the Alps. His reputation gained there led to his appointment as the first official guide of the Alpine Club of Canada, based in Banff, Alberta, in 1909. He assisted early surveying teams at the Rogers and Yellowhead passes. In 1911, he built the first ski jump in Banff and brought in recreational skiing. He led the first ascents of Mt. Robson (1913) and Mt. Farnham. In 1916, he developed new climbing techniques for the ascents of Mt. Louis, Mt. Howser, and the Bugaboo Spires. His solo snowshoe ascent of Mt. Jumbo (1919) was the first winter ascent of a major Canadian peak. His last major ascent, in the Purcells (1933), was of a peak which later was called after Kain, Mt. Conrad. Kain died of encephalitis in Cranbrook, B.C. in 1934.

A versatile Austrian-Canadian in the mountains business, as a guide and entrepreneur, is **Hans Gmoser**. Born in Upper Austria in 1932, he apprenticed as an electrician at VÖEST in Linz. Having emigrated to Canada in 1951, he began a mountain guide career in Banff in 1953. In 1957, he founded Canadian Mountain Holidays, Ltd. and in ensuing years ascended Mt. Logan and Mt. McKinley. In 1965, he initiated helicopter skiing in the Bugaboo Mountains, B.C., the first such operation anywhere in the world. In the decades since, he has extended heli-skiing and heli-hiking enterprises in Western Canada and built the first heli-skiing lodges. In 1987, he became a member of the Order of Canada.

A prominent Western Canadian entrepreneur is **Michael (Mike) Wiegele**. Born in 1938 in Feistritz (Carinthia), he came to Canada in 1959. In 1965, he took over the Lake Louise ski school. Looking for something more exciting, he set up a heli-skiing base in Valemount in the northern Cariboo in 1970. Business improved when film-maker Warren Miller gave it some publicity. When Wiegele noted that there were higher snow piles farther south, in Blue River, B.C., he moved there in 1974. Wiegele's fleet has grown to six helicopters, and most of his clientele is international. In Ontario, **Josl Huter**'s enterprise is more traditional. In 1963, he began to develop the ski resort of Mount St. Louis, north of Barrie, Ontario. The adjoining ski hill, Moonstone, belonged to a competitor whom Huter bought out in 1984. The joint resort now has two base lodges and two major ski hills, each with two peaks. In 1969, Huter installed Canada's first triple chair lift. Since 1966, there has also been a snow-making system.

An Austrian-American who is not a sports entrepreneur, but who combines a prominent engineering career with an important role in international skiing, is **Karl Martitsch**. Born in the 1920s in Ratnitz, Carinthia, he received a master's degree in engineering from the University of Graz (1949). From 1936 to 1950, he competed for Austria in all skiing disciplines: downhill, slalom, cross country and ski jumping. Emigrating to Canada in 1951, he worked for the Foundation Company of Canada, Ltd. till 1963 and then, till his retirement in 1988, for Stone & Webster, Ltd., after 1972 as vice-president. Around 1960, he built Canada's first 70m jump hill at Hiawatha Park, near Sault Ste. Marie. He played major roles in the design and construction of the ski-jumping complexes for the Winter Olympics of Lake Placid (1980) and Calgary (1988). Martitsch has had important roles in F.I.S., the international ski federation, serving on its council from 1979 to 1992.

Rudolph (Rudi) Liska was an Austrian who made a major contribution to Toronto's fashion world. Born in Austria in 1921, he served in the German army and became a prisoner of war. He came to Toronto in 1953 and immediately launched into the fashion business. He was one of the founders of, and the driving force behind, Toronto's Canadian-Austrian Society (1986). He died in Toronto in 1993. **Martin Scholler**, who influenced Montreal's plastics business, was born in Austria in 1933. He lived in Salzburg and came to Canada in 1951. He engaged in electroplating before emigrating. In Boucherville, Quebec he founded and still presides over National Pro Industries, Inc. The firm deals primarily in plastics. Among its many diverse products are car mats and diving suits.

A most remarkable alumnus of Queen's University is **Alfred Bader**. Born in 1924 in Vienna of a Jewish father—who died soon after Bader's birth—and a Catholic mother, he managed to get to England in late 1938 where a Mrs. Wolff took an interest in him and made sure he got an education. Transported to, and interned in, Canada in 1940 as an "enemy alien," he found out accidentally that Mrs. Wolff's son lived in Montreal. After his release, the Wolffs took him in. He was rejected by McGill because he exceeded their Jewish quota and by the University of Toronto because he had been interned. Queen's accepted him and he never forgot. After a Master's from Queen's and a Ph.D. from Harvard, he became a partner of the Aldrich Chemical Company, which he merged with the Sigma firm and took over himself. Sigma-Aldrich became a leading firm in quality chemicals. Serving on Queen's board of trustees, Bader endowed chairs in chemistry and art history and gave Queen's $2 million on the fiftieth anniversary of his admission to Queen's. After retiring as CEO of Sigma-Aldrich, he was removed from its board by his successor. Bader drowned his sorrow, bought himself a Rembrandt, and made Queen's University a most unusual gift. He had bought the southern English castle of Herstmonceaux for $8 million, renovated it for $4 million, and donated it to Queen's so that the university would have a European base for an enriching experience for some of its students.

The millions of computer users in Canada may want to know that the first pilot model of an electronic computer in Canada was designed and built by a Jewish immigrant from Austria. Born in Vienna in 1921, **Josef Kates (Katz)** came to Toronto in 1942. He joined the Imperial Optical Company which manufactured naval precision optics. In 1948, he designed for the Canadian National Exhibition "Bertie the Brain," Canada's first electronic game playing machine, and in 1954, he designed for Metro Toronto the world's first computer-controlled traffic signal system. He founded KCS, Ltd. in 1954 which, in 1967, joined with the consulting firm of Peat, Marvick, Mitchell and Co. to form corporations in Canada, the U.K. and the U.S. Since 1974, he has been president of Josef Kates Associates, Inc. He served on the Science Council of Canada from 1968 to 1974 and was its chairman from 1975 to 1978. From 1979 to 1985, he was Chancellor of the University of Waterloo.

Prominent in the pulp and paper industry was the Austrian-Canadian **Karl F. Landegger**. While president of the firm Parsons & Whittemore, in 1967, he founded the Prince Albert Pulp Co., which he developed into what appears to have been Saskatchewan's largest industrial establishment. Decorated by Austria, he died in 1976. Two Austrian-Canadian brothers became prominent manufacturers of investment castings. Born in the Styrian city of Bruck an der Mur, **Frank** (1923) and **Josef** (1925) **Valenta**, emigrated in 1951. Frank went to Toronto, Josef to Buenos Aires. In 1959 they were reunited in Montreal where they founded the firm of Cercast, Inc. Because of thriving business, they decided to separate the production of ferrous and non-ferrous castings in 1963. Frank stayed with Cercast and took over the non-ferrous business. Josef, however, founded Vestshell to specialize in ferrous castings.

The Austrian-Canadian **Roland Pirker** is important in Canadian film. Born in 1946 in Klagenfurt, he came to Canada in 1967. He worked for the CBC from 1972 to 1974 and for the National Museums of Canada from 1974 to 1981 as cinematographer, producer, director and editor. In 1981, he founded his own company, Rollframe Productions, Ltd. Rollframe has served, among others, Atomic Energy Canada, Bell Canada, the BBC, the CBC, Elections Canada, Health and Welfare Canada, the National Film Board of Canada, the National Arts Center, the Prime Minister's Office, and the World Health Organization. Pirker's production experience extends to the Canadian and American North, Europe, Asia and Africa.

The bibliophile and antiquarian **Bernard Altmann** was born in Vienna in 1907 of book-loving parents. Fleeing Vienna the day the Nazis came, he volunteered for the French army. In 1945, he arrived in Ottawa, where his brother was living, with two boxes of books, and he soon moved to Montreal. He founded Bernard Altmann Books, later called Montreal Book Auction. In 1951, he opened a store on Sherbrooke Street and specialized in Canadiana. He had great merit in protecting Canada's intellectual culture. The University of Saskatchewan gave him an honorary degree. Altmann died in Montreal in 1979.

George Hinterhoeller, an Austrian boat builder, came to Canada in 1952. His first job was as a power boat builder, but his real interest was designing and building sailboats. His great success was the Shark. Hinterhoeller Yachts built many Sharks in the 1960s, and the boat became internationally known. There are about 3,000 Sharks in existence; they sail in North America and Europe.

It is hardly surprising that an Austrian-Canadian would succeed in the wine business, as viticulture in Austria reputedly dates back to the Roman Emperor Probus in the third century. **Karl Kaiser**, born in Austria in 1941, learned a bit about wine-making when he attended a convent school. He came to Canada in 1969 and settled in the Niagara Peninsula, studying chemistry at Brock University. In 1973, he met the horticulturist Donald Ziraldo from St. Catherines, and two years later, they were in the wine-growing and -making business in Niagara-on-the-Lake. Inniskillin winery was so successful that Brock University conferred an honorary degree on Kaiser in 1994. The man who introduced Austrian wines to Canada is **Karl Gyaki**. Born in Oberwart, Burgenland, he became a tailor and was a successful soccer player. Feeling that Oberwart was too small for him, he did tailoring in various places in Austria and

Switzerland. He came to Canada in 1951 and again worked as a tailor. In 1958, he discovered accidentally that one could not get any Austrian wine in Ontario. This discovery led to his decision to enter the wine import business. In 1959, he founded the firm Gyaki Agencies, which became Canada's chief importer of Austrian wines, earning him an Austrian decoration and the informal title of "Ambassador of Austrian wine to Canada."

An important person in British Columbia real estate, who worked prominently in Western Canadian-Austrian relations, was **John Rudolf Hecht**, born 1911 in Vienna. He was president of Vancouver's Equitable Real Estate Investment Corp. Ltd., was Special Advisor to the Commissioner of the Northwest Territories and served as consultant to the International Finance Corporation in Washington, D.C. Hecht served many years as Honorary Consul General of Austria for British Columbia and the Yukon Territory. The founding president of Austrian Airlines immigrated to Canada in 1965. Born in 1919 in Budapest, **Sepp Froeschl** was a highly decorated Luftwaffe officer and became a colonel in the Austrian air reserve. He became an airline executive in Montreal where he has been engaged in Austrian and German community activities.

Joseph Kandler, born in Vienna in 1921 and immigrating to Canada in 1952, came as a tradesman and had an active career in Edmonton as a chartered accountant, leading to his becoming the chief financial officer of automotive firms. Very active in the community, he was appointed to the Board of Governors of the University of Alberta. When vice-president of Edmonton's Club Austria, he founded the Johann Strauss Foundation of Alberta (1975), dedicated to the support of the musical education of Canadian students by way of scholarships for advanced study of music in Austria. He also initiated the international student exchange between the University of Alberta's Faculty of Business and the Wirtschaftsuniversität Wien and partially endowed it. For these unusual diplomatic achievements, he was highly decorated by the Republic of Austria, the city of Vienna, and the Province of Alberta. Retiring to British Columbia, he founded, in 1985, the Johann Strauss Foundation of British Columbia.

Born in Austria and an honours graduate of Vienna's Technical University (1949), **Roland Bergmann** joined the Toronto firm of M.S. Yolles, now Hooper and Yolles, in 1955 and, after serving as Chief Engineer and Vice-President, became a partner in 1974. While the largest projects in which he was the Partner-in-Charge were outside Canada (World Financial Center, New York; Canary Wharf, London), he has been in charge of many Canadian construction projects, including Bell Trinity Square, First Canadian Place, and College Park, all in Toronto. A pharmaceutical executive, born in Vienna in 1940, is **Frank Michael Unger**. A Dozent at the University of Vienna who worked for Sandoz (Vienna) from 1980 to 1987, he became, in 1990, president of Chembiomed (Edmonton) and a member of the Alberta Research Council.

PUBLIC SERVICE

One Austrian-Canadian has been an outstanding public servant. The Honourable **Fred Kaufman**, C.M., Q.C., was born in Vienna in 1924. Like many other Jewish refugees, he went the *via dolorosa* of emigration to, and internment in, England and transport to, and internment in, Canada until his release in 1942. He was educated at Bishop's University and McGill and admitted to the bars of Quebec (1955), the Northwest Territories (1961), and Alberta (1968). Before this, he had a brief career as a part-time journalist. From 1962 to 1994, he taught at the McGill Faculties of Law and Management, and in the Concordia University Faculty of Commerce and Administration. Kaufman was Judge of the Quebec Court of Appeal from 1973 to 1991, serving as Acting Chief Justice of Quebec for part of 1988. He published widely and became a Member of the Order of Canada. Because of its relevance to this study, we quote his citation for the Order of Canada:

Arriving in Canada as a Youth Displaced by War, He Showed Perseverance and Courage, Becoming a Judge of the Quebec Court of Appeal, where His Judgements Were Models of Erudition, Clarity and Precision. He Has Had a Diverse Career as Brilliant Criminal Lawyer, a Teacher and a Writer, Dedicating His Life to Justice, Fairness and Freedom. Moreover, He Has Instilled in Others the Pursuit of these Ideals.

Kurt F. Paümann can best be described as a pioneering private diplomat. A descendant of an officer who was elevated to the noble rank of baron for his valiant conduct during Vienna's siege by the Turks in 1683, he was the son of Eduard Freiherr von Paümann, a high official at the Imperial Court. Born in 1901 in Vienna, he was forced to interrupt his law studies when his family was hit hard by the post-World War I inflation. With experience in banking and industry, he was a voluntary Hitler refugee who was interned in England as an "enemy alien." There, however, the *via dolorosa* ended for him, and he was able to bring his family to

Canada in late 1941. Settling in Montreal, he worked as auditor and office manager. By 1947, he was impressed by the lack of Austrian as well as Canadian efforts to establish diplomatic relations. He managed to get to Vienna in 1947 where he established important contacts in his determination to help set up diplomatic relations between Austria and Canada, an effort he then continued in Ottawa. The outcome of his endeavours was the establishment of an Austrian Consulate General in Ottawa under Friedrich Riedl-Riedenstein, with Paümann as Chancellor. Because of Riedl's illness, Paümann ended up in charge and worked on elevating the Consulate to a Legation. The change was made in 1952 with Walther Peinsipp as Chargé d'Affaires. One year later, Peinsipp terminated Paümann's appointment suddenly, claiming mutual agreement. Paümann, having become known as "Monsieur Autriche" in Ottawa, was stunned. In 1956 Kurt Waldheim, having come to Ottawa as Austrian Minister, finally apologized for the termination. In 1958, Paümann became Honorary Correspondent for the Austrian Federal Press Service. Twenty-three years later, Ambassador Tarter testified that he continued a special interest in Austria's relations with Canada and the work of the Embassy. Nearly thirty years ago, he wrote a chapter pioneering in what we are doing here, viz. writing a history of the contributions of Austrians to Canada's cultural, economic and social life. In 1995, he celebrated his 94th birthday, according to his daughter "impeccably dressed, and over a glass of champagne and Sachertorte."

A prominent Austrian-Canadian in Canada's public service is **Erika von Conta Bruce**. Born in Vienna in 1937, she studied there, receiving a Ph.D. in political economy in 1960. After editorial and journalistic work in Vienna and Munich, she came to Ottawa in 1967. From 1968 to 1973, she held major positions with the Canada Council. After foundation work in New York, she returned to Ottawa where (1982-87) she held major positions with the Senate and the Social Sciences and Humanities Research Council (SSHRC). Having served as Director of Information and Press (NATO) in Brussels (1990-94), she is now Director General, Corporate and Intergovernmental Affairs, Canadian Heritage, with the Government of Canada.

An Austrian-Canadian who was able to combine Austrian training in *Kunstgewerbe* (applied art) with a unique service to Canada is **Walter Ott**. Born in 1928, he came to Canada in 1952. After years of working in and teaching engraving, he joined the Royal Canadian Mint as engraver in 1964. From 1977 till 1985 (retirement), he served as the Mint's Chief

Engraver and Director of Art. His gold coins (1 oz., $^1/_4$ oz., $^1/_{10}$ oz.) are probably the purest in the world. He also designed and modeled medals, among others, of Pope John Paul II, Governor General Schreyer, and for the Supreme Court of Canada, the Royal Society of Canada, and the Montreal and Calgary Olympics. A similar role to that of Ott has been played by the designer **Ernst Roch**. Born in Osijek, Croatia, into an Austrian family, he came to Austria in 1944, studied design in Graz, and emigrated to Canada in 1953. Active as a designer in Montreal, he went into business in 1960 (Design Collaborative, then Signum Press, a publishing company, then Roch design, 1978). In 1962, he sketched the Queen (two sittings) in Buckingham Palace for Canada Post (1963 postage stamps) and designed the commemorative postage stamp of Sir Oliver Mowat (1967). A member of the Postage Stamp Design Advisory Committee of the Canadian Post Office Department (1975-1980), he designed, during the eighties, the commemorative postage stamp series "Early Canadian Locomotives," "Christmas 1988," and "Canadian Mushrooms."

A prince of the Roman Catholic Church, while born in Saskatchewan of parents who immigrated from Bukovina, definitely views himself as an Austrian-Canadian. The Most Reverend **Adam Exner**, OMI, Archbishop of Vancouver, was born in Killaly, Saskatchewan in 1928, ordained in Rome in 1957 and consecrated as Bishop of Kamloops, B.C. in 1974. From 1974 to 1980, he was Secretary of the Western Conference of Catholic Bishops. He was named Archbishop of Winnipeg in 1982 and Archbishop of Vancouver in 1991. Since 1993, he has been President of the Theology Commission of the Canadian Conference of Catholic Bishops. Exner speaks six languages and received, in 1960, a Doctorate of Theology from Ottawa University.

Our concluding observation is that Austrian-Canadians have indeed contributed to many aspects of Canada's culture, society and economy. Many fields of Canadian endeavour would have suffered at least slightly, and some distinctly more, had there been no Austrian immigration.

SOURCES

Armour, Drew. "Venerable Bibliophile: The Late Bernard Amtmann." *Canadian Antiques*, 2(1980), 27-29.

Biographisches Handbuch der deutschsprachigen Emigration nach 1933. Vol. 2.1 and 2.2. (Munich, 1980-83).

Canadian Who's Who. (Toronto, 1992, 1993, 1994).

Canadian Encyclopedia, 2nd ed. (Edmonton, 1988).

Debor, H.W., "Die Österreicher in Kanada." *Nordwesten,* April 25, 1967.

DeMont, John. "Electric Conductor" [Georg Tintner]. *Maclean's,* April 22, 1991: 59.

Enchin, Harvey. "Pants saver for car floor" [Martin Scholler]. *The Gazette* (Montreal), June 2, 1981.

Encyclopedia of Music in Canada. (Toronto, 1981, 1992).

Encyclopedia Canadiana. (Ottawa, 1957).

Everett-Green, Robert. "I've got something up my sleeve" [Nicholas Goldschmidt]. *The Globe and Mail,* December 6, 1988: A23.

Foss, Krista. "Victory of the Vines" [Karl Kaiser]. *Foodservice and Hospitality,* 24(10), 1991: 225-41.

Froeschle, Hartmut. "The German-Canadians. A Concise History." *German-Canadian Yearbook.* Vol. 12. Toronto, 1992, p. 60.

Garland, G.D. "Another Centenary: Poles of the Unknown in Our Earth." *Transactions of the Royal Society of Canada,* 20(1982), 359-68.

Gibbon, J.M. "Contributions of Austro-German Music to Canadian Culture." *Royal Society of Canada Transactions,* 43, 3rd series, Section 2, 1949: 57-71.

Harris, Christopher. "A generous inspiration to youthful musicians" [Greta Kraus]. *The Globe and Mail,* September 26, 1990: C5.

Hietsch, Otto, ed. *Österreich und die angelsächsische Welt: Kulturbegegnungen und Vergleiche.* Vol. 2. Wien, 1968,

International Who's Who in Music. 12th ed. Cambridge, 1994-95.

Jedlicka, Peter W. *Klub im Wandel: Festschrift zum 25-jährigen Jubiläum des Austrian Club "Edelweiss" Inc.* (Toronto, 1974).

Jelen, Walter. "Österreicher im zweitgrößten Land der Erde." *Montrealer Nachrichten,* April 15, 1967: 4.

Johnson, Arthur. "Man of Parts" [Frank Stronach]. *Canadian Business,* December 1992, 80-87.

Kallmann, Dr. Helmut. "The German Contribution to Music in Canada." *German-Canadian Yearbook,* Vol. 2. Toronto, 1975, pp. 152-66.

Koch, George. "Carving with Tin: Mike Wiegele's Quarter Century in the Cariboos." *Ski Canada,* Winter 1995: 894.

Lambton, Gunda. "Contributions of German Graphic Artists in the History of Canadian Printmaking." *German Canadian Yearbook,* Vol. 4. Toronto, 1979, pp. 180-204.

Lauzon, Michael. "National Pro making use of recycled ...?" [Martin Scholler]. *Plastics News,* April 2, 1990.

Lawley, Sarah. "A Maestro in the Maritimes" [Georg Tintner]. *Imperial Oil Review,* 78 (1990): 26-30.

Lees, Nick. "Forging links between nations" [Harald Schwarz]. *Edmonton Journal,* February 28, 1991: B12.

Liddell, Peter and Walter Riedel, eds. *Carl Weiselberger. Eine Auswahl seiner Schriften.* (Toronto, 1981), pp. 1-10.

Lownsbrough, John. "Music Man." *City and Country Home,* 8(5), June 1989: 118-26.

MacMillan, K. and John Beckwith. *Contemporary Canadian Composers.* Toronto, 1975.

Martin, Sandra. "Queen's and the Castle." *Saturday Night,* July/August 1994: 18-24.

Mautner, Lorenz. "Die Kanadisch-Österreichische Gesellschaft in Toronto." *German-Canadian Yearbook.* Vol. 6. (Toronto, 1981), pp. 258-60.

Miska, John. *Ethnic and Native Canadian Literature: A Bibliography.* (Toronto, 1990).

Neighbor, O.W. *The New Grove Dictionary of Music and Musicians.* 5th ed. (Washington, 1980).

Norris, John. *Strangers Entertained. A History of the Ethnic Groups of British Columbia* (British Columbia Centennial Committee, 1971), pp. 107-08.

Notes on the Canadian Family Tree. "Austrians." Ottawa, 1960, pp. 1-4.

Paümann, Kurt. "Der Einfluß österreichischer Einwanderer auf das Kulturleben in Kanada," in Otto Hietsch, ed. *Österreich und die angelsächsische Welt: Kulturbegegnungen und Vergleiche,* Vol. 2. (Vienna, 1968), pp. 188-201.

Placzek, Adolf K. , ed. *Macmillan Encyclopedia of Architects,* Vol. 4. (New York, 1982).

Polanyi-Levitt, Kari. *The Life and Work of Karl Polanyi: A Celebration.* (Montreal, 1990).

Priebert, Eckehart J. *Thank you, Canada.* (West Vancouver, 1990).

Riedel, Walter. "Charles Wassermann." *The Old World and the New.* (Toronto, 1984), pp. 124-43.

———. "An Austrian in Ottawa: Carl Weiselberger's Canadian Experience." *The Old World and the New.* (Toronto, 1984), pp. 107-23.

Ripley, Gordon and Anne Mercer. *Who's Who in Canadian Literature 1985-86.* (Toronto, 1985).

Robson, Barbara. "Diary recalls Jew's ordeal in Canada" [Harry Seidler]. *Winnipeg Free Press,* May 1988: 7.

Roger, Dieter. "Dr. Ferdinand Eckhardt und seine Frau Sophie-Carmen Eckhardt-Grammaté. 40. Jubiläum der Ankunft in Kanada." *Kanada Kurier,* 21. Oktober 1993: 45.

———. "Zum 80.Geburtstag Dr. Ferdinand Eckhardts, des langjährigen Direktors der Winnipeg Art Gallery." *German-Canadian Yearbook,* Vol. 7. (Toronto, 1983), pp. 148-54.

Rogers, R.R. "Walter Francis Hitschfeld." *Transactions of the Royal Society of Canada,* Series 5/Volume 2, 1987: 239-41.

Sachs, Harvey. "She Shall Have Music" [Greta Kraus]. *Saturday Night,* July-August 1994: 24-27, 60.

Seliger, Helfried. "Charles Wassermann: Life and Oeuvre in the Service of Mutual Understanding." *The Old World and the New.* (Toronto, 1984), pp. 124-43.

Slonimsky, Nicolas, ed. *Baker's Biographical Dictionary of Musicians.* (New York, 1984).

Smith, Harold. "Eli Kassner: A biography." *Guitar Canada,* 2(4), 1989: 16.

Stoffman, Daniel. "Stalled" [Frank Stronach]. *Report on Business Magazine,* April 1990: 46-52.

Taylor, Kate. "Someone to sing about" [Nicholas Goldschmidt]. *The Globe and Mail,* May 29, 1993: C4.

Van Herk, Aritha. "Henry Kreisel: 1922-1991." *Canadian Literature* 131 (1991), 261-63.

Van Alphen, Tony. "Stronach takes aim at politics." *The Ottawa Citizen,* September 26, 1988: B12.

APPENDIX

Amtmann, Willy, b. Vienna, 1910. Historian, violinist. Played in the Ottawa Philharmonic and taught at Carleton University. Wrote on music in Quebec, 1600-1800.

Asknasy, Anna Helene, b. Vienna, 1893. Writer.

Bauer, Hans. Conductor. 1963-69, Director of Music, University of Waterloo, then Professor of Violin. Since 1992 Professor of Violin at the University of Western Ontario.

Benko, Jo. Glazed enamel designer.

Birnbaum, Solomon. Philologist and paleographer.

Blach, Adolf Ernst, b. Vienna, 1926; to Canada, 1956. Engineer. Studied after military service. Not permitted to finish studies, he emigrated to Montreal. Earned doctorate at Sir George Williams University (now Concordia University). Taught at Concordia, wrote two books and many articles.

Bolf, Matthias, b. Vienna, 1720, married in Portneuf.

Brosz, Helmut Gunter, b. Vienna, 1942. Forensic engineer. President and CEO, Brosz and Associates, Markham, Ontario.

Bruck, Peter A., b. Vienna, 1950. Professor and Director of Communications, Culture and Society, Carleton University, 1985. Professor and Head, International Research Programme, Economy and Future of Print Media, University of Salzburg.

Clement, André. Son of Gilbert Clement (b. Vienna). Married 1720 in Portneuf.

de Buda, Yvonne. Professor emerita of Family and Community Medicine at the University of Toronto.

Dollfuss, Rudolf. Psychiatrist. Educated in Montreal. Practiced in Montreal and Vancouver. Son of Chancellor Engelbert Dollfuss.

Ebner, Josef, to Canada, 1970. Hotelier. Manager, Delta Chelsea Inn, Toronto.

Famira, Helmut, b. Tyrol. Professor of German at Concordia University, Montreal.

Firestone, O.J., b. Austria-Hungary, 1913. Economist. Taught at the University of Ottawa. Became also known as an economic advisor to the Government of Saskatchewan.

Freud, Alexander, b. Vienna, 1866. Economist.

Friesen, Ilse, b. Vienna, 1940. Studied art history in Vienna, Munich and Innsbruck. Came to Canada in 1965. Art historian. Has taught at Winnipeg and Wilfried Laurier University.

Frisch, Anton, b. Naples, Italy. Lyricist. Published four anthologies of poems in English, one in German (Vienna, 1952).

Fuerst, Karin. English-German translator. Works as consultant. Co-editor of memoirs of Ferdinand Eckhardt.

Furst, Joseph. Opera Festival Company of Toronto.

Gartner, Emil, b. Vienna, 1914; to Canada, 1938; d. Toronto, 1960. Choral conductor. Directed Jewish Folk Choir of Toronto and choir of Beth Shalom Synagogue.

Goigner, Herman, b. Veitsch, Styria, 1944; to Canada, 1969. Painter, art teacher. Studied history and political science at the University of Calgary, but worked in hotel industry till 1983. Active in Edmonton art world. Began to exhibit in 1988.

Gorth, Sully. Theater set designer. Toronto.

Graf, Peter, b. Vienna, 1944; to Canada, 1967. Restaurant manager. Grew up in Zurndorf, Burgenland. To Vienna in 1958; attended Hotel- und Gastgewerbeschule. Interned in Vienna's Rathauskeller and Hotel Imperial. From 1962 to 1966, work on the Channel Islands. Manager of Carleton University Faculty Club and Ottawa Country Club. Since 1976, Manager, Faculty Club, University of Alberta.

Griesseier, Hermann, b. Styria. Member, Ottawa Schrammel Quartett.

Gruber, Hans, b. Vienna, 1925; to Canada, 1939. Conductor. 1948-63, conductor of Victoria Symphony Orchestra.

Grunsky, Wolfgang. Cellist, Toronto Symphony.

Guschlbauer, Franz, b. Vienna; to Canada, 1969. Metal printer. In 1979, founded Franjo Metal Spinning, Inc. Firm has the only computerized metal printing machines in Quebec.

Hafner, Karl-Franz, b. Graz; to Canada, 1954. Since late 50's, Technical Officer of Physics Department, Carleton University. Participated in designing Carleton's Herzberg Physics Building and constructed the university's Foucault Pendulum (1970).

Halpern, Hans. President, Amik Systems Ltd.

Hammerschmid, Leo, to Canada at age six. Retired engineer. Author of a privately published book on Empress Zita. Decorated by Austria.

Hargassner, Helmut, b. Weng, Upper Austria, 1940; to Canada, 1960. Jeweler and chief European purchaser for Birk's Jewellers.

Hauser, Alexis, b. Vienna, 1947; to Canada, 1981. Conductor. Studied under Karajan. Music Director, London (Ontario) Symphony Orchestra, 1981.

Heinisch, Gerhard. Surgeon in Winnipeg.

Heinzle, Richard. Came to Canada in 1982. Conductor and Music Director. Founder of Vivace Orchestra, Ottawa.

Helleiner, Christopher Walter, b. Vienna, 1930. Professor of Biochemistry, Dalhousie University.

Herler, Melchior. Wood carver in Vancouver.

Hoenig, Julius, b. Prague, 1916. Professor of Psychiatry, Memorial University of Newfoundland.

Holzbauer, Otto, b. Benesov (now Czech Republic), 1927. Lived in Austria several years before and after World War II; to Canada, 1976. Businessman. House painter and mason in Austria, then businessman in Germany. In Canada, baker. Vice-president of MO-NA Food Enterprises (1992) in Edmonton, "the first Canadian wild mushroom company." Imports mushrooms from all over Austria, and exports them all over the world.

Kanits, Walter. CBC programs on folk songs.

Karlweis, Marta, b. Vienna, 1889; d. 1965. Writer and psychoanalyst. Wife of writer Jakob Wassermann and mother of writer Charles Ulric Wassermann.

Kaufmann, Christof, b. Salzburg, 1930. Architect and retired city planner in Winnipeg.

Kaufmann, Wilhelm, b. Salzburg. Portrait and landscape painter.

Klinkhoff, Walter. Appraiser and dealer in antiquities in Montreal. Interned in Canada during World War II. Finished engineering studies in Vienna, then returned to Montreal. Brought paintings along and sold them all so successfully that he opened an art gallery.

Kling, Paul, b. Troppau, Austrian Silesia, 1928; to Canada in seventies. Violinist, professor. Studied in Vienna, Brno, Prague. Played in Vienna Symphony. 1977, Professor of Music, University of Victoria. Introduced many contemporary Austrian composers to Canada.

Koch, Erich. Author of *Deemed Suspect*, an internment autobiography.

Koller, Reinhold. Montreal furniture designer.

Kraemer, Angelo. Opera Players of B.C.

Kraus, J. John, b. Galicia, 1894; to Canada, 1896; d. Prince Albert, 1950. Educated in law at the University of Saskatchewan. Was Registrar at the Prince Alberta Land Titles Office, 1938-1950.

Kremsner, Angela. Leading roles with Opera Players of British Columbia.

Kreyszig, Walter Kurt. Professor of Music, University of Saskatchewan.

Kriegel, Friedrich, d. 1994. Professor at Victoria College, University of Toronto. Co-author of cultural reader *2000 Jahre deutsches Leben*.

Kuchar, Joseph. Holds more than 200 international patents, including on the carbon-free copying process.

Ladner, Gerhart B., b. Vienna, 1905. Art historian.

Landegger, Carl C. Industrialist. Chairman and President of St. Anne Pulp and Paper Co. Ltd. and of Prince Albert Pulp Co.

Landseygner, Johann. Merchant, m. 1786.

Lavicka, Herwig, b. Baden bei Wien, 1928; to Canada, 1952. Owns a photostudio in Calgary. Very active in the German-speaking community.

Leismer, Hubert. b. Bohemia, 1897. Writer, poet.

Lister, Mark, to Canada, 1951. Studied *Bodenkultur*, lost most of his Jewish family. First president of the Österreichische Gesellschaft Montreal. Active in efforts to bring Jewish farmers to Canada.

Lukuvka, Josef Franz, b. Lassee, Austria, 1915; to Canada, 1954, d. Winnipeg, 1993. Barber and hairdresser in Winnipeg. Won a Grand Championship in New York.

MacHardy, Karin J. Historian. Studied at the Universities of Western Ontario and California (Berkeley). Teaches at the University of Waterloo. Focus of research is Central European social history, with emphasis on early modern Austria.

Maier, Franz. Photographer. Known for his news and nature photography in Western Ontario.

May, Karl, to Canada, 1952. Printer.

Mayerhoffer, Vincent Philip, b. Raab (Hungary), 1785; to Canada, 1819. Franciscan priest in Austrian army against Napoleon. 1819 to York County. Became Anglican missionary.

Meixner, Frank, b. Oberndorf near Salzburg, 1933; to Canada, 1955. Businessman in Calgary. Very active in Austrian community, president of Austrian Club since 1967.

Morawetz, Oskar, b. near Prague, 1917; to Canada, 1940. Composer. In 1953, Professor of Music, University of Toronto.

Moser, Walter. Professor of Comparative Literature, Université de Montréal.

Neumann, A.L. Surgeon in Winnipeg.

Niederleitner, Joe, b. Klosterneuburg, 1928; to Canada, 1963. Forester and businessman. After the war, policeman in Klagenfurt. Knew English and worked with British military police. Founding member of Club Austria in Edmonton; its president for many years since 1967.

Ockermüller, Hans, b. Shanghai; to Canada, early fifties. In insurance business. 1963, Austrian Vice Consul in Calgary; 1970, Consul; 1988, Consul General.

Ott, Walter. Professor of Educational Foundations, University of New Brunswick. Son of engraver Walter Ott.

Pacher, Horst. Printer in Winnipeg.

Pacher, Judith. Manitoba psychiatrist.

Philippovich, Eugen von. In 1905 (?) wrote a travelogue about his travels to western Canada.

Pilis, Andy von. Dairy farmer in Saskatoon region.

Piller, Helmut, b. 1935; to Canada, 1953. Surveyor. In 1979 founded surveying firm in Toronto.

Platzer, Alois, b. Styria. Member, Ottawa Schrammel Quaretett.

Pollhammer, Hugo and Theresia. The family operates a large agricultural enterprise in Manitoba.

Pollmer, Gert. Graphic designer, CBC (since 1952).

Puerstl, Willi. Ski jumper.

Raschke, John R., b. Vienna, 1931; to Canada, 1954. Began work with Toronto-Dominion Bank in 1955, did important work with immigrants. 1968-1971 in Vienna with Bankhaus Mayer-Loos & Co., to bring bank up to North American standards. Returned to Toronto in 1971. Since 1992 with Banca Commerciale Italiano of Canada. Very active in Canadian Austrian Society of Toronto; its president since 1981.

Redler, Richard, b. Bregenz, 1906. Instructor at Ashbury College, Ottawa.

Richter, Francis Xavier, b. Friedland, Bohemia. Ranched in Similkameen Valley.

Richter, Francis Xavier, Jr., ("Frank"). B.C. Minister of Agriculture and Mines.

Riml, Otto. Physician. Specialist on convalescence from polio.

Roch, Hans Sr., b. Wiener Neustadt, 1896; to Canada, 1954; d. 1972. Artist. In 1907, moved to Osijek, now Croatia. Made numerous drawings and linocuts in Yugoslavia and Italy. In 1944, managed to escape back to Austria. Joined his three sons in Canada in 1954. Continued work in Austria and Canada. Exhibits in Yugoslavia, Germany, Austria, and Canada.

Roch, John, b. 1920; to Canada, 1954. Introduced and disseminated non-destructive testing by means of ultrasound and x-rays.

Roch, Joe, b. 1931; to Canada, 1954. Was manager of American Airlines in-flight catering services in Toronto and New York. Now, manager of executive dining services, Toronto headquarters, Royal Bank.

Rummel, Erika. Professor of History, Wilfried Laurier University.

Sabidussi, Dr. M. Professor of Mathematics, Université de Montréal.

Salvendy, John T., b. Budapest, 1937; to Canada, 1967. Psychiatrist. Educated in Vienna. Professor of Psychiatry at the University of Toronto, 1989. Wrote book on Crown Prince Rudolf; many other publications.

Schaible, Juliane, b. Winnipeg, 1962. B.A., M.B.A., University of Manitoba. International business consultant. Consultant to the Canadian Council of Ministers of the Environment.

Schardl, Albert J. Composer. Wrote symphony in Toronto.

Scheer, Herfried, to Canada in the early fifties. Was Professor of German, Concordia University. Studied *Germanistik* in Canada (Alberta, McGill).

Schima, Joseph, to Canada in the thirties. Founded Continental Gallery (art gallery) in Montreal as representative of Thonet, a Viennese furniture firm. Widow Vilma managed gallery after his death.

Schirmer, Kurt E., b. Vienna, 1927; to Canada, 1953. Ophthamologist. Till 1960, in Toronto and Sudbury. Active in ophthalmic research, mainly laser technology, at St. Mary's Hospital, Hampstead, Quebec.

Schludermann, Eduard F. Physician. Decorated by Austria for multicultural activities.

Schludermann, Eduard Harry. Son of E.F. Schludermann. Psychology professor at the University of Manitoba.

Schneid, Otto, b. Slovakia, 1900. Artist, art historian, painter, sculptor.

Schwarz, Felix. Painter of *Bauernmalerei*.

Semelka, Gunther, b. Vienna, 1923; to Canada, 1951. Physician. Educated in Innsbruck, interned in Wisconsin (1949-51). Since 1956 at St. Boniface Hospital in Winnipeg. Specializes in anaesthesia and chronic pain.

Spencer, Hanna, b. Kladno (Bohemia) 1931. Professor of German, University of Western Ontario.

Stearns, Anna, b. Skala, Galicia, 1904. Professor of Ethnology, Université de Montréal.

Steiger, Fred. Painter. Parliament in St. John's, Newfoundland, displays his paintings of Newfoundland's premiers and Speakers.

Steiner, Adolf. Violinist. Played with the Montreal Symphony in the late fifties and early sixties.

Sterling, Bryan B., b. Vienna, 1922. Writer.

Sterling, Theodor David, b. Vienna, 1923; to Canada, 1972. Computing scientist. Hitler refugee to U.S. In 1972, appointed Chair of Computing Science at Simon Fraser University.

Stockinger, Friedrich, to Canada, 1938. Austrian officer in World War I. First Austrian trade delegate, Toronto. Was consultant to RCMP and CPR.

Suschnigg, Peter. Sociologist. Studied in New Zealand and at York University and teaches at Laurentian University. Reserach centers on the sociology of work. Came to Canada from New Zealand in 1981.

Swinton, Kurt Rudolf, to Canada, 1940. Transported to Canada as "enemy alien," then admitted to Canadian Army. 1945, Lieutenant Colonel. President of Encyclopedia Britannica of Canada. Chairman, Canadian Conference on Education.

Vinzenz, Fred, b. Vienna, 1934; to Canada, 1953. Chartered accountant. Odd jobs and correspondence education, culminating in C.A., 1965. First with Salada Foods, then Ralston Purina, finally (1985) with Pioneer Electronics of Canada; became Executive Vice-President (1990).

von Feltz, b. Radstadt; to Canada, 1738. Physician. Military doctor in Montreal. Later, Seigneur of Isle St. Paul.

Waizman, Louis, b. Salzburg, 1863; to Canada, 1893, d. 1951. Composer, music teacher, Mozarteum graduate (1884). Taught, among others, Percy Faith.

Wazda, Eva. Managing Director and publisher of the German-Canadian Business and Trade Directory, Toronto.

Weber, Greta. Press chief of Lufthansa in Canada.

Weichsler, Richard. Broadcaster in Vancouver. Made videocassette "Österreicher in Britisch Kolumbien."

Weiss, Ivo. Furniture designer in Ottawa.

Weswaldi, Günther, to Canada, 1965. Businessman in Toronto. In 1986, he opened a restaurant, then an import-export firm. 1982, variety theater (Varieté).

Wexler, Joseph. Furrier, m. 1764.

Wiener, Lore Maria, b. Vienna. Fashion designer in Vancouver.

Wirth, Gerald, b. Upper Austria, 1965; to Canada, 1991. Former Head Chorister, conductor and artistic director of the Vienna Choir Boys. In 1991, art director of Calgary Boys Choir.

Wolkenstein, Christopher, b. Innsbruck, 1922; to Canada, 1954. Anaesthetist. Descendant of poet Oswald von Wolkenstein (1377-1445). As son of anti-Nazi, was interned in England and transported to Australia. Studied medicine in Melbourne, Vienna, London, and New York. 1954-88, Department of Anesthesiology, Health Sciences Center; taught at University of Manitoba.

Wunsch, Wilhelm. Engineer, member of Free Austrian movement.

Wynne, Robert. Was Professor of History, University of Waterloo.

Wyslouzil, Edmund, b. Kitzbühel. Member, Ottawa Schrammel Quartett.

Wyslouzil, Hans, b. Kitzbühel. Member, Ottawa Schrammel Quartett.

Zeller, Frank Joseph William, b. Croatia, 1915; to Canada, 1952. Lawyer and notary. With Manitoba Telephone Company, 1958-80 (retirement). Is now lawyer and notary for German-speaking community in Winnipeg.

Zschokke, Hermann, b. 1838. In 1880, traveled from Vienna to U.S. and Canada. Published travelogue *Nach Nordamerika und Kanada* (1881?).